C-4322   CAREER EXAMINATION SERIES

*This is your*
*PASSBOOK for...*

# Grant Writer

*Test Preparation Study Guide*
*Questions & Answers*

NATIONAL LEARNING CORPORATION®

# COPYRIGHT NOTICE

This book is SOLELY intended for, is sold ONLY to, and its use is RESTRICTED to individual, bona fide applicants or candidates who qualify by virtue of having seriously filed applications for appropriate license, certificate, professional and/or promotional advancement, higher school matriculation, scholarship, or other legitimate requirements of education and/or governmental authorities.

This book is NOT intended for use, class instruction, tutoring, training, duplication, copying, reprinting, excerption, or adaptation, etc., by:

1) Other publishers
2) Proprietors and/or Instructors of "Coaching" and/or Preparatory Courses
3) Personnel and/or Training Divisions of commercial, industrial, and governmental organizations
4) Schools, colleges, or universities and/or their departments and staffs, including teachers and other personnel
5) Testing Agencies or Bureaus
6) Study groups which seek by the purchase of a single volume to copy and/or duplicate and/or adapt this material for use by the group as a whole without having purchased individual volumes for each of the members of the group
7) Et al.

Such persons would be in violation of appropriate Federal and State statutes.

PROVISION OF LICENSING AGREEMENTS – Recognized educational, commercial, industrial, and governmental institutions and organizations, and others legitimately engaged in educational pursuits, including training, testing, and measurement activities, may address request for a licensing agreement to the copyright owners, who will determine whether, and under what conditions, including fees and charges, the materials in this book may be used them.  In other words, a licensing facility exists for the legitimate use of the material in this book on other than an individual basis.  However, it is asseverated and affirmed here that the material in this book CANNOT be used without the receipt of the express permission of such a licensing agreement from the Publishers. Inquiries re licensing should be addressed to the company, attention rights and permissions department.

All rights reserved, including the right of reproduction in whole or in part, in any form or by any means, electronic or mechanical, including photocopying, recording, or by any information storage and retrieval system, without permission in writing from the Publisher.

Copyright © 2025 by

# National Learning Corporation

212 Michael Drive, Syosset, NY 11791
(516) 921-8888 • www.passbooks.com
E-mail: info@passbooks.com

# PASSBOOK® SERIES

THE *PASSBOOK® SERIES* has been created to prepare applicants and candidates for the ultimate academic battlefield – the examination room.

At some time in our lives, each and every one of us may be required to take an examination – for validation, matriculation, admission, qualification, registration, certification, or licensure.

Based on the assumption that every applicant or candidate has met the basic formal educational standards, has taken the required number of courses, and read the necessary texts, the *PASSBOOK® SERIES* furnishes the one special preparation which may assure passing with confidence, instead of failing with insecurity. Examination questions – together with answers – are furnished as the basic vehicle for study so that the mysteries of the examination and its compounding difficulties may be eliminated or diminished by a sure method.

This book is meant to help you pass your examination provided that you qualify and are serious in your objective.

The entire field is reviewed through the huge store of content information which is succinctly presented through a provocative and challenging approach – the question-and-answer method.

A climate of success is established by furnishing the correct answers at the end of each test.

You soon learn to recognize types of questions, forms of questions, and patterns of questioning. You may even begin to anticipate expected outcomes.

You perceive that many questions are repeated or adapted so that you can gain acute insights, which may enable you to score many sure points.

You learn how to confront new questions, or types of questions, and to attack them confidently and work out the correct answers.

You note objectives and emphases, and recognize pitfalls and dangers, so that you may make positive educational adjustments.

Moreover, you are kept fully informed in relation to new concepts, methods, practices, and directions in the field.

You discover that you are actually taking the examination all the time: you are preparing for the examination by "taking" an examination, not by reading extraneous and/or supererogatory textbooks.

In short, this PASSBOOK®, used directedly, should be an important factor in helping you to pass your test.

# GRANT WRITER

DUTIES AND RESPONSIBILITIES:
   Primary responsibilities include preparation of proposals and grant applications, and performance of responsible professional and administrative work in researching, identifying, developing and responding to public and private grant opportunities in the areas of Agriculture/Food/Farming, Animal Welfare, Arts and Cultural Programs, Business Incubation/Development, Christian Programs, Youth and Children, Civil Rights, Community Development, Crime Legal Law, Disaster Relief, Education, Employment/Jobs, Energy and Environment, Healthcare Services, Housing, Human Services, Medical/Research, Mental Health, Public Affairs, Recreation/Sports, Social Services, Technology.   Work is performed under broad direction of the Grants Director with the majority of work performed independently.

   Researches and identifies new government, corporate, foundations and private funding prospects.
- Generates proposals and supporting documents in response to solicitations.
- Generates revenues for Client programs and services through timely submission of well-researched, well written and well-documented grant/fund-raising proposals.
- If required supervise other consultants hired by Clients for specific writing purposes.
- Maintains and implements funding calendar activities, including cultivation activities.
- Writes reports to government, corporate, foundations and other funders.
- Acts as liaison with program staff. (If needed)
- Identifies funding opportunities and new program areas to match client's priorities, using research tools.
- Serves as a liaison to all funding agencies or organizations. (If needed)
- Engages with program officers at organizations to solicit invitations to submit proposals.
- Special projects as needed.

COMPETENCIES:
   To perform the job successfully, an individual should demonstrate some or all of the following competencies:
- **Analytical** - Synthesizes complex or diverse information; collects and researches data; uses intuition and experience to complement data; designs work flows and procedures.
- **Design** - Generates creative solutions; translates concepts and information into images; demonstrates attention to detail.
- **Problem Solving** - Identifies and resolves problems in a timely manner; gathers and analyzes information skillfully; develops alternative solutions; works well in group problem solving situations; uses reason even when dealing with emotional topics.
- **Technical Skills** - Assesses own strengths and weaknesses; pursues training and development opportunities; strives to continuously build knowledge and skills; shares expertise with others.
- **Customer Service** - Manages difficult or emotional customer situations; responds promptly to customer needs; solicits customer feedback to improve service; responds to requests for service and assistance; meets commitments.
- **Interpersonal Skills** - Focuses on solving conflict, not blaming; maintains confidentiality; listens to others without interrupting; keeps emotions under control; remains open to others' ideas and tries new things.
- **Oral Communication** - Speaks clearly and persuasively in positive or negative situations; listens and gets clarification; responds well to questions; demonstrates group presentation skills; participates in meetings.
- **Written Communication** - Writes clearly and informatively; varies writing style to meet

needs; presents numerical data effectively; able to read and interpret written information.
- **Teamwork** - Balances team and individual responsibilities; exhibits objectivity and openness to others' views; gives and welcomes feedback; contributes to building a positive team spirit; puts success of team above own interests; able to build morale and group commitments to goals and objectives; supports everyone's efforts to succeed.
- **Visionary Leadership** - Inspires respect and trust; mobilizes others to fulfill the vision.
- **Change Management** - Develops workable implementation plans; communicates changes effectively; builds commitment and overcomes resistance; prepares and supports those affected by change; monitors transition and evaluates results.
- **Leadership** - Exhibits confidence in self and others; inspires and motivates others to perform well; effectively influences actions and opinions of others; accepts feedback from others; gives appropriate recognition to others
- **Quality Management** - Looks for ways to improve and promote quality; demonstrates accuracy and thoroughness.
- **Business Acumen** - Understands business implications of decisions; displays orientation to profitability; demonstrates knowledge of market and competition; aligns work with strategic goals.
- **Cost Consciousness** - Works within approved budget; develops and implements cost saving measures; contributes to profits and revenue; conserves organizational resources.
- **Diversity** - Demonstrates knowledge of NPO's guidelines; shows respect and sensitivity for cultural differences; educates others on the value of diversity; promotes a harassment-free environment.
- **Ethics** - Treats people with respect; keeps commitments; inspires the trust of others; works with integrity and ethically; upholds organizational values.
- **Organizational Support** - Follows policies and procedures; completes administrative tasks correctly and on time; supports organization's goals and values: benefits organization through outside activities; supports affirmative action policies and respects diversity.
- **Strategic Thinking** - Understands organization's strengths and weaknesses; analyzes market and competition; identifies external threats and opportunities; adapts strategy to changing conditions.
- **Judgment** - Displays willingness to make decisions; exhibits sound and accurate judgment; supports and explains reasoning for decisions; includes appropriate people in decision-making process; makes timely decisions.
- **Motivation** - Sets and achieves challenging goals; demonstrates persistence and overcomes obstacles; measures self against standard of excellence; takes calculated risks to accomplish goals.
- **Planning/Organizing** - Prioritizes and plans work activities; uses time efficiently; plans for additional resources; sets goals and objectives; organizes or schedules other people and their tasks; develops realistic action plans.
- **Professionalism** - Approaches others in a tactful manner; reacts well under pressure; treats others with respect and consideration regardless of their status or position; accepts responsibility for own actions; follows through on commitments.
- **Quality** - Demonstrates accuracy and thoroughness; looks for ways to improve and promote quality; applies feedback to improve performance; monitors own work to ensure quality.
- **Quantity** - Strives to increase productivity.
- **Adaptability** - Adapts to changes in the work environment; manages competing demands; Changes approach or method to best fit the situation; Able to deal with frequent change, delays or unexpected events.
- **Attendance/Punctuality** - Ensures work responsibilities are covered when absent; arrives at meetings and appointments on time. (if applicable)
- **Dependability** - Follows instructions; responds to management direction; takes responsibility

for own actions; keeps commitments; commits to long hours of work when necessary to reach goals; completes tasks on time or notifies appropriate person with an alternate plan.
- **Initiative** - Volunteers readily; undertakes self-development activities; seeks increased responsibilities; takes independent actions and calculated risks; looks for and takes advantage of opportunities; asks for and offers help when needed.
- **Innovation** - Displays original thinking and creativity; meets challenges with resourcefulness; generates suggestions for improving work; develops innovative approaches and ideas; presents ideas and information in a manner that gets others' attention.

MINIMUM QUALIFICATIONS:
To perform this job successfully, an individual must be able to perform each essential duty satisfactorily.
The requirements listed below are representative of the knowledge, skills, and/or abilities required. Reasonable accommodations may be made to enable individuals with disabilities to perform the essential functions.
- **Knowledge, Skills and Abilities** - Comprehensive knowledge of standard office practices, procedures, equipment, and techniques; knowledge of adult learning techniques.
- **Education and/or Experience** - Bachelor's degree with a minimum of three years related experience in grant writing and contract administration.
- **Language Skills** - Ability to read and interpret documents such as safety rules, operating and maintenance instructions and procedure manuals; ability to write routine reports and correspondence; ability to speak effectively before groups of customers or employees of an organization.
- **Mathematical Skills** - Ability to calculate figures and amounts such as discounts, interest, commissions, proportions, percentages, area, circumference, and volume; ability to apply concepts of basic algebra and geometry.
- **Reasoning Ability** - Ability to solve practical problems and deal with a variety of concrete variables in situations where only limited standardization exists; ability to interpret a variety of instructions furnished in written, oral, diagram, or schedule form.
- **Computer Skills** - Experience with and knowledge of computer operation; knowledge of Microsoft Office Suite (Word, Excel, PowerPoint, Outlook, etc.), and database applications.

SUBJECT OF EXAMINATION
The written test designed to evaluate knowledge, skills and/or abilities in the following areas:
1. Evaluating conclusions in light of known facts;
2. Preparing written material;
3. Understanding and interpreting tabular material; and
4. Understanding and interpreting written material.

# HOW TO TAKE A TEST

I. YOU MUST PASS AN EXAMINATION

A. *WHAT EVERY CANDIDATE SHOULD KNOW*

Examination applicants often ask us for help in preparing for the written test. What can I study in advance? What kinds of questions will be asked? How will the test be given? How will the papers be graded?

As an applicant for a civil service examination, you may be wondering about some of these things. Our purpose here is to suggest effective methods of advance study and to describe civil service examinations.

Your chances for success on this examination can be increased if you know how to prepare. Those "pre-examination jitters" can be reduced if you know what to expect. You can even experience an adventure in good citizenship if you know why civil service exams are given.

B. *WHY ARE CIVIL SERVICE EXAMINATIONS GIVEN?*

Civil service examinations are important to you in two ways. As a citizen, you want public jobs filled by employees who know how to do their work. As a job seeker, you want a fair chance to compete for that job on an equal footing with other candidates. The best-known means of accomplishing this two-fold goal is the competitive examination.

Exams are widely publicized throughout the nation. They may be administered for jobs in federal, state, city, municipal, town or village governments or agencies.

Any citizen may apply, with some limitations, such as the age or residence of applicants. Your experience and education may be reviewed to see whether you meet the requirements for the particular examination. When these requirements exist, they are reasonable and applied consistently to all applicants. Thus, a competitive examination may cause you some uneasiness now, but it is your privilege and safeguard.

C. *HOW ARE CIVIL SERVICE EXAMS DEVELOPED?*

Examinations are carefully written by trained technicians who are specialists in the field known as "psychological measurement," in consultation with recognized authorities in the field of work that the test will cover. These experts recommend the subject matter areas or skills to be tested; only those knowledges or skills important to your success on the job are included. The most reliable books and source materials available are used as references. Together, the experts and technicians judge the difficulty level of the questions.

Test technicians know how to phrase questions so that the problem is clearly stated. Their ethics do not permit "trick" or "catch" questions. Questions may have been tried out on sample groups, or subjected to statistical analysis, to determine their usefulness.

Written tests are often used in combination with performance tests, ratings of training and experience, and oral interviews. All of these measures combine to form the best-known means of finding the right person for the right job.

## II. HOW TO PASS THE WRITTEN TEST

### A. NATURE OF THE EXAMINATION

To prepare intelligently for civil service examinations, you should know how they differ from school examinations you have taken. In school you were assigned certain definite pages to read or subjects to cover. The examination questions were quite detailed and usually emphasized memory. Civil service exams, on the other hand, try to discover your present ability to perform the duties of a position, plus your potentiality to learn these duties. In other words, a civil service exam attempts to predict how successful you will be. Questions cover such a broad area that they cannot be as minute and detailed as school exam questions.

In the public service similar kinds of work, or positions, are grouped together in one "class." This process is known as *position-classification*. All the positions in a class are paid according to the salary range for that class. One class title covers all of these positions, and they are all tested by the same examination.

### B. FOUR BASIC STEPS

#### 1) Study the announcement

How, then, can you know what subjects to study? Our best answer is: "Learn as much as possible about the class of positions for which you've applied." The exam will test the knowledge, skills and abilities needed to do the work.

Your most valuable source of information about the position you want is the official exam announcement. This announcement lists the training and experience qualifications. Check these standards and apply only if you come reasonably close to meeting them.

The brief description of the position in the examination announcement offers some clues to the subjects which will be tested. Think about the job itself. Review the duties in your mind. Can you perform them, or are there some in which you are rusty? Fill in the blank spots in your preparation.

Many jurisdictions preview the written test in the exam announcement by including a section called "Knowledge and Abilities Required," "Scope of the Examination," or some similar heading. Here you will find out specifically what fields will be tested.

#### 2) Review your own background

Once you learn in general what the position is all about, and what you need to know to do the work, ask yourself which subjects you already know fairly well and which need improvement. You may wonder whether to concentrate on improving your strong areas or on building some background in your fields of weakness. When the announcement has specified "some knowledge" or "considerable knowledge," or has used adjectives like "beginning principles of…" or "advanced … methods," you can get a clue as to the number and difficulty of questions to be asked in any given field. More questions, and hence broader coverage, would be included for those subjects which are more important in the work. Now weigh your strengths and weaknesses against the job requirements and prepare accordingly.

#### 3) Determine the level of the position

Another way to tell how intensively you should prepare is to understand the level of the job for which you are applying. Is it the entering level? In other words, is this the position in which beginners in a field of work are hired? Or is it an intermediate or advanced level? Sometimes this is indicated by such words as "Junior" or "Senior" in the class title. Other jurisdictions use Roman numerals to designate the level – Clerk I, Clerk II, for example. The word "Supervisor" sometimes appears in the title. If the level is not indicated by the title, check the description of duties. Will you be working under very close supervision, or will you have responsibility for independent decisions in this work?

### 4) Choose appropriate study materials

Now that you know the subjects to be examined and the relative amount of each subject to be covered, you can choose suitable study materials. For beginning level jobs, or even advanced ones, if you have a pronounced weakness in some aspect of your training, read a modern, standard textbook in that field. Be sure it is up to date and has general coverage. Such books are normally available at your library, and the librarian will be glad to help you locate one. For entry-level positions, questions of appropriate difficulty are chosen – neither highly advanced questions, nor those too simple. Such questions require careful thought but not advanced training.

If the position for which you are applying is technical or advanced, you will read more advanced, specialized material. If you are already familiar with the basic principles of your field, elementary textbooks would waste your time. Concentrate on advanced textbooks and technical periodicals. Think through the concepts and review difficult problems in your field.

These are all general sources. You can get more ideas on your own initiative, following these leads. For example, training manuals and publications of the government agency which employs workers in your field can be useful, particularly for technical and professional positions. A letter or visit to the government department involved may result in more specific study suggestions, and certainly will provide you with a more definite idea of the exact nature of the position you are seeking.

## III. KINDS OF TESTS

Tests are used for purposes other than measuring knowledge and ability to perform specified duties. For some positions, it is equally important to test ability to make adjustments to new situations or to profit from training. In others, basic mental abilities not dependent on information are essential. Questions which test these things may not appear as pertinent to the duties of the position as those which test for knowledge and information. Yet they are often highly important parts of a fair examination. For very general questions, it is almost impossible to help you direct your study efforts. What we can do is to point out some of the more common of these general abilities needed in public service positions and describe some typical questions.

### 1) General information

Broad, general information has been found useful for predicting job success in some kinds of work. This is tested in a variety of ways, from vocabulary lists to questions about current events. Basic background in some field of work, such as sociology or economics, may be sampled in a group of questions. Often these are principles which have become familiar to most persons through exposure rather than through formal training. It is difficult to advise you how to study for these questions; being alert to the world around you is our best suggestion.

### 2) Verbal ability

An example of an ability needed in many positions is verbal or language ability. Verbal ability is, in brief, the ability to use and understand words. Vocabulary and grammar tests are typical measures of this ability. Reading comprehension or paragraph interpretation questions are common in many kinds of civil service tests. You are given a paragraph of written material and asked to find its central meaning.

3) Numerical ability

Number skills can be tested by the familiar arithmetic problem, by checking paired lists of numbers to see which are alike and which are different, or by interpreting charts and graphs. In the latter test, a graph may be printed in the test booklet which you are asked to use as the basis for answering questions.

4) Observation

A popular test for law-enforcement positions is the observation test. A picture is shown to you for several minutes, then taken away. Questions about the picture test your ability to observe both details and larger elements.

5) Following directions

In many positions in the public service, the employee must be able to carry out written instructions dependably and accurately. You may be given a chart with several columns, each column listing a variety of information. The questions require you to carry out directions involving the information given in the chart.

6) Skills and aptitudes

Performance tests effectively measure some manual skills and aptitudes. When the skill is one in which you are trained, such as typing or shorthand, you can practice. These tests are often very much like those given in business school or high school courses. For many of the other skills and aptitudes, however, no short-time preparation can be made. Skills and abilities natural to you or that you have developed throughout your lifetime are being tested.

Many of the general questions just described provide all the data needed to answer the questions and ask you to use your reasoning ability to find the answers. Your best preparation for these tests, as well as for tests of facts and ideas, is to be at your physical and mental best. You, no doubt, have your own methods of getting into an exam-taking mood and keeping "in shape." The next section lists some ideas on this subject.

## IV. KINDS OF QUESTIONS

Only rarely is the "essay" question, which you answer in narrative form, used in civil service tests. Civil service tests are usually of the short-answer type. Full instructions for answering these questions will be given to you at the examination. But in case this is your first experience with short-answer questions and separate answer sheets, here is what you need to know:

### 1) Multiple-choice Questions

Most popular of the short-answer questions is the "multiple choice" or "best answer" question. It can be used, for example, to test for factual knowledge, ability to solve problems or judgment in meeting situations found at work.

A multiple-choice question is normally one of three types—
- It can begin with an incomplete statement followed by several possible endings. You are to find the one ending which *best* completes the statement, although some of the others may not be entirely wrong.
- It can also be a complete statement in the form of a question which is answered by choosing one of the statements listed.

- It can be in the form of a problem – again you select the best answer.

Here is an example of a multiple-choice question with a discussion which should give you some clues as to the method for choosing the right answer:

When an employee has a complaint about his assignment, the action which will *best* help him overcome his difficulty is to
   A. discuss his difficulty with his coworkers
   B. take the problem to the head of the organization
   C. take the problem to the person who gave him the assignment
   D. say nothing to anyone about his complaint

In answering this question, you should study each of the choices to find which is best. Consider choice "A" – Certainly an employee may discuss his complaint with fellow employees, but no change or improvement can result, and the complaint remains unresolved. Choice "B" is a poor choice since the head of the organization probably does not know what assignment you have been given, and taking your problem to him is known as "going over the head" of the supervisor. The supervisor, or person who made the assignment, is the person who can clarify it or correct any injustice. Choice "C" is, therefore, correct. To say nothing, as in choice "D," is unwise. Supervisors have and interest in knowing the problems employees are facing, and the employee is seeking a solution to his problem.

## 2) True/False Questions

The "true/false" or "right/wrong" form of question is sometimes used. Here a complete statement is given. Your job is to decide whether the statement is right or wrong.

SAMPLE: A roaming cell-phone call to a nearby city costs less than a non-roaming call to a distant city.

This statement is wrong, or false, since roaming calls are more expensive.

This is not a complete list of all possible question forms, although most of the others are variations of these common types. You will always get complete directions for answering questions. Be sure you understand *how* to mark your answers – ask questions until you do.

## V. RECORDING YOUR ANSWERS

Computer terminals are used more and more today for many different kinds of exams.
For an examination with very few applicants, you may be told to record your answers in the test booklet itself. Separate answer sheets are much more common. If this separate answer sheet is to be scored by machine – and this is often the case – it is highly important that you mark your answers correctly in order to get credit.

An electronic scoring machine is often used in civil service offices because of the speed with which papers can be scored. Machine-scored answer sheets must be marked with a pencil, which will be given to you. This pencil has a high graphite content which responds to the electronic scoring machine. As a matter of fact, stray dots may register as answers, so do not let your pencil rest on the answer sheet while you are pondering the correct answer. Also, if your pencil lead breaks or is otherwise defective, ask for another.

Since the answer sheet will be dropped in a slot in the scoring machine, be careful not to bend the corners or get the paper crumpled.

The answer sheet normally has five vertical columns of numbers, with 30 numbers to a column. These numbers correspond to the question numbers in your test booklet. After each number, going across the page are four or five pairs of dotted lines. These short dotted lines have small letters or numbers above them. The first two pairs may also have a "T" or "F" above the letters. This indicates that the first two pairs only are to be used if the questions are of the true-false type. If the questions are multiple choice, disregard the "T" and "F" and pay attention only to the small letters or numbers.

Answer your questions in the manner of the sample that follows:

32. The largest city in the United States is
    A. Washington, D.C.
    B. New York City
    C. Chicago
    D. Detroit
    E. San Francisco

1) Choose the answer you think is best. (New York City is the largest, so "B" is correct.)
2) Find the row of dotted lines numbered the same as the question you are answering. (Find row number 32)
3) Find the pair of dotted lines corresponding to the answer. (Find the pair of lines under the mark "B.")
4) Make a solid black mark between the dotted lines.

## VI. BEFORE THE TEST

Common sense will help you find procedures to follow to get ready for an examination. Too many of us, however, overlook these sensible measures. Indeed, nervousness and fatigue have been found to be the most serious reasons why applicants fail to do their best on civil service tests. Here is a list of reminders:

- Begin your preparation early – Don't wait until the last minute to go scurrying around for books and materials or to find out what the position is all about.
- Prepare continuously – An hour a night for a week is better than an all-night cram session. This has been definitely established. What is more, a night a week for a month will return better dividends than crowding your study into a shorter period of time.
- Locate the place of the exam – You have been sent a notice telling you when and where to report for the examination. If the location is in a different town or otherwise unfamiliar to you, it would be well to inquire the best route and learn something about the building.
- Relax the night before the test – Allow your mind to rest. Do not study at all that night. Plan some mild recreation or diversion; then go to bed early and get a good night's sleep.
- Get up early enough to make a leisurely trip to the place for the test – This way unforeseen events, traffic snarls, unfamiliar buildings, etc. will not upset you.
- Dress comfortably – A written test is not a fashion show. You will be known by number and not by name, so wear something comfortable.

- Leave excess paraphernalia at home – Shopping bags and odd bundles will get in your way. You need bring only the items mentioned in the official notice you received; usually everything you need is provided. Do not bring reference books to the exam. They will only confuse those last minutes and be taken away from you when in the test room.
- Arrive somewhat ahead of time – If because of transportation schedules you must get there very early, bring a newspaper or magazine to take your mind off yourself while waiting.
- Locate the examination room – When you have found the proper room, you will be directed to the seat or part of the room where you will sit. Sometimes you are given a sheet of instructions to read while you are waiting. Do not fill out any forms until you are told to do so; just read them and be prepared.
- Relax and prepare to listen to the instructions
- If you have any physical problem that may keep you from doing your best, be sure to tell the test administrator. If you are sick or in poor health, you really cannot do your best on the exam. You can come back and take the test some other time.

## VII. AT THE TEST

The day of the test is here and you have the test booklet in your hand. The temptation to get going is very strong. Caution! There is more to success than knowing the right answers. You must know how to identify your papers and understand variations in the type of short-answer question used in this particular examination. Follow these suggestions for maximum results from your efforts:

### 1) Cooperate with the monitor

The test administrator has a duty to create a situation in which you can be as much at ease as possible. He will give instructions, tell you when to begin, check to see that you are marking your answer sheet correctly, and so on. He is not there to guard you, although he will see that your competitors do not take unfair advantage. He wants to help you do your best.

### 2) Listen to all instructions

Don't jump the gun! Wait until you understand all directions. In most civil service tests you get more time than you need to answer the questions. So don't be in a hurry. Read each word of instructions until you clearly understand the meaning. Study the examples, listen to all announcements and follow directions. Ask questions if you do not understand what to do.

### 3) Identify your papers

Civil service exams are usually identified by number only. You will be assigned a number; you must not put your name on your test papers. Be sure to copy your number correctly. Since more than one exam may be given, copy your exact examination title.

### 4) Plan your time

Unless you are told that a test is a "speed" or "rate of work" test, speed itself is usually not important. Time enough to answer all the questions will be provided, but this does not mean that you have all day. An overall time limit has been set. Divide the total time (in minutes) by the number of questions to determine the approximate time you have for each question.

### 5) Do not linger over difficult questions

If you come across a difficult question, mark it with a paper clip (useful to have along) and come back to it when you have been through the booklet. One caution if you do this – be sure to skip a number on your answer sheet as well. Check often to be sure that you have not lost your place and that you are marking in the row numbered the same as the question you are answering.

### 6) Read the questions

Be sure you know what the question asks! Many capable people are unsuccessful because they failed to *read* the questions correctly.

### 7) Answer all questions

Unless you have been instructed that a penalty will be deducted for incorrect answers, it is better to guess than to omit a question.

### 8) Speed tests

It is often better NOT to guess on speed tests. It has been found that on timed tests people are tempted to spend the last few seconds before time is called in marking answers at random – without even reading them – in the hope of picking up a few extra points. To discourage this practice, the instructions may warn you that your score will be "corrected" for guessing. That is, a penalty will be applied. The incorrect answers will be deducted from the correct ones, or some other penalty formula will be used.

### 9) Review your answers

If you finish before time is called, go back to the questions you guessed or omitted to give them further thought. Review other answers if you have time.

### 10) Return your test materials

If you are ready to leave before others have finished or time is called, take ALL your materials to the monitor and leave quietly. Never take any test material with you. The monitor can discover whose papers are not complete, and taking a test booklet may be grounds for disqualification.

## VIII. EXAMINATION TECHNIQUES

1) Read the general instructions carefully. These are usually printed on the first page of the exam booklet. As a rule, these instructions refer to the timing of the examination; the fact that you should not start work until the signal and must stop work at a signal, etc. If there are any *special* instructions, such as a choice of questions to be answered, make sure that you note this instruction carefully.

2) When you are ready to start work on the examination, that is as soon as the signal has been given, read the instructions to each question booklet, underline any key words or phrases, such as *least, best, outline, describe* and the like. In this way you will tend to answer as requested rather than discover on reviewing your paper that you *listed without describing*, that you selected the *worst* choice rather than the *best* choice, etc.

3) If the examination is of the objective or multiple-choice type – that is, each question will also give a series of possible answers: A, B, C or D, and you are called upon to select the best answer and write the letter next to that answer on your answer paper – it is advisable to start answering each question in turn. There may be anywhere from 50 to 100 such questions in the three or four hours allotted and you can see how much time would be taken if you read through all the questions before beginning to answer any. Furthermore, if you come across a question or group of questions which you know would be difficult to answer, it would undoubtedly affect your handling of all the other questions.

4) If the examination is of the essay type and contains but a few questions, it is a moot point as to whether you should read all the questions before starting to answer any one. Of course, if you are given a choice – say five out of seven and the like – then it is essential to read all the questions so you can eliminate the two that are most difficult. If, however, you are asked to answer all the questions, there may be danger in trying to answer the easiest one first because you may find that you will spend too much time on it. The best technique is to answer the first question, then proceed to the second, etc.

5) Time your answers. Before the exam begins, write down the time it started, then add the time allowed for the examination and write down the time it must be completed, then divide the time available somewhat as follows:
    - If 3-1/2 hours are allowed, that would be 210 minutes. If you have 80 objective-type questions, that would be an average of 2-1/2 minutes per question. Allow yourself no more than 2 minutes per question, or a total of 160 minutes, which will permit about 50 minutes to review.
    - If for the time allotment of 210 minutes there are 7 essay questions to answer, that would average about 30 minutes a question. Give yourself only 25 minutes per question so that you have about 35 minutes to review.

6) The most important instruction is to *read each question* and make sure you know what is wanted. The second most important instruction is to *time yourself properly* so that you answer every question. The third most important instruction is to *answer every question*. Guess if you have to but include something for each question. Remember that you will receive no credit for a blank and will probably receive some credit if you write something in answer to an essay question. If you guess a letter – say "B" for a multiple-choice question – you may have guessed right. If you leave a blank as an answer to a multiple-choice question, the examiners may respect your feelings but it will not add a point to your score. Some exams may penalize you for wrong answers, so in such cases *only*, you may not want to guess unless you have some basis for your answer.

7) Suggestions
    a. Objective-type questions
        1. Examine the question booklet for proper sequence of pages and questions
        2. Read all instructions carefully
        3. Skip any question which seems too difficult; return to it after all other questions have been answered
        4. Apportion your time properly; do not spend too much time on any single question or group of questions

5. Note and underline key words – *all, most, fewest, least, best, worst, same, opposite*, etc.
6. Pay particular attention to negatives
7. Note unusual option, e.g., unduly long, short, complex, different or similar in content to the body of the question
8. Observe the use of "hedging" words – *probably, may, most likely*, etc.
9. Make sure that your answer is put next to the same number as the question
10. Do not second-guess unless you have good reason to believe the second answer is definitely more correct
11. Cross out original answer if you decide another answer is more accurate; do not erase until you are ready to hand your paper in
12. Answer all questions; guess unless instructed otherwise
13. Leave time for review

b. Essay questions
1. Read each question carefully
2. Determine exactly what is wanted. Underline key words or phrases.
3. Decide on outline or paragraph answer
4. Include many different points and elements unless asked to develop any one or two points or elements
5. Show impartiality by giving pros and cons unless directed to select one side only
6. Make and write down any assumptions you find necessary to answer the questions
7. Watch your English, grammar, punctuation and choice of words
8. Time your answers; don't crowd material

8) Answering the essay question

Most essay questions can be answered by framing the specific response around several key words or ideas. Here are a few such key words or ideas:

M's: manpower, materials, methods, money, management
P's: purpose, program, policy, plan, procedure, practice, problems, pitfalls, personnel, public relations

    a. Six basic steps in handling problems:
       1. Preliminary plan and background development
       2. Collect information, data and facts
       3. Analyze and interpret information, data and facts
       4. Analyze and develop solutions as well as make recommendations
       5. Prepare report and sell recommendations
       6. Install recommendations and follow up effectiveness

    b. Pitfalls to avoid
       1. *Taking things for granted* – A statement of the situation does not necessarily imply that each of the elements is necessarily true; for example, a complaint may be invalid and biased so that all that can be taken for granted is that a complaint has been registered

2. *Considering only one side of a situation* – Wherever possible, indicate several alternatives and then point out the reasons you selected the best one
3. *Failing to indicate follow up* – Whenever your answer indicates action on your part, make certain that you will take proper follow-up action to see how successful your recommendations, procedures or actions turn out to be
4. *Taking too long in answering any single question* – Remember to time your answers properly

## IX. AFTER THE TEST

Scoring procedures differ in detail among civil service jurisdictions although the general principles are the same. Whether the papers are hand-scored or graded by machine we have described, they are nearly always graded by number. That is, the person who marks the paper knows only the number – never the name – of the applicant. Not until all the papers have been graded will they be matched with names. If other tests, such as training and experience or oral interview ratings have been given, scores will be combined. Different parts of the examination usually have different weights. For example, the written test might count 60 percent of the final grade, and a rating of training and experience 40 percent. In many jurisdictions, veterans will have a certain number of points added to their grades.

After the final grade has been determined, the names are placed in grade order and an eligible list is established. There are various methods for resolving ties between those who get the same final grade – probably the most common is to place first the name of the person whose application was received first. Job offers are made from the eligible list in the order the names appear on it. You will be notified of your grade and your rank as soon as all these computations have been made. This will be done as rapidly as possible.

People who are found to meet the requirements in the announcement are called "eligibles." Their names are put on a list of eligible candidates. An eligible's chances of getting a job depend on how high he stands on this list and how fast agencies are filling jobs from the list.

When a job is to be filled from a list of eligibles, the agency asks for the names of people on the list of eligibles for that job. When the civil service commission receives this request, it sends to the agency the names of the three people highest on this list. Or, if the job to be filled has specialized requirements, the office sends the agency the names of the top three persons who meet these requirements from the general list.

The appointing officer makes a choice from among the three people whose names were sent to him. If the selected person accepts the appointment, the names of the others are put back on the list to be considered for future openings.

That is the rule in hiring from all kinds of eligible lists, whether they are for typist, carpenter, chemist, or something else. For every vacancy, the appointing officer has his choice of any one of the top three eligibles on the list. This explains why the person whose name is on top of the list sometimes does not get an appointment when some of the persons lower on the list do. If the appointing officer chooses the second or third eligible, the No. 1 eligible does not get a job at once, but stays on the list until he is appointed or the list is terminated.

# X. HOW TO PASS THE INTERVIEW TEST

The examination for which you applied requires an oral interview test. You have already taken the written test and you are now being called for the interview test – the final part of the formal examination.

You may think that it is not possible to prepare for an interview test and that there are no procedures to follow during an interview. Our purpose is to point out some things you can do in advance that will help you and some good rules to follow and pitfalls to avoid while you are being interviewed.

### What is an interview supposed to test?

The written examination is designed to test the technical knowledge and competence of the candidate; the oral is designed to evaluate intangible qualities, not readily measured otherwise, and to establish a list showing the relative fitness of each candidate – as measured against his competitors – for the position sought. Scoring is not on the basis of "right" and "wrong," but on a sliding scale of values ranging from "not passable" to "outstanding." As a matter of fact, it is possible to achieve a relatively low score without a single "incorrect" answer because of evident weakness in the qualities being measured.

Occasionally, an examination may consist entirely of an oral test – either an individual or a group oral. In such cases, information is sought concerning the technical knowledges and abilities of the candidate, since there has been no written examination for this purpose. More commonly, however, an oral test is used to supplement a written examination.

### Who conducts interviews?

The composition of oral boards varies among different jurisdictions. In nearly all, a representative of the personnel department serves as chairman. One of the members of the board may be a representative of the department in which the candidate would work. In some cases, "outside experts" are used, and, frequently, a businessman or some other representative of the general public is asked to serve. Labor and management or other special groups may be represented. The aim is to secure the services of experts in the appropriate field.

However the board is composed, it is a good idea (and not at all improper or unethical) to ascertain in advance of the interview who the members are and what groups they represent. When you are introduced to them, you will have some idea of their backgrounds and interests, and at least you will not stutter and stammer over their names.

### What should be done before the interview?

While knowledge about the board members is useful and takes some of the surprise element out of the interview, there is other preparation which is more substantive. It *is* possible to prepare for an oral interview – in several ways:

**1) Keep a copy of your application and review it carefully before the interview**

This may be the only document before the oral board, and the starting point of the interview. Know what education and experience you have listed there, and the sequence and dates of all of it. Sometimes the board will ask you to review the highlights of your experience for them; you should not have to hem and haw doing it.

**2) Study the class specification and the examination announcement**

Usually, the oral board has one or both of these to guide them. The qualities, characteristics or knowledges required by the position sought are stated in these documents. They offer valuable clues as to the nature of the oral interview. For example, if the job involves supervisory responsibilities, the announcement will usually indicate that knowledge of modern supervisory methods and the qualifications of the candidate as a supervisor will be tested. If so, you can expect such questions, frequently in the form of a hypothetical situation which you are expected to solve. NEVER go into an oral without knowledge of the duties and responsibilities of the job you seek.

### 3) Think through each qualification required

Try to visualize the kind of questions you would ask if you were a board member. How well could you answer them? Try especially to appraise your own knowledge and background in each area, *measured against the job sought*, and identify any areas in which you are weak. Be critical and realistic – do not flatter yourself.

### 4) Do some general reading in areas in which you feel you may be weak

For example, if the job involves supervision and your past experience has NOT, some general reading in supervisory methods and practices, particularly in the field of human relations, might be useful. Do NOT study agency procedures or detailed manuals. The oral board will be testing your understanding and capacity, not your memory.

### 5) Get a good night's sleep and watch your general health and mental attitude

You will want a clear head at the interview. Take care of a cold or any other minor ailment, and of course, no hangovers.

*What should be done on the day of the interview?*

Now comes the day of the interview itself. Give yourself plenty of time to get there. Plan to arrive somewhat ahead of the scheduled time, particularly if your appointment is in the fore part of the day. If a previous candidate fails to appear, the board might be ready for you a bit early. By early afternoon an oral board is almost invariably behind schedule if there are many candidates, and you may have to wait. Take along a book or magazine to read, or your application to review, but leave any extraneous material in the waiting room when you go in for your interview. In any event, relax and compose yourself.

The matter of dress is important. The board is forming impressions about you – from your experience, your manners, your attitude, and your appearance. Give your personal appearance careful attention. Dress your best, but not your flashiest. Choose conservative, appropriate clothing, and be sure it is immaculate. This is a business interview, and your appearance should indicate that you regard it as such. Besides, being well groomed and properly dressed will help boost your confidence.

Sooner or later, someone will call your name and escort you into the interview room. *This is it.* From here on you are on your own. It is too late for any more preparation. But remember, you asked for this opportunity to prove your fitness, and you are here because your request was granted.

*What happens when you go in?*

The usual sequence of events will be as follows: The clerk (who is often the board stenographer) will introduce you to the chairman of the oral board, who will introduce you to the other members of the board. Acknowledge the introductions before you sit down. Do not be surprised if you find a microphone facing you or a stenotypist sitting by. Oral interviews are usually recorded in the event of an appeal or other review.

Usually the chairman of the board will open the interview by reviewing the highlights of your education and work experience from your application – primarily for the benefit of the other members of the board, as well as to get the material into the record. Do not interrupt or comment unless there is an error or significant misinterpretation; if that is the case, do not hesitate. But do not quibble about insignificant matters. Also, he will usually ask you some question about your education, experience or your present job – partly to get you to start talking and to establish the interviewing "rapport." He may start the actual questioning, or turn it over to one of the other members. Frequently, each member undertakes the questioning on a particular area, one in which he is perhaps most competent, so you can expect each member to participate in the examination. Because time is limited, you may also expect some rather abrupt switches in the direction the questioning takes, so do not be upset by it. Normally, a board member will not pursue a single line of questioning unless he discovers a particular strength or weakness.

After each member has participated, the chairman will usually ask whether any member has any further questions, then will ask you if you have anything you wish to add. Unless you are expecting this question, it may floor you. Worse, it may start you off on an extended, extemporaneous speech. The board is not usually seeking more information. The question is principally to offer you a last opportunity to present further qualifications or to indicate that you have nothing to add. So, if you feel that a significant qualification or characteristic has been overlooked, it is proper to point it out in a sentence or so. Do not compliment the board on the thoroughness of their examination – they have been sketchy, and you know it. If you wish, merely say, "No thank you, I have nothing further to add." This is a point where you can "talk yourself out" of a good impression or fail to present an important bit of information. Remember, *you close the interview yourself.*

The chairman will then say, "That is all, Mr. _____, thank you." Do not be startled; the interview is over, and quicker than you think. Thank him, gather your belongings and take your leave. Save your sigh of relief for the other side of the door.


*How to put your best foot forward*

Throughout this entire process, you may feel that the board individually and collectively is trying to pierce your defenses, seek out your hidden weaknesses and embarrass and confuse you. Actually, this is not true. They are obliged to make an appraisal of your qualifications for the job you are seeking, and they want to see you in your best light. Remember, they must interview all candidates and a non-cooperative candidate may become a failure in spite of their best efforts to bring out his qualifications. Here are 15 suggestions that will help you:

1) **Be natural – Keep your attitude confident, not cocky**

If you are not confident that you can do the job, do not expect the board to be. Do not apologize for your weaknesses, try to bring out your strong points. The board is interested in a positive, not negative, presentation. Cockiness will antagonize any board member and make him wonder if you are covering up a weakness by a false show of strength.

2) **Get comfortable, but don't lounge or sprawl**

Sit erectly but not stiffly. A careless posture may lead the board to conclude that you are careless in other things, or at least that you are not impressed by the importance of the occasion. Either conclusion is natural, even if incorrect. Do not fuss with your clothing, a pencil or an ashtray. Your hands may occasionally be useful to emphasize a point; do not let them become a point of distraction.

3) **Do not wisecrack or make small talk**

This is a serious situation, and your attitude should show that you consider it as such. Further, the time of the board is limited – they do not want to waste it, and neither should you.

### 4) Do not exaggerate your experience or abilities
In the first place, from information in the application or other interviews and sources, the board may know more about you than you think. Secondly, you probably will not get away with it. An experienced board is rather adept at spotting such a situation, so do not take the chance.

### 5) If you know a board member, do not make a point of it, yet do not hide it
Certainly you are not fooling him, and probably not the other members of the board. Do not try to take advantage of your acquaintanceship – it will probably do you little good.

### 6) Do not dominate the interview
Let the board do that. They will give you the clues – do not assume that you have to do all the talking. Realize that the board has a number of questions to ask you, and do not try to take up all the interview time by showing off your extensive knowledge of the answer to the first one.

### 7) Be attentive
You only have 20 minutes or so, and you should keep your attention at its sharpest throughout. When a member is addressing a problem or question to you, give him your undivided attention. Address your reply principally to him, but do not exclude the other board members.

### 8) Do not interrupt
A board member may be stating a problem for you to analyze. He will ask you a question when the time comes. Let him state the problem, and wait for the question.

### 9) Make sure you understand the question
Do not try to answer until you are sure what the question is. If it is not clear, restate it in your own words or ask the board member to clarify it for you. However, do not haggle about minor elements.

### 10) Reply promptly but not hastily
A common entry on oral board rating sheets is "candidate responded readily," or "candidate hesitated in replies." Respond as promptly and quickly as you can, but do not jump to a hasty, ill-considered answer.

### 11) Do not be peremptory in your answers
A brief answer is proper – but do not fire your answer back. That is a losing game from your point of view. The board member can probably ask questions much faster than you can answer them.

### 12) Do not try to create the answer you think the board member wants
He is interested in what kind of mind you have and how it works – not in playing games. Furthermore, he can usually spot this practice and will actually grade you down on it.

### 13) Do not switch sides in your reply merely to agree with a board member
Frequently, a member will take a contrary position merely to draw you out and to see if you are willing and able to defend your point of view. Do not start a debate, yet do not surrender a good position. If a position is worth taking, it is worth defending.

**14) Do not be afraid to admit an error in judgment if you are shown to be wrong**

The board knows that you are forced to reply without any opportunity for careful consideration. Your answer may be demonstrably wrong. If so, admit it and get on with the interview.

**15) Do not dwell at length on your present job**

The opening question may relate to your present assignment. Answer the question but do not go into an extended discussion. You are being examined for a *new* job, not your present one. As a matter of fact, try to phrase ALL your answers in terms of the job for which you are being examined.

*Basis of Rating*

Probably you will forget most of these "do's" and "don'ts" when you walk into the oral interview room. Even remembering them all will not ensure you a passing grade. Perhaps you did not have the qualifications in the first place. But remembering them will help you to put your best foot forward, without treading on the toes of the board members.

Rumor and popular opinion to the contrary notwithstanding, an oral board wants you to make the best appearance possible. They know you are under pressure – but they also want to see how you respond to it as a guide to what your reaction would be under the pressures of the job you seek. They will be influenced by the degree of poise you display, the personal traits you show and the manner in which you respond.


ABOUT THIS BOOK

This book contains tests divided into Examination Sections. Go through each test, answering every question in the margin. We have also attached a sample answer sheet at the back of the book that can be removed and used. At the end of each test look at the answer key and check your answers. On the ones you got wrong, look at the right answer choice and learn. Do not fill in the answers first. Do not memorize the questions and answers, but understand the answer and principles involved. On your test, the questions will likely be different from the samples. Questions are changed and new ones added. If you understand these past questions you should have success with any changes that arise. Tests may consist of several types of questions. We have additional books on each subject should more study be advisable or necessary for you. Finally, the more you study, the better prepared you will be. This book is intended to be the last thing you study before you walk into the examination room. Prior study of relevant texts is also recommended. NLC publishes some of these in our Fundamental Series. Knowledge and good sense are important factors in passing your exam. Good luck also helps. So now study this Passbook, absorb the material contained within and take that knowledge into the examination. Then do your best to pass that exam.

# EXAMINATION SECTION

# EXAMINATION SECTION
## TEST 1

DIRECTIONS: Each question or incomplete statement is followed by several suggested answers or completions. Select the one that BEST answers the question or completes the statement. *PRINT THE LETTER OF THE CORRECT ANSWER IN THE SPACE AT THE RIGHT.*

1. When conducting a needs assessment for the purpose of education planning, an agency's FIRST step is to identify or provide
    A. a profile of population characteristics
    B. barriers to participation
    C. existing resources
    D. profiles of competing resources

    1.____

2. Research has demonstrated that of the following, the MOST effective medium for communicating with external publics is(are)
    A. video news releases
    B. television
    C. radio
    D. newspapers

    2.____

3. Basic ideas behind the effort to influence the attitudes and behaviors of a constituency include each of the following EXCEPT the idea that
    A. words, rather than actions or events, are most likely to motivate
    B. demands for action are a usual response
    C. self-interest usually figures heavily into public involvement
    D. the reliability of change programs is difficult to assess

    3.____

4. An agency representative is trying to craft a pithy message to constituents in order to encourage the use of agency program resources.
Choosing an audience for such messages is easiest when the message
    A. is project- or behavior-based
    B. is combined with other messages
    C. is abstract
    D. has a broad appeal

    4.____

5. Of the following factors, the MOST important to the success of an agency's external education or communication programs is the
    A. amount of resources used to implement them
    B. public's prior experiences with the agency
    C. real value of the program to the public
    D. commitment of the internal audience

    5.____

6. A representative for a state agency is being interviewed by a reporter from a local news network. The representative is being asked to defend a program that is extremely unpopular in certain parts of the municipality.
When a constituency is known to be opposed to a position, the MOST useful communication strategy is to present

    6.____

A. only the arguments that are consistent with constituents' views
B. only the agency's side of the issue
C. both sides of the argument as clearly as possible
D. both sides of the argument, omitting key information about the opposing position

7. The MOST significant barriers to effective agency community relations include
   I. widespread distrust of communication strategies
   II. the media's "watchdog" stance
   III. public apathy
   IV. statutory opposition

   The CORRECT answer is:
   A. I only   B. I and II   C. II and III   D. III and IV

7.____

8. In conducting an education program, many agencies use workshops and seminars in a classroom setting.
   Advantages of classroom-style teaching over other means of educating the public include each of the following, EXCEPT
   A. enabling an instructor to verify learning through testing and interaction with the target audience
   B. enabling hands-on practice and other participatory learning techniques
   C. ability to reach an unlimited number of participants in a given length of time
   D. ability to convey the latest, most up-to-date information

8.____

9. The _____ model of community relations is characterized by an attempt to persuade the public to adopt the agency's point of view.
   A. two-way symmetric          B. two-way asymmetric
   C. public information         D. press agency/publicity

9.____

10. Important elements of an internal situation analysis include the
    I. list of agency opponents          II. communication audit
    III. updated organizational almanac  IV. stakeholder analysis

    The CORRECT answer is:
    A. I and II   B. I, II, and III   C. II and III   D. I, II, III and IV

10.____

11. Government agency information efforts typically involve each of the following objectives, EXCEPT to
    A. implement changes in the policies of government agencies to align with public opinion
    B. communicate the work of agencies
    C. explain agency techniques in a way that invites input from citizens
    D. provide citizen feedback to government administrators

11.____

12. Factors that are likely to influence the effectiveness of an educational campaign include the
    I. level of homogeneity among intended participants
    II. number and types of media used
    III. receptivity of the intended participants
    IV. level of specificity in the message or behavior to be taught

    The CORRECT answer is:
    A. I and II    B. I, II, and III    C. II and III    D. I, II, III, and IV

13. An agency representative is writing instructional objectives that will later help to measure the effectiveness of an educational program.
    Which of the following verbs, included in an objective, would be MOST helpful for the purpose of measuring effectiveness?
    A. Know    B. Identify    C. Learn    D. Comprehend

14. A state education agency wants to encourage participation in a program that has just received a boost through new federal legislation. The program is intended to include participants from a wide variety of socioeconomic and other demographic characteristics. The agency wants to launch a broad-based program that will inform virtually every interested party in the state about the program's new circumstances.
    In attempting to deliver this message to such a wide-ranging constituency, the agency's BEST practice would be to
    A. broadcast the same message through as many different media channels as possible
    B. focus on one discrete segment of the public at a time
    C. craft a message whose appeal is as broad as the public itself
    D. let the program's achievements speak for themselves and rely on word-of-mouth

15. Advantages associated with using the World Wide Web as an educational tool include
    I. an appeal to younger generations of the public
    II. visually-oriented, interactive learning
    III. learning that is not confined by space, time, or institutional association
    IV. a variety of methods for verifying use and learning

    The CORRECT answer is:
    A. I only    B. I and II    C. I, II, and III    D. I, II, II, and IV

16. In agencies involved in health care, community relations is a critical function because it
    A. serves as an intermediary between the agency and consumers
    B. generates a clear mission statement for agency goals and priorities
    C. ensures patient privacy while satisfying the media's right to information
    D. helps marketing professionals determine the wants and needs of agency constituents

17. After an extensive campaign to promote its newest program to constituents, an agency learns that most of the audience did not understand the intended message.
MOST likely, the agency has
   A. chosen words that were intended to inform, rather than persuade
   B. not accurately interpreted what the audience really needed to know
   C. overestimated the ability of the audience to receive and process the message
   D. compensated for noise that may have interrupted the message

18. The necessary elements that lead to conviction and motivation in the minds of participants in an educational or information program include each of the following, EXCEPT the _____ of the message.
   A. acceptability
   B. intensity
   C. single-channel appeal
   D. pervasiveness

19. Printed materials are often at the core of educational programs provided by public agencies.
The PRIMARY disadvantage associated with print is that it
   A. does not enable comprehensive treatment of a topic
   B. is generally unreliable in term of assessing results
   C. is often the most expensive medium available
   D. is constrained by time

20. Traditional thinking on public opinion holds that there is about _____ percent of the public who are pivotal to shifting the balance and momentum of opinion—they are concerned about an issue, but not fanatical, and interested enough to pay attention to a reasoned discussion.
   A. 2    B. 10    C. 33    D. 51

21. One of the most useful guidelines for influencing attitude change among people is to
   A. invite the target audience to come to you, rather than approaching them
   B. use moral appeals as the primary approach
   C. use concrete images to enable people to see the results of behaviors or indifference
   D. offer tangible rewards to people for changes in behavior

22. An agency is attempting to evaluate the effectiveness of its educational program. For this purpose, it wants to observe several focus groups discussing the same program.
Which of the following would NOT be a guideline for the use of focus groups?
   A. Focus groups should only include those who have participated in the program.
   B. Be sure to accurately record the discussion.
   C. The same questions should be asked at each focus group meeting.
   D. It is often helpful to have a neutral, non-agency employee facilitate discussions.

23. Research consistently shows that _____ is the determinant most likely to make a newspaper editor run a news release.
    A. novelty    B. prominence    C. proximity    D. conflict

24. Which of the following is NOT one of the major variables to take into account when considering a population-needs assessment?
    A. State of program development    B. Resources available
    C. Demographics                    D. Community attitudes

25. The FIRST step in any communications audit is to
    A. develop a research instrument
    B. determine how the organization currently communicates
    C. hire a contractor
    D. determine which audience to assess

# KEY (CORRECT ANSWERS)

| | | | | |
|---|---|---|---|---|
| 1. | A | | 11. | A |
| 2. | D | | 12. | D |
| 3. | A | | 13. | B |
| 4. | A | | 14. | B |
| 5. | D | | 15. | C |
| 6. | C | | 16. | A |
| 7. | D | | 17. | B |
| 8. | C | | 18. | C |
| 9. | B | | 19. | B |
| 10. | C | | 20. | B |

21. C
22. A
23. C
24. C
25. D

# TEST 2

DIRECTIONS: Each question or incomplete statement is followed by several suggested answers or completions. Select the one that BEST answers the question or completes the statement. *PRINT THE LETTER OF THE CORRECT ANSWER IN THE SPACE AT THE RIGHT.*

1. A public relations practitioner at an agency has just composed a press release highlighting a program's recent accomplishments and success stories.
   In pitching such releases to print outlets, the practitioner should
   I. e-mail, mail, or send them by messenger
   II. address them to "editor" or "news director"
   III. have an assistant call all media contacts by telephone
   IV. ask reporters or editors how they prefer to receive them

   The CORRECT answer is:
   A. I and II     B. I and IV     C. II, III, and IV     D. III only

2. The "output goals" of an educational program are MOST likely to include
   A. specified ratings of services by participants on a standardized scale
   B. observable effects on a given community or clientele
   C. the number of instructional hours provided
   D. the number of participants served

3. An agency wants to evaluate satisfaction levels among program participants, and mails out questionnaires to everyone who has been enrolled in the last year.
   The PRIMARY problem associated with this method of evaluative research is that it
   A. poses a significant inconvenience for respondents
   B. is inordinately expensive
   C. does not allow for follow-up or clarification questions
   D. usually involves a low response rate

4. A communications audit is an important tool for measuring
   A. the depth of penetration of a particular message or program
   B. the cost of the organization's information campaigns
   C. how key audiences perceive an organization
   D. the commitment of internal stakeholders

5. The "ABCs" of written learning objectives include each of the following, EXCEPT
   A. Audience     B. Behavior     C. Conditions     D. Delineation

6. When attempting to change the behaviors of constituents, it is important to keep in mind that
   I. most people are skeptical of communications that try to get them to change their behaviors
   II. in most cases, a person selects the media to which he exposes himself
   III. people tend to react defensively to messages or programs that rely on fear as a motivating factor
   IV. programs should aim for the broadest appeal possible in order to include as many participants as possible

   The CORRECT answer is:
   A. I and II  B. I, II and III  C. II and III  D. I, II, III, and IV

7. The "laws" of public opinion include the idea that it is
   A. useful for anticipating emergencies
   B. not sensitive to important events
   C. basically determined by self-interest
   D. sustainable through persistent appeals

8. Which of the following types of evaluations is used to measure public attitudes before and after an information/educational program?
   A. Retrieval study
   B. Copy test
   C. Quota sampling
   D. Benchmark study

9. The PRIMARY source for internal communications is(are) usually
   A. flow charts
   B. meetings
   C. voice mail
   D. printed publications

10. An agency representative is putting together informational materials—brochures and a newsletter—outlining changes in one of the state's biggest benefits programs.
    In assembling print materials as a medium for delivering information to the public, the representative should keep in mind each of the following trends:
    I. For various reasons, the reading capabilities of the public are in general decline
    II. Without tables and graphs to help illustrate the changes, it is unlikely that the message will be delivered effectively
    III. Professionals and career-oriented people are highly receptive to information written in the form of a journal article or empirical study
    IV. People tend to be put off by print materials that use itemized and bulleted (●) lists

    The CORRECT answer is:
    A. I and II  B. I, II and III  C. II and III  D. I, II, III, and IV

11. Which of the following steps in a problem-oriented information campaign would typically be implemented FIRST?
    A. Deciding on tactics
    B. Determining a communications strategy
    C. Evaluating the problem's impact
    D. Developing an organizational strategy

11.____

12. A common pitfall in conducting an educational program is to
    A. aim it at the wrong target audience
    B. overfund it
    C. leave it in the hands of people who are in the business of education, rather than those with expertise in the business of the organization
    D. ignore the possibility that some other organization is meeting the same educational need for the target audience

12.____

13. The key factors that affect the credibility of an agency's educational program include
    A. organization
    B. scope
    C. sophistication
    D. penetration

13.____

14. Research on public opinion consistently demonstrates that it is
    A. easy to move people toward a strong opinion on anything, as long as they are approached directly through their emotions
    B. easier to move people away from an opinion they currently hold than to have them form an opinion about something they have not previously cared about
    C. easy to move people toward a strong opinion on anything, as long as the message appeals to their reason and intellect
    D. difficult to move people toward a strong opinion on anything, no matter what the approach

14.____

15. In conducting an education program, many agencies use meetings and conferences to educate an audience about the organization and its programs. Advantages associated with this approach include
    I. a captive audience that is known to be interested in the topic
    II. ample opportunities for verifying learning
    III. cost-efficient meeting space
    IV. the ability to provide information on a wider variety of subjects

    The CORRECT answer is:
    A. I and II   B. I, III and IV   C. II and III   D. I, II, III and IV

15.____

16. An agency is attempting to evaluate the effectiveness of its educational programs. For this purpose, it wants to observe several focus groups discussing particular programs.
    For this purpose, a focus group should never number more than _____ participants.
    A. 5   B. 10   C. 15   D. 20

16.____

17. A _____ speech is written so that several agency members can deliver it to different audiences with only minor variations.
    A. basic    B. printed    C. quota    D. pattern

17.____

18. Which of the following statements about public opinion is generally considered to be FALSE?
    A. Opinion is primarily reactive rather than proactive.
    B. People have more opinions about goals than about the means by which to achieve them.
    C. Facts tend to shift opinion in the accepted direction when opinion is not solidly structured.
    D. Public opinion is based more on information than desire.

18.____

19. An agency is trying to promote its educational program.
    As a general rule, the agency should NOT assume that
    A. people will only participate if they perceive an individual benefit
    B. promotions need to be aimed at small, discrete groups
    C. if the program is good, the audience will find out about it
    D. a variety of methods, including advertising, special events, and direct mail, should be considered

19.____

20. In planning a successful educational program, probably the first and most important question for an agency to ask is:
    A. What will be the content of the program?
    B. Who will be served by the program?
    C. When is the best time to schedule the program?
    D. Why is the program necessary?

20.____

21. Media kits are LEAST likely to contain
    A. fact sheets              B. memoranda
    C. photographs with captions    D. news releases

21.____

22. The use of pamphlets and booklets as media for communication with the public often involves the disadvantage that
    A. the messages contained within them are frequently nonspecific
    B. it is difficult to measure their effectiveness in delivering the message
    C. there are few opportunities for people to refer to them
    D. color reproduction is poor

22.____

23. The MOST important prerequisite of a good educational program is an
    A. abundance of resources to implement it
    B. individual staff unit formed for the purpose of program delivery
    C. accurate needs assessment
    D. uneducated constituency

23.____

24. After an education program has been delivered, an agency conducts a program evaluation to determine whether its objectives have been met.
General rules about how to conduct such an education program valuation include each of the following, EXCEPT that it
    A. must be done immediately after the program has been implemented
    B. should be simple and easy to use
    C. should be designed so that tabulation of responses can take place quickly and inexpensively
    D. should solicit mostly subjective, open-ended responses if the audience was large

25. Using electronic media such as television as means of educating the public is typically recommended ONLY for agencies that
    I. have a fairly simple message to begin with
    II. want to reach the masses, rather than a targeted audience
    III. have substantial financial resources
    IV. accept that they will not be able to measure the results of the campaign with much precision

    The CORRECT answer is:
    A. I and II      B. I, II and III      C. II and IV      D. I, II, III and IV

## KEY (CORRECT ANSWERS)

| | | | |
|---|---|---|---|
| 1. | B | 11. | C |
| 2. | C | 12. | D |
| 3. | D | 13. | A |
| 4. | C | 14. | D |
| 5. | D | 15. | B |
| 6. | B | 16. | B |
| 7. | C | 17. | D |
| 8. | D | 18. | D |
| 9. | D | 19. | C |
| 10. | A | 20. | D |

| | |
|---|---|
| 21. | B |
| 22. | B |
| 23. | C |
| 24. | D |
| 25. | D |

# EVALUATING CONCLUSIONS IN LIGHT OF KNOWN FACTS
## EXAMINATION SECTION
## TEST 1

DIRECTIONS: Each question or incomplete statement is followed by several suggested answers or completions. Select the one that BEST answers the question or completes the statement. *PRINT THE LETTER OF THE CORRECT ANSWER IN THE SPACE AT THE RIGHT.*

Questions 1-9.

DIRECTIONS: In Questions 1 through 9, you will read a set of facts and a conclusion drawn from them. The conclusion may be valid or invalid, based on the facts—it's your task to determine the validity of the conclusion.

For each question, select the letter before the statement that BEST expresses the relationship between the given facts and the conclusion that has been drawn from them. Your choices are:
- A. The facts prove the conclusion;
- B. The facts disprove the conclusion; or
- C. The facts neither prove nor disprove the conclusion.

1. FACTS: If the supervisor retires, James, the assistant supervisor, will not be transferred to another department. James will be promoted to supervisor if he is not transferred. The supervisor retired.

    CONCLUSION: James will be promoted to supervisor.
    - A. The facts prove the conclusion.
    - B. The facts disprove the conclusion.
    - C. The facts neither prove nor disprove the conclusion.

    1.____

2. FACTS: In the town of Luray, every player on the softball team works at Luray National Bank. In addition, every player on the Luray softball team wear glasses.

    CONCLUSIONS: At least some of the people who work at Luray National Bank wear glasses.
    - A. The facts prove the conclusion.
    - B. The facts disprove the conclusion.
    - C. The facts neither prove nor disprove the conclusion.

    2.____

3. FACTS: The only time Henry and June go out to dinner is on an evening when they have childbirth classes. Their childbirth classes meet on Tuesdays and Thursdays.

    3.____

CONCLUSION: Henry and June never go out to dinner on Friday or Saturday.
A. The facts prove the conclusion.
B. The facts disprove the conclusion.
C. The facts neither prove nor disprove the conclusion.

4. FACTS: Every player on the field hockey team has at least one bruise. Everyone on the field hockey team also has scarred knees.

   CONCLUSION: Most people with both bruises and scarred knees are field hockey players.
   A. The facts prove the conclusion.
   B. The facts disprove the conclusion.
   C. The facts neither prove nor disprove the conclusion.

4.____

5. FACTS: In the chess tournament, Lance will win his match against Jane if Jane wins her match against Mathias. If Lance wins his match against Jane, Christine will not win her match against Jane.

   CONCLUSION: Christine will not win her match against Jane if Jane wins her match against Mathias.
   A. The facts prove the conclusion.
   B. The facts disprove the conclusion.
   C. The facts neither prove nor disprove the conclusion.

5.____

6. FACTS: No green lights on the machine are indicators for the belt drive status. Not all of the lights on the machine's upper panel are green. Some lights on the machine's lower panel are green.

   CONCLUSION: The green lights on the machine's lower panel may be indicators for the belt drive status.
   A. The facts prove the conclusion.
   B. The facts disprove the conclusion.
   C. The facts neither prove nor disprove the conclusion.

6.____

7. FACTS: At a small, one-room country school, there are eight students: Amy, Ben, Carla, Dan, Elliot, Francine, Greg, and Hannah. Each student is in either the 6th, 7th, or 8th grade. Either two or three students are in each grade. Amy, Dan, and Francine are all in different grades. Ben and Elliot are both in the 7th grade. Hannah and Carl are in the same grade.

   CONCLUSION: Exactly three students are in the 7th grade.
   A. The facts prove the conclusion.
   B. The facts disprove the conclusion.
   C. The facts neither prove nor disprove the conclusion.

7.____

8. FACTS: Two married couples are having lunch together. Two of the four people are German and two are Russian, but in each couple the nationality of the spouse is not necessarily the same as the other's. One person in the group is a teacher, the other a lawyer, one an engineer, and the other a writer. The teacher is a Russian man. The writer is Russian, and her husband is an engineer. One of the people, Mr. Stern, is German.

   CONCLUSION: Mr. Stern's wife is a writer.
   A. The facts prove the conclusion.
   B. The facts disprove the conclusion.
   C. The facts neither prove nor disprove the conclusion.

   8.____

9. FACTS: The flume ride at the county fair is open only to children who are at least 36 inches tall. Lisa is 30 inches tall. John is shorter than Henry, but more than 10 inches taller than Lisa.

   CONCLUSION: Lisa is the only one who can't ride the flume ride.
   A. The facts prove the conclusion.
   B. The facts disprove the conclusion.
   C. The facts neither prove nor disprove the conclusion.

   9.____

Questions 10-17.

DIRECTIONS: Questions 10 through 17 are based on the following reading passage. It is not your knowledge of the particular topic that is being tested, but your ability to reason based on what you have read. The passage is likely to detail several proposed courses of action and factors affecting these proposals. The reading passage is followed by a conclusion or outcome based on the facts in the passage, or a description of a decision taken regarding the situation. The conclusion is followed by a number of statements that have a possible connection to the conclusion. For each statement, you are to determine whether:
   A. The statement proves the conclusion.
   B. The statement supports the conclusion but does not prove it.
   C. The statement disproves the conclusion.
   D. The statement weakens the conclusion but does not disprove it.
   E. The statement has no relevance to the conclusion.

Remember that the conclusion after the passage is to be accepted as the outcome of what actually happened, and that you are being asked to evaluate the impact each statement would have had on the conclusion.

PASSAGE:

The Grand Army of Foreign Wars, a national veteran's organization, is struggling to maintain its National Home, where the widowed spouses and orphans of deceased members are housed together in a small village-like community. The Home is open to spouses and children who are bereaved for any reason, regardless of whether the member's death was related to military service, but a new global conflict has led to a dramatic surge in the number of members' deaths: many veterans who re-enlisted for the conflict have been killed in action.

The Grand Army of Foreign Wars is considering several options for handling the increased number of applications for housing at the National Home, which has been traditionally supported by membership due. At its national convention, it will choose only one of the following:

The first idea is a one-time $50 tax on all members, above and beyond the dues they pay already. Since the organization has more than a million member, this tax should be sufficient for the construction and maintenance of new housing for applicants on the existing grounds of the National Home. The idea is opposed, however, by some older members who live on fixed incomes. These members object in principle to the taxation of Grand Army members. The Grand Army has never imposed a tax on its members.

The second idea is to launch a national fundraising drive the public relations campaign that will attract donations for the National Home. Several national celebrities are members of the organization, and other celebrities could be attracted to the cause. Many Grand Army members are wary of this approach, however: in the past, the net receipts of some fundraising efforts have been relatively insignificant, given the costs of staging them.

A third approach, suggested by many of the younger members, is to have new applicants share some of the costs of construction and maintenance. The spouses and children would pay an up-front "enrollment" fee, based on a sliding scale proportionate to their income and assets, and then a monthly fee adjusted similarly to contribute to maintenance costs. Many older members are strongly opposed to this idea, as it is in direct contradiction to the principles on which the organization was founded more than a century ago.

The fourth option is simply to maintain the status quo, focus the organization's efforts on supporting the families who already live at the National Home, and wait to accept new applicants based on attrition.

CONCLUSION: At its annual national convention, the Grand Army of Foreign Wars votes to impose a one-time tax of $10 on each member for the purpose of expanding and supporting the National Home to welcome a larger number of applicants. The tax is considered to be the solution most likely to produce the funds needed to accommodate the growing number of applicants.

10. Actuarial studies have shown that because the Grand Army's membership consists mostly of older veterans from earlier wars, the organization's membership will suffer a precipitous decline in numbers in about five years.
    A. The statement proves the conclusion.
    B. The statement supports the conclusion but does not prove it.
    C. The statement disproves the conclusion.
    D. The statement weakens the conclusion but does not disprove it.
    E. The statement has no relevance to the conclusion.

11. After passage of the funding measure, a splinter group of older members appeals for the "sliding scale" provision to be applied to the tax, so that some members may be allowed to contribute less based on their income.
    A. The statement proves the conclusion.
    B. The statement supports the conclusion but does not prove it.
    C. The statement disproves the conclusion.
    D. The statement weakens the conclusion but does not disprove it.
    E. The statement has no relevance to the conclusion.

5 (#1)

12. The original charter of the Grand Army of Foreign Wars specifically states that the organization will not levy taxes or duties on its members beyond its modest annual dues. It takes a super-majority of attending delegates at the national convention to make alterations to the charter.
    A. The statement proves the conclusion.
    B. The statement supports the conclusion but does not prove it.
    C. The statement disproves the conclusion.
    D. The statement weakens the conclusion but does not disprove it.
    E. The statement has no relevance to the conclusion.

12.____

13. Six months before Grand Army of Foreign Wars' national convention, the Internal Revenue Service rules that because it is an organization that engages in political lobbying, the Grand Army must no longer enjoy its own federal tax-exempt status.
    A. The statement proves the conclusion.
    B. The statement supports the conclusion but does not prove it.
    C. The statement disproves the conclusion.
    D. The statement weakens the conclusion but does not disprove it.
    E. The statement has no relevance to the conclusion.

13.____

14. Two months before the national convention, Dirk Rockwell, arguably the country's most famous film actor, announces in a nationally televised interview that he has been saddened to learn of the plight of the National Home, and that he is going to make it his own personal crusade to see that it is able to house and support a greater number of widowed spouses and orphans in the future.
    A. The statement proves the conclusion.
    B. The statement supports the conclusion but does not prove it.
    C. The statement disproves the conclusion.
    D. The statement weakens the conclusion but does not disprove it.
    E. The statement has no relevance to the conclusion.

14.____

15. The Grand Army's final estimate is that the cost of expanding the National Home to accommodate the increased number of applicants will be about $61 million.
    A. The statement proves the conclusion.
    B. The statement supports the conclusion but does not prove it.
    C. The statement disproves the conclusion.
    D. The statement weakens the conclusion but does not disprove it.
    E. The statement has no relevance to the conclusion.

15.____

16. Just before the national convention, the Federal Department of Veterans Affairs announces steep cuts in the benefits package that is currently offered to the widowed spouses and orphans of veterans.
    A. The statement proves the conclusion.
    B. The statement supports the conclusion but does not prove it.
    C. The statement disproves the conclusion.
    D. The statement weakens the conclusion but does not disprove it.
    E. The statement has no relevance to the conclusion.

16.____

17. After the national convention, the Grand Army of Foreign Wars begins charging a modest "start-up" fee to all families who apply for residence at the national home.
    A. The statement proves the conclusion.
    B. The statement supports the conclusion but does not prove it.
    C. The statement disproves the conclusion.
    D. The statement weakens the conclusion but does not disprove it.
    E. The statement has no relevance to the conclusion.

Questions 18-25.

DIRECTIONS: Questions 18 through 25 each provide four factual statements and a conclusion based on these statements. After reading the entire question, you will decide whether:
   A. The conclusion is proved by statements I-IV;
   B. The conclusion is disproved by statements I-IV.
   C. The facts are not sufficient to prove or disprove the conclusion.

18. FACTUAL STATEMENTS:
    I. In the Field Day high jump competition, Martha jumped higher than Frank.
    II. Carl jumped higher than Ignacio.
    III. Ignacio jumped higher than Frank.
    IV. Dan jumped higher than Carl.

    CONCLUSION: Frank finished last in the high jump competition.
    A. The conclusion is proved by statements I-IV;
    B. The conclusion is disproved by statements I-IV.
    C. The facts are not sufficient to prove or disprove the conclusion.

19. FACTUAL STATEMENTS:
    I. The door to the hammer mill chamber is locked if light 6 is red.
    II. The door to the hammer mill chamber is locked only when the mill is operating.
    III. If the mill is not operating, light 6 is blue.
    IV. Light 6 is blue.

    CONCLUSION: The door to the hammer mill chamber is locked.
    A. The conclusion is proved by statements I-IV;
    B. The conclusion is disproved by statements I-IV.
    C. The facts are not sufficient to prove or disprove the conclusion.

20. FACTUAL STATEMENTS:
    I. Ziegfried, the lion tamer at the circus, has demanded ten additional minutes of performance time during each show.
    II. If Ziegfried is allowed his ten additional minutes per show, he will attempt to teach Kimba the tiger to shoot a basketball.
    III. If Kimba learns how to shoot a basketball, then Ziegfried was not given his ten additional minutes.
    IV. Ziegfried was given his ten additional minutes.

CONCLUSION: Despite Ziegfried's efforts, Kimba did not learn how to shoot a basketball.
   A. The conclusion is proved by statements I-IV;
   B. The conclusion is disproved by statements I-IV.
   C. The facts are not sufficient to prove or disprove the conclusion.

21. FACTUAL STATEMENTS:
   I. If Stan goes to counseling, Sara won't divorce him.
   II. If Sara divorces Stan, she'll move back to Texas.
   III. If Sara doesn't divorce Stan, Irene will be disappointed.
   IV. Stan goes to counseling.

   CONCLUSION: Irene will be disappointed.
   A. The conclusion is proved by statements I-IV;
   B. The conclusion is disproved by statements I-IV.
   C. The facts are not sufficient to prove or disprove the conclusion.

22. FACTUAL STATEMENTS:
   I. If Delia is promoted to district manager, Claudia will have to be promoted to team leader.
   II. Delia will be promoted to district manager unless she misses her fourth-quarter sales quota.
   III. If Claudia is promoted to team leader, Thomas will be promoted to assistant team leader.
   IV. Delia meets her fourth-quarter sales quota.

   CONCLUSION: Thomas is promoted to assistant team leader.
   A. The conclusion is proved by statements I-IV;
   B. The conclusion is disproved by statements I-IV.
   C. The facts are not sufficient to prove or disprove the conclusion.

23. FACTUAL STATEMENTS:
   I. Clone D is identical to Clone B.
   II. Clone B is not identical to Clone A.
   III. Clone D is not identical to Clone C.
   IV. Clone E is not identical to the clones that are identical to Clone B.

   CONCLUSION: Clone E is identical to Clone D.
   A. The conclusion is proved by statements I-IV;
   B. The conclusion is disproved by statements I-IV.
   C. The facts are not sufficient to prove or disprove the conclusion.

24. FACTUAL STATEMENTS:
   I. In the Stafford Tower, each floor is occupied by a single business.
   II. Big G Staffing is on a floor between CyberGraphics and MainEvent.
   III. Gasco is on the floor directly below CyberGraphics and three floors above Treehorn Audio.
   IV. MainEvent is five floors below EZ Tax and four floors below Treehorn Audio.

CONCLUSION: EZ Tax is on a floor between Gasco and MainEvent.
  A. The conclusion is proved by statements I-IV;
  B. The conclusion is disproved by statements I-IV.
  C. The facts are not sufficient to prove or disprove the conclusion.

25. FACTUAL STATEMENTS:
  I. Only county roads lead to Nicodemus.
  II. All the roads from Hill City to Graham County are federal highways.
  III. Some of the roads from Plainville lead to Nicodemus.
  IV. Some of the roads running from Hill City lead to Strong City.

  CONCLUSION: Some of the roads from Plainville are county roads.
  A. The conclusion is proved by statements I-IV;
  B. The conclusion is disproved by statements I-IV.
  C. The facts are not sufficient to prove or disprove the conclusion.

# KEY (CORRECT ANSWERS)

| | | | | |
|---|---|---|---|---|
| 1. | A | | 11. | A |
| 2. | A | | 12. | D |
| 3. | A | | 13. | E |
| 4. | C | | 14. | D |
| 5. | A | | 15. | B |
| 6. | B | | 16. | B |
| 7. | A | | 17. | C |
| 8. | A | | 18. | A |
| 9. | A | | 19. | B |
| 10. | E | | 20. | A |

| | |
|---|---|
| 21. | A |
| 22. | A |
| 23. | B |
| 24. | A |
| 25. | A |

# SOLUTIONS TO PROBLEMS

1. **CORRECT ANSWER: A**
   Given Statement 3, we deduce that James will not be transferred to another department. By Statement 2, we can conclude that James will be promoted.

2. **CORRECT ANSWER: A**
   Since every player on the softball team wears glasses, these individuals compose some of the people who work at the bank. Although not every person who works at the bank plays softball, those bank employees who do play softball wear glasses.

3. **CORRECT ANSWER: A**
   If Henry and June go out to dinner, we conclude that it must be on Tuesday or Thursday, which are the only two days when they have childbirth classes. This implies that if it is not Tuesday or Thursday, then this couple does not go out to dinner.

4. **CORRECT ANSWER: C**
   We can only conclude that if a person plays on the field hockey team, then he or she has both bruises and scarred knees. But there are probably a great number of people who have both bruises and scarred knees but do not play on the field hockey team. The given conclusion can neither be proven or disproven.

5. **CORRECT ANSWER: A**
   From statement 1, if Jane beats Mathias, then Lance will beat Jane. Using statement 2, we can then conclude that Christine will not win her match against Jane.

6. **CORRECT ANSWER: B**
   Statement 1 tells us that no green light can be an indicator of the belt drive status. Thus, the given conclusion must be false.

7. **CORRECT ANSWER: A**
   We already know that Ben and Elliot are in the 7$^{th}$ grade. Even though Hannah and Carl are in the same grade, it cannot be the 7$^{th}$ grade because we would then have at least four students in this 7$^{th}$ grade. This would contradict the third statement, which states that either two or three students are in each grade. Since Amy, Dan, and Francine are in different grade, exactly one of them must be in the 7$^{th}$ grade. Thus, Ben, Elliot, and exactly one of Amy, Dan, and Francine are the three students in the 7$^{th}$ grade.

8. **CORRECT ANSWER: A**
   One man is a teacher, who is Russian. We know that the writer is female and is Russian. Since her husband is an engineer, he cannot be the Russian teacher. Thus, her husband is of German descent, namely Mr. Stern. This means that Mr. Stern's wife is the writer. Note that one couple consists of a male Russian teacher and a female German lawyer. The other couple consists of a male German engineer and a female Russian writer.

10 (#1)

9.  CORRECT ANSWER: A
    Since John is more than 10 inches taller than Lisa, his height is at least 46 inches. Also, John is shorter than Henry, so Henry's height must be greater than 46 inches. Thus, Lisa is the only one whose height is less than 36 inches. Therefore, she is the only one who is not allowed on the flume ride.

18. CORRECT ANSWER: A
    Dan jumped higher than Carl, who jumped higher than Ignacio, who jumped higher than Frank. Since Martha jumped higher than Frank, every person jumped higher than Frank. Thus, Frank finished last.

19. CORRECT ANSWER: B
    If the light is red, then the door is locked. If the door is locked, then the mill is operating. Reversing the logical sequence of these statements, if the mill is not operating, then the door is not locked, which means that the light is blue. Thus, the given conclusion is disproved.

20. CORRECT ANSWER: A
    Using the contrapositive of statement III, Ziegfried was given his ten additional minutes, then Kimba did not learn how to shoot a basketball. Since statement IV is factual, the conclusion is proved.

21. CORRECT ANSWER: A
    From Statements IV and I, we conclude that Sara doesn't divorce Stan. Then statement III reveals that Irene will be disappointed. Thus, the conclusion is proved.

22. CORRECT ANSWER: A
    Statement II can be rewritten as "Delia is promoted to district manager or she misses her sales quota." Furthermore, this statement is equivalent to "If Delia makes her sales quota, then she is promoted to district manager." From statement I, we conclude that Claudia is promoted to team leader. Finally, by statement III, Thomas is promoted to assistant team leader.

23. CORRECT ANSWER: B
    By statement IV, Clone E is not identical to any clones identical to Clone B. Statement I tells us that Clones B and D are identical. Therefore, Clone E cannot be identical to Clone D. The conclusion is disproved.

24. CORRECT ANSWER: A
    Based on all four statements, CyberGraphics is somewhere below MainEvent. Gasco is one floor below CyberGraphics. EZ Tax is two floors below Gasco. Treehorn Audio is one floor below EZ Tax. MainEvent is four floors below Treehorn Audio. Thus, EZ Tax is two floors below Gasco and five floors above MainEvent. The conclusion is proved.

25. CORRECT ANSWER: A
    From statement III, we know that some of the roads from Plainville lead to Nicodemus. But statement I tells us that only county roads lead to Nicodemus. Therefore, some of the roads from Plainville must be county roads. The conclusion is proved.

# TEST 2

DIRECTIONS: Each question or incomplete statement is followed by several suggested answers or completions. Select the one that BEST answers the question or completes the statement. *PRINT THE LETTER OF THE CORRECT ANSWER IN THE SPACE AT THE RIGHT.*

Questions 1-9.

DIRECTIONS: In Questions 1 through 9, you will read a set of facts and a conclusion drawn from them. The conclusion may be valid or invalid, based on the facts—it's your task to determine the validity of the conclusion.

For each question, select the letter before the statement that BEST expresses the relationship between the given facts and the conclusion that has been drawn from them. Your choices are:
    A. The facts prove the conclusion;
    B. The facts disprove the conclusion; or
    C. The facts neither prove nor disprove the conclusion.

1. FACTS: Some employees in the testing department are statisticians. Most of the statisticians who work in the testing department are projection specialists. Tom Wilks works in the testing department.

   CONCLUSION: Tom Wilks is a statistician.
       A. The facts prove the conclusion.
       B. The facts disprove the conclusion.
       C. The facts neither prove nor disprove the conclusion.

2. FACTS: Ten coins are split among Hank, Lawrence, and Gail. If Lawrence gives his coins to Hank, then Hank will have more coins than Gail. If Gail gives her coins to Lawrence, then Lawrence will have more coins than Hank.

   CONCLUSION: Hank has six coins.
       A. The facts prove the conclusion.
       B. The facts disprove the conclusion.
       C. The facts neither prove nor disprove the conclusion.

3. FACTS: Nobody loves everybody. Janet loves Ken. Ken loves everybody who loves Janet.

   CONCLUSION: Everybody loves Janet.
       A. The facts prove the conclusion.
       B. The facts disprove the conclusion.
       C. The facts neither prove nor disprove the conclusion.

4. **FACTS:** Most of the Torres family lives in East Los Angeles. Many people in East Los Angeles celebrate Cinco de Mayo. Joe is a member of the Torres family.

   **CONCLUSION:** Joe lives in East Los Angeles.
   A. The facts prove the conclusion.
   B. The facts disprove the conclusion.
   C. The facts neither prove nor disprove the conclusion.

   4.\_\_\_\_

5. **FACTS:** Five professionals each occupy one story of a five-story office building. Dr. Kane's office is above Dr. Assad's. Dr. Johnson's office is between Dr. Kane's and Dr. Conlon's. Dr. Steen's office is between Dr. Conlon's and Dr. Assad's. Dr. Johnson is on the fourth story.

   **CONCLUSION:** Dr. Kane occupies the top story.
   A. The facts prove the conclusion.
   B. The facts disprove the conclusion.
   C. The facts neither prove nor disprove the conclusion.

   5.\_\_\_\_

6. **FACTS:** To be eligible for membership in the Yukon Society, a person must be able to either tunnel through a snowbank while wearing only a T-shirt and short, or hold his breath for two minutes under water that is 50°F. Ray can only hold his breath for a minute and a half.

   **CONCLUSION:** Ray can still become a member of the Yukon Society by tunneling through a snowbank while wearing a T-shirt and shorts.
   A. The facts prove the conclusion.
   B. The facts disprove the conclusion.
   C. The facts neither prove nor disprove the conclusion.

   6.\_\_\_\_

7. **FACTS:** A mark is worth five plunks. You can exchange four sharps for a tinplot. It takes eight marks to buy a sharp.

   **CONCLUSION:** A sharp is the most valuable.
   A. The facts prove the conclusion.
   B. The facts disprove the conclusion.
   C. The facts neither prove nor disprove the conclusion.

   7.\_\_\_\_

8. **FACTS:** There are gibbons, as well as lemurs, who like to play in the trees at the monkey house. All those who like to play in the trees at the monkey house are fed lettuce and bananas.

   **CONCLUSION:** Lemurs and gibbons are types of monkeys.
   A. The facts prove the conclusion.
   B. The facts disprove the conclusion.
   C. The facts neither prove nor disprove the conclusion.

   8.\_\_\_\_

9. FACTS: None of the Blackfoot tribes is a Salishan Indian tribe. Salishan Indians came from the northern Pacific Coast. All Salishan Indians live each of the Continental Divide.  9._____

CONCLUSION: No Blackfoot tribes live east of the Continental Divide.
- A. The facts prove the conclusion.
- B. The facts disprove the conclusion.
- C. The facts neither prove nor disprove the conclusion.

Questions 10-17.

DIRECTIONS: Questions 10 through 17 are based on the following reading passage. It is not your knowledge of the particular topic that is being tested, but your ability to reason based on what you have read. The passage is likely to detail several proposed courses of action and factors affecting these proposals. The reading passage is followed by a conclusion or outcome based on the facts in the passage, or a description of a decision taken regarding the situation. The conclusion is followed by a number of statements that have a possible connection to the conclusion. For each statement, you are to determine whether:
- A. The statement proves the conclusion.
- B. The statement supports the conclusion but does not prove it.
- C. The statement disproves the conclusion.
- D. The statement weakens the conclusion but does not disprove it.
- E. The statement has no relevance to the conclusion.

Remember that the conclusion after the passage is to be accepted as the outcome of what actually happened, and that you are being asked to evaluate the impact each statement would have had on the conclusion.

PASSAGE:

On August 12, Beverly Willey reported that she was in the elevator late on the previous evening after leaving her office on the 16th floor of a large office building. In her report, she states that a man got on the elevator at the 11th floor, pulled her off the elevator, assaulted her, and stole her purse. Ms. Willey reported that she had seen the man in the elevators and hallways of the building before. She believes that the man works in the building. Her description of him is as follows: he is tall, unshaven, with wavy brown hair and a scar on his left cheek. He walks with a pronounced limp, often dragging his left foot behind his right.

CONCLUSION: After Beverly Willey makes her report, the police arrest a 43-year-old man, Barton Black, and charge him with her assault.

10. Barton Black is a former Marine who served in Vietnam, where he sustained shrapnel wounds to the left side of his face and suffered nerve damage in his left leg.
    A. The statement proves the conclusion.
    B. The statement supports the conclusion but does not prove it.
    C. The statement disproves the conclusion.
    D. The statement weakens the conclusion but does not disprove it.
    E. The statement has no relevance to the conclusion.

11. When they arrived at his residence to question him, detectives were greeted at the door by Barton Black, who was tall and clean-shaven.
    A. The statement proves the conclusion.
    B. The statement supports the conclusion but does not prove it.
    C. The statement disproves the conclusion.
    D. The statement weakens the conclusion but does not disprove it.
    E. The statement has no relevance to the conclusion.

12. Barton Black was booked into the county jail several days after Beverly Willey's assault.
    A. The statement proves the conclusion.
    B. The statement supports the conclusion but does not prove it.
    C. The statement disproves the conclusion.
    D. The statement weakens the conclusion but does not disprove it.
    E. The statement has no relevance to the conclusion.

13. Upon further investigation, detectives discover that Beverly Willey does not work at the office building.
    A. The statement proves the conclusion.
    B. The statement supports the conclusion but does not prove it.
    C. The statement disproves the conclusion.
    D. The statement weakens the conclusion but does not disprove it.
    E. The statement has no relevance to the conclusion.

14. Upon further investigation, detectives discover that Barton Black does not work at the office building.
    A. The statement proves the conclusion.
    B. The statement supports the conclusion but does not prove it.
    C. The statement disproves the conclusion.
    D. The statement weakens the conclusion but does not disprove it.
    E. The statement has no relevance to the conclusion.

15. In the spring of the following year, Barton Black is convicted of assaulting Beverly Willey on August 11.
    A. The statement proves the conclusion.
    B. The statement supports the conclusion but does not prove it.
    C. The statement disproves the conclusion.
    D. The statement weakens the conclusion but does not disprove it.
    E. The statement has no relevance to the conclusion.

5 (#2)

16. During their investigation of the assault, detectives determine that Beverly Willey was assaulted on the 12th floor of the office building.
    A. The statement proves the conclusion.
    B. The statement supports the conclusion but does not prove it.
    C. The statement disproves the conclusion.
    D. The statement weakens the conclusion but does not disprove it.
    E. The statement has no relevance to the conclusion.

16.____

17. The day after Beverly Willey's assault, Barton Black fled the area and was never seen again.
    A. The statement proves the conclusion.
    B. The statement supports the conclusion but does not prove it.
    C. The statement disproves the conclusion.
    D. The statement weakens the conclusion but does not disprove it.
    E. The statement has no relevance to the conclusion.

17.____

Questions 18-25.

DIRECTIONS: Questions 18 through 25 each provide four factual statements and a conclusion based on these statements. After reading the entire question, you will decide whether:
  A. The conclusion is proved by statements I-IV;
  B. The conclusion is disproved by statements I-IV.
  C. The facts are not sufficient to prove or disprove the conclusion.

18. FACTUAL STATEMENTS:
    I. Among five spice jars on the shelf, the sage is to the right of the parsley.
    II. The pepper is to the left of the basil.
    III. The nutmeg is between the sage and the pepper.
    IV. The pepper is the second spice from the left.

    CONCLUSION: The safe is the farthest to the right.
    A. The conclusion is proved by statements I-IV;
    B. The conclusion is disproved by statements I-IV.
    C. The facts are not sufficient to prove or disprove the conclusion.

18.____

19. FACTUAL STATEMENTS:
    I. Gear X rotates in a clockwise direction if Switch C is in the OFF position.
    II. Gear X will rotate in a counter-clockwise direction is Switch C is ON.
    III. If Gear X is rotating in a clockwise direction, then Gear Y will not be rotating at all.
    IV. Switch C is ON.

    CONCLUSION: Gear X is rotating in a counter-clockwise direction.
    A. The conclusion is proved by statements I-IV;
    B. The conclusion is disproved by statements I-IV.
    C. The facts are not sufficient to prove or disprove the conclusion.

19.____

20. FACTUAL STATEMENTS:
   I. Lane will leave for the Toronto meeting today only if Terence, Rourke, and Jackson all file their marketing reports by the end of the work day.
   II. Rourke will file her report on time only if Ganz submits last quarter's data.
   III. If Terence attends the security meeting, he will attend it with Jackson, and they will not file their marketing reports by the end of the work day.

   CONCLUSION: Lane will leave for the Toronto meeting today.
   A. The conclusion is proved by statements I-IV;
   B. The conclusion is disproved by statements I-IV.
   C. The facts are not sufficient to prove or disprove the conclusion.

21. FACTUAL STATEMENTS:
   I. Bob is in second place in the Boston Marathon.
   II. Gregory is winning the Boston Marathon.
   III. There are four miles to go in the race, and Bob is gaining on Gregory at the rate of 100 yards every minute.
   IV. There are 1760 yards in a mile and Gregory's usual pace during the Boston Marathon is one mile every six minutes.

   CONCLUSION: Bob wins the Boston Marathon.
   A. The conclusion is proved by statements I-IV;
   B. The conclusion is disproved by statements I-IV.
   C. The facts are not sufficient to prove or disprove the conclusion.

22. FACTUAL STATEMENTS:
   I. Four brothers are named Earl, John, Gary, and Pete.
   II. Earl and Pete are unmarried.
   III. John is shorter than the youngest of the four.
   IV. The oldest brother is married, and is also the tallest.

   CONCLUSION: Gary is the oldest brother.
   A. The conclusion is proved by statements I-IV;
   B. The conclusion is disproved by statements I-IV.
   C. The facts are not sufficient to prove or disprove the conclusion.

23. FACTUAL STATEMENTS:
   I. Brigade X is ten miles from the demilitarized zone.
   II. If General Woundwort gives the order, Brigade X will advance to the demilitarized zone, but not quickly enough to reach the zone before the conflict begins.
   III. Brigade Y, five miles behind Brigade X, will not advance unless General Woundwort gives the order.
   IV. Brigade Y advances.

7 (#2)

CONCLUSION: Brigade X reaches the demilitarized zone before the conflict begins.
  A. The conclusion is proved by statements I-IV;
  B. The conclusion is disproved by statements I-IV.
  C. The facts are not sufficient to prove or disprove the conclusion.

24. FACTUAL STATEMENTS:
  I. Jerry has decided to take a cab from Fullerton to Elverton.
  II. Chubby Cab charges $5 plus $3 a mile.
  III. Orange Cab charges $7.50 but gives free mileage for the first 5 miles.
  IV. After the first 5 miles, Orange Cab charges $2.50 a mile.

  CONCLUSION: Orange Cab is the cheaper fare from Fullerton to Elverton.
  A. The conclusion is proved by statements I-IV;
  B. The conclusion is disproved by statements I-IV.
  C. The facts are not sufficient to prove or disprove the conclusion.

25. FACTUAL STATEMENTS:
  I. Dan is never in class when his friend Lucy is absent.
  II. Lucy is never absent unless her mother is sick.
  III. If Lucy is in class, Sergio is in class also.
  IV. Sergio is never in class when Dalton is absent.

  CONCLUSION: If Lucy is absent, Dalton may be in class.
  A. The conclusion is proved by statements I-IV;
  B. The conclusion is disproved by statements I-IV.
  C. The facts are not sufficient to prove or disprove the conclusion.

## KEY (CORRECT ANSWERS)

| | | | | |
|---|---|---|---|---|
| 1. | C | | 11. | E |
| 2. | B | | 12. | B |
| 3. | B | | 13. | D |
| 4. | C | | 14. | E |
| 5. | A | | 15. | A |
| | | | | |
| 6. | A | | 16. | E |
| 7. | B | | 17. | C |
| 8. | C | | 18. | B |
| 9. | C | | 19. | A |
| 10. | B | | 20. | C |

| | |
|---|---|
| 21. | C |
| 22. | A |
| 23. | B |
| 24. | A |
| 25. | B |

# SOLUTIONS TO PROBLEMS

1. **CORRECT ANSWER: C**
Statement 1 only tells us that some employees who work in the Testing Department are statisticians. This means that we need to allow the possibility that at least one person in this department is not a statistician. Thus, if a person works in the Testing Department, we cannot conclude whether or not this individual is a statistician.

2. **CORRECT ANSWER: B**
If Hank had six coins, then the total of Gail's collection and Lawrence's collection would be four. Thus, if Gail gave all her coins to Lawrence, Lawrence would only have four coins. Thus, it would be impossible for Lawrence to have more coins than Hank.

3. **CORRECT ANSWER: B**
Statement 1 tells us that nobody loves everybody. If everybody loved Janet, then Statement 3 would imply that Ken loves everybody. This would contradict statement 1. The conclusion is disproved.

4. **CORRECT ANSWER: C**
Although most of the Torres family lives in East Los Angeles, we can assume that some members of this family do not live in East Los Angeles. Thus, we cannot prove or disprove that Joe, who is a member of the Torres family, lives in East Los Angeles.

5. **CORRECT ANSWER: A**
Since Dr. Johnson is on the $4^{th}$ floor, either (a) Dr. Kane is on the $5^{th}$ floor and Dr. Conlon is on the $3^{rd}$ floor, or (b) Dr. Kane is on the $3^{rd}$ floor and Dr. Conlon is on the $5^{th}$ floor. If option (b) were correct, then since Dr. Assad would be on the $1^{st}$ floor, it would be impossible for Dr. Steen's office to be between Dr. Conlon and Dr. Assad's office. Therefore, Dr. Kane's office must be on the $5^{th}$ floor. The order of the doctors' offices, from $5^{th}$ floor down to the $1^{st}$ floor is: Dr. Kane, Dr. Johnson, Dr. Conlon, Dr. Steen, Dr. Assad.

6. **CORRECT ANSWER: A**
Ray does not satisfy the requirement of holding his breath for two minutes under water, since he can only hold is breath for one minute in that setting. But if he tunnels through a snowbank with just a T-shirt and shorts, he will satisfy the eligibility requirement. Note that the eligibility requirement contains the key word "or." So only one of the two clauses separated by "or" need to be fulfilled.

7. **CORRECT ANSWER: B**
Statement 2 says that four sharps is equivalent to one tinplot. This means that a tinplot is worth more than a sharp. The conclusion is disproved. We note that the order of these items, from most valuable to least valuable are: tinplot, sharp, mark, plunk.

8. **CORRECT ANSWER: C**
We can only conclude that gibbons and lemurs are fed lettuce and bananas. We can neither prove nor disprove that these animals are types of monkeys.

9. **CORRECT ANSWER: C**
We know that all Salishan Indians live east of the Continental Divide. But some non-members of this tribe of Indians may also live east of the Continental Divide. Since none of the members of the Blackfoot tribe belong to the Salishan Indian tribe, we cannot draw any conclusion about the location of the Blackfoot tribe with respect to the Continental Divide.

18. **CORRECT ANSWER: B**
Since the pepper is second from the left and the nutmeg is between the sage and the pepper, the positions 2, 3, and 4 (from the left) are pepper, nutmeg, sage. By statement II, the basil must be in position 5, which implies that the parsley is in position 1. Therefore, the basil, not the sage, is farthest to the right. The conclusion disproved.

19. **CORRECT ANSWER: A**
Statement II assures us that if switch C is ON, then Gear X is rotating in a counterclockwise direction. The conclusion is proved.

20. **CORRECT ANSWER: C**
Based on Statement IV, followed by Statement II, we conclude that Ganz and Rourke will file their reports on time. Statement III reveals that if Terence and Jackson attend the security meeting, they will fail to file their reports on time. We have no further information if Terence and Jackson attended the security meeting, so we are not able to either confirm or deny that their reports were filed on time. This implies that we cannot know for certain that Lane will leave for his meeting in Toronto.

21. **CORRECT ANSWER: C**
Although Bob is in second place behind Gregory, we cannot deduce how far behind Gregory he is running. At Gregory's current pace, he will cover four miles in 24 minutes. If Bob were only 100 yards behind Gregory, he would catch up to Gregory in one minute. But if Bob were very far behind Gregory, for example 5 miles, this is the equivalent of (5)(1760) = 8800 yards. Then Bob would need 8800/100 = 88 minutes to catch up to Gregory. Thus, the given facts are not sufficient to draw a conclusion.

22. **CORRECT ANSWER: A**
Statement II tells us that neither Earl nor Pete could be the oldest; also, either John or Gary is married. Statement IV reveals that the oldest brother is both married and the tallest. By Statement III, John cannot be the tallest. Since John is not the tallest, he is not the oldest. Thus, the oldest brother must be Gary. The conclusion is proved.

23. **CORRECT ANSWER: B**
By Statements III and IV, General Woundwort must have given the order to advance. Statement II then tells us that Brigade X will advance to the demilitarized zone, but not soon enough before the conflict begins. Thus, the conclusion is disproved.

24. CORRECT ANSWER: A
If the distance is 5 miles or less, then the cost for the Orange Cab is only $7.50, whereas the cost for the Chubby Cab is $5 + 3x, where x represents the number of miles traveled. For 1 to 5 miles, the cost of the Chubby Cab is between $8 and $20. This means that for a distance of 5 miles, the Orange Cab costs $7.50, whereas the Chubby Cab costs $20. After 5 miles, the cost per mile of the Chubby Cab exceeds the cost per mile of the Orange Cab. Thus, regardless of the actual distance between Fullerton and Elverton, the cost for the Orange Cab will be cheaper than that of the Chubby Cab.

25. CORRECT ANSWER: B
It looks like "Dalton" should be replaced by "Dan" in the conclusion. Then by statement I, if Lucy is absent, Dan is never in class. Thus, the conclusion is disproved.

# EVALUATING CONCLUSIONS IN LIGHT OF KNOWN FACTS
# EXAMINATION SECTION
# TEST 1

DIRECTIONS: Each question or incomplete statement is followed by several suggested answers or completions. Select the one that BEST answers the question or completes the statement. *PRINT THE LETTER OF THE CORRECT ANSWER IN THE SPACE AT THE RIGHT.*

Questions 1-9.

DIRECTIONS: In Questions 1 through 9, you will read a set of facts and a conclusion drawn from them. The conclusion may be valid or invalid, based on the facts. It is your task to determine the validity of the conclusion.
For each question, select the letter before the statement that BEST expresses the relationship between the given facts and the conclusion that has been drawn from them. Your choices are:
A. The facts prove the conclusion.
B. The facts disprove the conclusion; or
C. The facts neither prove nor disprove the conclusion.

1. FACTS: Lauren must use Highway 29 to get to work. Lauren has a meeting today at 9:00 A.M. If she misses the meeting, Lauren will probably lose a major account. Highway 29 is closed all day today for repairs.

    CONCLUSION: Lauren will not be able to get to work.

    A. The facts prove the conclusion.
    B. The facts disprove the conclusion.
    C. The facts neither prove nor disprove the conclusion.

2. FACTS: The Tumbleweed Follies, a traveling burlesque show, is looking for a new line dancer. The position requires both singing and dancing skills. If the show cannot fill the position by Friday, it will begin to look for a magician to fill the time slot currently held by the line dancers. Willa, who wants to audition for the line dancing position, can sing, but cannot dance.

    CONCLUSION: Willa is qualified to audition for the part of line dancer.

    A. The facts prove the conclusion.
    B. The facts disprove the conclusion.
    C. The facts neither prove nor disprove the conclusion.

3. FACTS: Terry owns two dogs, Spike and Stan. One of the dogs is short-haired and has blue eyes. One dog as a pink nose. The blue-eyed dog never barks. One of the dogs has white fur on its paws. Sam has long hair.

   CONCLUSION: Spike never barks.

   A. The facts prove the conclusion.
   B. The facts disprove the conclusion.
   C. The facts neither prove nor disprove the conclusion.

4. FACTS: No science teachers are members of the PTA. Some English teachers are members of the PTA. Some English teachers in the PTA also wear glasses. Every PTA member is required to sit on the dunking stool at the student carnival except for those who wear glasses, who will be exempt. Those who are exempt, however, will have to officiate the hamster races. All of the English teachers in the PTA who do not wear glasses are married.

   CONCLUSION: All the married English teachers in the PTA will set on the dunking stool at the student carnival.

   A. The facts prove the conclusion.
   B. The facts disprove the conclusion.
   C. The facts neither prove nor disprove the conclusion.

5. FACTS: If the price of fuel is increased and sales remain constant, oil company profits will increase. The price of fuel was increased, and market experts project that sales levels are likely to be maintained.

   CONCLUSION: The price of fuel will increase.

   A. The facts prove the conclusion.
   B. The facts disprove the conclusion.
   C. The facts neither prove nor disprove the conclusion.

6. FACTS: Some members of the gymnastics team are double-jointed, and some members of the gymnastics team ae also on the lacrosse team. Some double-jointed members of the gymnastics team are also coaches. All gymnastics team members perform floor exercises, except the coaches. All the double-jointed members of the gymnastics team who are not coaches are freshmen.

   CONCLUSION: Some double-jointed freshmen are coaches.

   A. The facts prove the conclusion.
   B. The facts disprove the conclusion.
   C. The facts neither prove nor disprove the conclusion.

3 (#1)

7. FACTS: Each member of the International Society speaks at least one foreign language, but no member speaks more than four foreign languages. Five members speak Spanish; three speak Mandarin; four speak French; four speak German; and five speak a foreign language other than Spanish, Mandarin, French, or German.

   CONCLUSION: The lowest possible number of members in the International Society is eight.

   A. The facts prove the conclusion.
   B. The facts disprove the conclusion.
   C. The facts neither prove nor disprove the conclusion.

   7.____

8. FACTS: Mary keeps seven cats in her apartment. Only three of the cats will eat the same kind of food. Mary wants to keep at least one extra bag of each kind of food.

   CONCLUSION: The minimum number of bags Mary will need to keep as extra is 7.

   A. The facts prove the conclusion.
   B. The facts disprove the conclusion.
   C. The facts neither prove nor disprove the conclusion.

   8.____

9. FACTS: In Ed and Marie's exercise group, everyone likes the treadmill or the stationary bicycle, or both, but Ed does not like the stationary bicycle. Marie has not expressed a preference, but spends most of her time on the stationary bicycle.

   CONCLUSION: Everyone in the group who does not like the treadmill likes the stationary bicycle.

   A. The facts prove the conclusion.
   B. The facts disprove the conclusion.
   C. The facts neither prove nor disprove the conclusion.

   9.____

Questions 10-17.

DIRECTIONS: Questions 10 through 17 are based on the following reading passage. It is not your knowledge of the particular topic that is being tested, but your ability to reason based on what you have read. The passage is likely to detail several proposed courses of action and factors affecting these proposals. The reading passage is followed by a conclusion or outcome based on the facts in the passage, or a description of a decision taken regarding the situation. The conclusion is followed by a number of statements that have a possible connection to the conclusion. For each statement, you are to determine whether:

A. The statement proves the conclusion.
B. The statement supports the conclusion but does not prove it.
C. The statement disproves the conclusion.
D. The statement weakens the conclusion but does not disprove it.
E. The statement has no relevance to the conclusion.

Remember that the conclusion after the passage is to be accepted as the outcome of what actually happened, and that you are being asked to evaluate the impact each statement would have had on the conclusion.

PASSAGE

The Owyhee Mission School District's Board of Directors is hosting a public meeting to debate the merits of the proposed abolition of all bilingual education programs within the district. The group that has made the proposal believes the programs, which teach immigrant children academic subjects in their native language until they have learned English well enough to join mainstream classes, inhibit the ability of students to acquire English quickly and succeed in school and in the larger American society. Such programs, they argue, are also a wasteful drain on the district's already scant resources.

At the meeting, several teachers and parents stand to speak out against the proposal. The purpose of an education, they say, should be to build upon, rather than dismantle, a minority child's language and culture. By teaching children in academic subjects in their native tongues, while simultaneously offering English language instruction, schools can meet the goals of learning English and progressing through academic subjects along with their peers.

Hiram Nguyen, a representative of the parents whose children are currently enrolled in bilingual education, stands at the meeting to express the parents' wishes. The parents have been polled, he says, and are overwhelmingly of the opinion that while language and culture are important to them, they are not things that will disappear from the students' lives if they are no longer taught in the classroom. The most important issue for the parents is whether their children will succeed in school and be competitive in the larger American society. If bilingual education can be demonstrated to do that, then the parents are in favor of continuing it.

At the end of the meeting, a proponent of the plan, Oscar Ramos, stands to clarify some misconceptions about the proposal. It does not call for a "sink or swim" approach, he says, but allows for an interpreter to be present in mainstream classes to explain anything a student finds too complex or confusing.

The last word of the meeting is given to Delia Cruz, a bilingual teacher at one of the district's elementary schools. A student is bound to find anything complex or confusing, she says, if it is spoken in a language he has never heard before. It is more wasteful to place children in classrooms where they don't understand anything, she says, than it is to try to teach them something useful as they are learning the English language.

CONCLUSION: After the meeting, the Owyhee Mission School District's Board of Directors votes to terminate all the district's bilingual education programs at the end of the current academic year, but to maintain the current level of funding to each of the schools that have programs cut.

5 (#1)

10. A poll conducted by the *Los Angeles Times* at approximately the same time as the Board's meeting indicated that 75% of the people were opposed to bilingual education; among Latinos, opposition was 84%.
    A. The statement proves the conclusion.
    B. The statement supports the conclusion but does not prove it.
    C. The statement disproves the conclusion.
    D. The statement weakens the conclusion but does not disprove it.
    E. The statement has no relevance to the conclusion.

    10._____

11. Of all the studies connected on bilingual education programs, 64% indicate that students learned English grammar better in "sink or swim" classes without any special features than they did in bilingual education classes.
    A. The statement proves the conclusion.
    B. The statement supports the conclusion but does not prove it.
    C. The statement disproves the conclusion.
    D. The statement weakens the conclusion but does not disprove it.
    E. The statement has no relevance to the conclusion.

    11._____

12. In the academic year that begins after the Board's vote, Montgomery Burns Elementary, an Owyhee Mission District school, launches a new bilingual program for the children of Somali immigrants.
    A. The statement proves the conclusion.
    B. The statement supports the conclusion but does not prove it.
    C. The statement disproves the conclusion.
    D. The statement weakens the conclusion but does not disprove it.
    E. The statement has no relevance to the conclusion.

    12._____

13. In the previous academic year, under severe budget restraints, the Owyhee Mission District cut all physical education, music, and art classes, but its funding for bilingual education classes increased by 18%.
    A. The statement proves the conclusion.
    B. The statement supports the conclusion but does not prove it.
    C. The statement disproves the conclusion.
    D. The statement weakens the conclusion but does not disprove it.
    E. The statement has no relevance to the conclusion.

    13._____

14. Before the Board votes, a polling consultant conducts randomly sampled assessments of immigrant students who enrolled in Owyhee District schools at a time when they did not speak any English at all. Ten years after graduating from high school, 44% of those who received bilingual education were professionals – doctors, lawyers, educators, engineers, etc. Of those who did not receive bilingual education, 38% were professionals.
    A. The statement proves the conclusion.
    B. The statement supports the conclusion but does not prove it.
    C. The statement disproves the conclusion.
    D. The statement weakens the conclusion but does not disprove it.
    E. The statement has no relevance to the conclusion.

    14._____

15. Over the past several years, the scores of Owyhee District students have gradually declined, and enrollment numbers have followed as anxious parents transferred their children to other schools or applied for a state-funded voucher program.
    A. The statement proves the conclusion.
    B. The statement supports the conclusion but does not prove it.
    C. The statement disproves the conclusion.
    D. The statement weakens the conclusion but does not disprove it.
    E. The statement has no relevance to the conclusion.

16. California and Massachusetts, two of the most liberal states in the country, have each passed ballot measures banning bilingual education in public schools.
    A. The statement proves the conclusion.
    B. The statement supports the conclusion but does not prove it.
    C. The statement disproves the conclusion.
    D. The statement weakens the conclusion but does not disprove it.
    E. The statement has no relevance to the conclusion.

17. In the academic year that begins after the Board's vote, no Owyhee Mission Schools are conducting bilingual instruction.
    A. The statement proves the conclusion.
    B. The statement supports the conclusion but does not prove it.
    C. The statement disproves the conclusion.
    D. The statement weakens the conclusion but does not disprove it.
    E. The statement has no relevance to the conclusion.

Questions 18-25.

DIRECTIONS: Questions 18 through 25 each provide four factual statements and a conclusion based on these statements. After reading the entire question, you will decide whether:
   A. The conclusion is proved by Statements 1-4;
   B. The conclusion is disproved by Statements 1-4;
   C. The facts are not sufficient to prove or disprove the conclusion.

18. FACTUAL STATEMENTS:
    1) Gear X rotates in a clockwise direction if Switch C is in the OFF position.
    2) Gear X will rotate in a counter-clockwise direction if Switch C is ON.
    3) If Gear X is rotating in a clockwise direction, then Gear Y will not be rotating at all.
    4) Switch C is OFF.

    CONCLUSION: Gear Y is rotating.

    A. The conclusion is proved by Statements 1-4;
    B. The conclusion is disproved by Statements 1-4;
    C. The facts are not sufficient to prove or disprove the conclusion.

19. **FACTUAL STATEMENTS:**                                                                                                   19._____
    1) Mark is older than Jim but younger than Dan.
    2) Fern is older than Mark but younger than Silas.
    3) Dan is younger than Silas but older than Edward.
    4) Edward is older than Mark but younger than Fern.

    CONCLUSION: Dan is older than Fern.

    A. The conclusion is proved by Statements 1-4;
    B. The conclusion is disproved by Statements 1-4;
    C. The facts are not sufficient to prove or disprove the conclusion.

20. **FACTUAL STATEMENTS:**                                                                                                   20._____
    1) Each of Fred's three sofa cushions lies on top of four lost coins.
    2) The cushion on the right covers two pennies and two dimes.
    3) The middle cushion covers two dimes and two quarters.
    4) The cushion on the left covers two nickels and two quarters.

    CONCLUSION: To be guaranteed of retrieving at least one coin of each denomination, and without looking at any of the coins, Frank must take three coins each from under the cushions on the right and the left.

    A. The conclusion is proved by Statements 1-4;
    B. The conclusion is disproved by Statements 1-4;
    C. The facts are not sufficient to prove or disprove the conclusion.

21. **FACTUAL STATEMENTS:**                                                                                                   21._____
    1) The door to the hammer mill chamber is locked if light 6 is red.
    2) The door to the hammer mill chamber is locked only when the mill is operating.
    3) If the mill is not operating, light 6 is blue.
    4) The door to the hammer mill chamber is locked.

    CONCLUSION: The mill is in operation.

    A. The conclusion is proved by Statements 1-4;
    B. The conclusion is disproved by Statements 1-4;
    C. The facts are not sufficient to prove or disprove the conclusion.

22. **FACTUAL STATEMENTS:**                                                                                                   22._____
    1) In a five-story office building, where each story is occupied by a single professional, Dr. Kane's office is above Dr. Assad's.
    2) Dr. Johnson's office is between Dr. Kane's and Dr. Conlon's.
    3) Dr. Steen's office is between Dr. Conlon's and Dr. Assad's.
    4) Dr. Johnson is on the fourth story.

    CONCLUSION: Dr. Steen occupies the second story.

A. The conclusion is proved by Statements 1-4;
B. The conclusion is disproved by Statements 1-4;
C. The facts are not sufficient to prove or disprove the conclusion.

23. FACTUAL STATEMENTS:
    1) On Saturday, farmers Hank, Earl, Roy, and Cletus plowed a total of 520 acres.
    2) Hank plowed twice as many acres as Roy.
    3) Roy plowed half as much as the farmer who plowed the most.
    4) Cletus plowed 160 acres.

    CONCLUSION: Hank plowed 200 acres.
    A. The conclusion is proved by Statements 1-4;
    B. The conclusion is disproved by Statements 1-4;
    C. The facts are not sufficient to prove or disprove the conclusion.

24. FACTUAL STATEMENTS:
    1) Four travelers – Tina, Jodie, Alex, and Oscar – each traveled to a different island – Aruba, Jamaica, Nevis, and Barbados – but not necessarily respectively.
    2) Tina did not travel as far to Jamaica as Jodie traveled to her island.
    3) Oscar traveled twice as far as Alex, who traveled the same distance as the traveler who went to Aruba.
    4) Oscar went to Barbados.

    CONCLUSION: Oscar traveled the farthest.

    A. The conclusion is proved by Statements 1-4;
    B. The conclusion is disproved by Statements 1-4;
    C. The facts are not sufficient to prove or disprove the conclusion.

25. FACTUAL STATEMENT:
    1) In the natural history museum, every Native American display that contains pottery also contains beadwork.
    2) Some of the displays containing lodge replicas also contain beadwork.
    3) The display on the Choctaw, a Native American tribe, contains pottery.
    4) The display on the Modoc, a Native American tribe, contains only two of these items.

    CONCLUSION: If the Modoc display contains pottery, it does not contain lodge replicas.

    A. The conclusion is proved by Statements 1-4;
    B. The conclusion is disproved by Statements 1-4;
    C. The facts are not sufficient to prove or disprove the conclusion.

## KEY (CORRECT ANSWERS)

1. A
2. B
3. A
4. A
5. C

6. B
7. B
8. B
9. A
10. B

11. B
12. C
13. B
14. D
15. E

16. E
17. A
18. B
19. C
20. A

21. A
22. A
23. C
24. A
25. A

# TEST 2

DIRECTIONS: Each question or incomplete statement is followed by several suggested answers or completions. Select the one that BEST answers the question or completes the statement. *PRINT THE LETTER OF THE CORRECT ANSWER IN THE SPACE AT THE RIGHT.*

Questions 1-9.

DIRECTIONS: In Questions 1 through 9, you will read a set of facts and a conclusion drawn from them. The conclusion may be valid or invalid, based on the facts. It is your task to determine the validity of the conclusion.
For each question, select the letter before the statement that BEST expresses the relationship between the given facts and the conclusion that has been drawn from them. Your choices are:
   A. The facts prove the conclusion.
   B. The facts disprove the conclusion; or
   C. The facts neither prove nor disprove the conclusion.

1. FACTS: If the maximum allowable income for Medicaid recipients is increased, the number of Medicaid recipients will increase. If the number of Medicaid recipients increases, more funds must be allocated to the Medicaid program, which will require a tax increase. Taxes cannot be approved without the approval of the legislature. The legislature probably will not approve a tax increase.

   CONCLUSION: The maximum allowable income for Medicaid recipients will increase.

   A. The facts prove the conclusion.
   B. The facts disprove the conclusion; or
   C. The facts neither prove nor disprove the conclusion.

2. FACTS: All the dentists on the baseball team are short. Everyone in the dugout is a dentist, but not everyone in the dugout is short. The baseball team is not made up of people of any particular profession.

   CONCLUSION: Some people who are not dentists are in the dugout.

   A. The facts prove the conclusion.
   B. The facts disprove the conclusion; or
   C. The facts neither prove nor disprove the conclusion.

3. FACTS: A taxi company's fleet is divided into two fleets. Fleet One contains cabs A, B, C, and D. Fleet Two contains E, F, G, and H. Each cab is either yellow or green. Five of the cabs are yellow. Cabs A and E are not both yellow. Either Cab C or F, or both, are not yellow. Cabs B and H are either both yellow or both green.

   CONCLUSION: Cab H is green.

1.\_\_\_\_

2.\_\_\_\_

3.\_\_\_\_

2 (#2)

    A. The facts prove the conclusion.
    B. The facts disprove the conclusion; or
    C. The facts neither prove nor disprove the conclusion.

4. FACTS: Most people in the skydiving club are not afraid of heights. Everyone in the skydiving club makes three parachute jumps a month.

   CONCLUSION: At least one person who is afraid of heights makes three parachute jumps a month.

       A. The facts prove the conclusion.
       B. The facts disprove the conclusion; or
       C. The facts neither prove nor disprove the conclusion.

5. FACTS: If the Board approves the new rule, the agency will move to a new location immediately. If the agency moves, five new supervisors will be immediately appointed. The Board has approved the new proposal.

   CONCLUSION: No new supervisors were appointed.

       A. The facts prove the conclusion.
       B. The facts disprove the conclusion; or
       C. The facts neither prove nor disprove the conclusion.

6. FACTS: All the workers at the supermarket chew gum when they sack groceries. Sometimes Lance, a supermarket worker, doesn't chew gum at all when he works. Another supermarket worker, Jenny, chews gum the whole time she is at work.

   CONCLUSION: Jenny always sacks groceries when she is at work.

7. FACTS: Lake Lottawatta is bigger than Lake Tacomi. Lake Tacomi and Lake Ottawa are exactly the same size. All lakes in Montana are bigger than Lake Ottawa.

   CONCLUSION: Lake Lottawatta is in Montana.

       A. The facts prove the conclusion.
       B. The facts disprove the conclusion; or
       C. The facts neither prove nor disprove the conclusion.

8. FACTS: Two men, Cox and Taylor, are playing poker at a table. Taylor has a pair of aces in his hand. One man is smoking a cigar. One of them has no pairs in his hand and is wearing an eye patch. The man wearing the eye patch is smoking a cigar. One man is bald.

   CONCLUSION: Cox is smoking a cigar.

A. The facts prove the conclusion.
B. The facts disprove the conclusion; or
C. The facts neither prove nor disprove the conclusion.

9. FACTS: All Kwakiutls are Wakashan Indians. All Wakashan Indians originated on Vancouver Island. The Nootka also originated on Vancouver Island.

   CONCLUSION: Kwakiutls originated on Vancouver Island.

   A. The facts prove the conclusion.
   B. The facts disprove the conclusion; or
   C. The facts neither prove nor disprove the conclusion.

9.____

Questions 10-17.

DIRECTIONS: Questions 10 through 17 are based on the following reading passage. It is not your knowledge of the particular topic that is being tested, but your ability to reason based on what you have read. The passage is likely to detail several proposed courses of action and factors affecting these proposals. The reading passage is followed by a conclusion or outcome based on the facts in the passage, or a description of a decision taken regarding the situation. The conclusion is followed by a number of statements that have a possible connection to the conclusion. For each statement, you are to determine whether:
A. The statement proves the conclusion.
B. The statement supports the conclusion but does not prove it.
C. The statement disproves the conclusion.
D. The statement weakens the conclusion but does not disprove it.
E. The statement has no relevance to the conclusion.

Remember that the conclusion after the passage is to be accepted as the outcome of what actually happened, and that you are being asked to evaluate the impact each statement would have had on the conclusion.

## PASSAGE

The World Wide Web portal and search engine, HipBot, is considering becoming a subscription-only service, locking out nonsubscribers from the content on its web site. HipBot currently relies solely on advertising revenues.

HipBot's content director says that by taking in an annual fee from each customer, the company can both increase profits and provide premium content that no other portal can match.

The marketing director disagrees, saying that there is no guarantee that anyone who now visits the web site for free will agree to pay for the privilege of visiting it again. Most will probably simply use the other major portals. Also, HipBot's advertising clients will not be happy when they learn that the site will be viewed by a more limited number of people.

4 (#2)

CONCLUSION: In January of 2016, the CEO of HipBot decides to keep the portal open to all web users, with some limited "premium content" available to subscribers who don't mind paying a little extra to access it. The company will aim to maintain, or perhaps increase, its advertising revenue.

10. In an independent marketing survey, 62% of respondents said they "strongly agree" with the following statement: "I almost never pay attention to advertisements that appear on the World Wide Web."
    A. The statement proves the conclusion.
    B. The statement supports the conclusion but does not prove it.
    C. The statement disproves the conclusion.
    D. The statement weakens the conclusion but does not disprove it.
    E. The statement has no relevance to the conclusion.

10.____

11. When it learns about the subscription-only debate going on at HipBot, Wernham Hogg Entertainment, one of HipBot's most reliable clients, says it will withdraw its ads and place them on a free web portal if HipBot decides to limit its content to subscribers. Wernham Hogg pays HipBot about $6 million annually – about 12% of HipBot's gross revenues – to run its ads online.
    A. The statement proves the conclusion.
    B. The statement supports the conclusion but does not prove it.
    C. The statement disproves the conclusion.
    D. The statement weakens the conclusion but does not disprove it.
    E. The statement has no relevance to the conclusion.

11.____

12. At the end of the second quarter of FY 2016, after continued stagnant profits, the CEO of HipBot assembles a blue ribbon commission to gather and analyze data on the costs, benefits, and feasibility of adding a limited amount of "premium" content to the HipBot portal.
    A. The statement proves the conclusion.
    B. The statement supports the conclusion but does not prove it.
    C. The statement disproves the conclusion.
    D. The statement weakens the conclusion but does not disprove it.
    E. The statement has no relevance to the conclusion.

12.____

13. In the following fiscal year, Wernham Hogg Entertainment, satisfied with the "hit counts" on HipBot's free web site, spends another $1 million on advertisements that will appear on web pages that are available to HipBot's "premium subscribers.
    A. The statement proves the conclusion.
    B. The statement supports the conclusion but does not prove it.
    C. The statement disproves the conclusion.
    D. The statement weakens the conclusion but does not disprove it.
    E. The statement has no relevance to the conclusion.

13.____

14. HipBot's information technology director reports that the engineers in his department have come up with a feature that will search not only individual web pages, but tie into other web-based search engines, as well, and then comb through all these results to find those most relevant to the user's search.

14.____

A. The statement proves the conclusion.
B. The statement supports the conclusion but does not prove it.
C. The statement disproves the conclusion.
D. The statement weakens the conclusion but does not disprove it.
E. The statement has no relevance to the conclusion.

15. In an independent marketing survey, 79% of respondents said they "strongly agree" with the following statement: "Many web sites are so dominated by advertisements these days that it is increasingly frustrating to find the content I want to read or see."
    A. The statement proves the conclusion.
    B. The statement supports the conclusion but does not prove it.
    C. The statement disproves the conclusion.
    D. The statement weakens the conclusion but does not disprove it.
    E. The statement has no relevance to the conclusion.

15.____

16. After three years of studies at the federal level, the Department of Commerce releases a report suggesting that, in general, the only private "subscriber-only" web sites that do well financially are those with a very specialized user population.
    A. The statement proves the conclusion.
    B. The statement supports the conclusion but does not prove it.
    C. The statement disproves the conclusion.
    D. The statement weakens the conclusion but does not disprove it.
    E. The statement has no relevance to the conclusion.

16.____

17. HipBot's own marketing research indicates that the introduction of premium content has the potential to attract new users to the HipBot portal.
    A. The statement proves the conclusion.
    B. The statement supports the conclusion but does not prove it.
    C. The statement disproves the conclusion.
    D. The statement weakens the conclusion but does not disprove it.
    E. The statement has no relevance to the conclusion.

17.____

Questions 18-25.

DIRECTIONS: Questions 18 through 25 each provide four factual statements and a conclusion based on these statements. After reading the entire question, you will decide whether:
  A. The conclusion is proved by Statements 1-4;
  B. The conclusion is disproved by Statements 1-4;
  C. The facts are not sufficient to prove or disprove the conclusion.

18. FACTUAL STATEMENTS:
    1) If the alarm goes off, Sam will wake up.
    2) If Tandy wakes up before 4:00, Linda will leave the bedroom and sleep on the couch.
    3) If Linda leaves the bedroom, she'll check the alarm to make sure it is working.
    4) The alarm goes off.

    CONCLUSION: Tandy woke up before 4:00.

    A. The conclusion is proved by Statements 1-4;
    B. The conclusion is disproved by Statements 1-4;
    C. The facts are not sufficient to prove or disprove the conclusion.

19. FACTUAL STATEMENTS:
    1) Four brothers are named Earl, John, Gary, and Pete.
    2) Earl and Pete are unmarried.
    3) John is shorter than the youngest of the four.
    4) The oldest brother is married, and is also the tallest.

    CONCLUSION: Pete is the youngest brother.

    A. The conclusion is proved by Statements 1-4;
    B. The conclusion is disproved by Statements 1-4;
    C. The facts are not sufficient to prove or disprove the conclusion.

20. FACTUAL STATEMENTS:
    1) Automobile engines are cooled either by air or by liquid.
    2) If the engine is small and simple enough, air from a belt-driven fan will cool it sufficiently.
    3) Most newer automobile engines are too complicated to be air-cooled.
    4) Air-cooled engines are cheaper and easier to build then liquid-cooled engines.

    CONCLUSION: Most newer automobile engines use liquid coolant.

    A. The conclusion is proved by Statements 1-4;
    B. The conclusion is disproved by Statements 1-4;
    C. The facts are not sufficient to prove or disprove the conclusion.

21. FACTUAL STATEMENTS:
    1) Erica will only file a lawsuit if she is injured while parasailing.
    2) If Rick orders Trip to run a rope test, Trip will check the rigging.
    3) If the rigging does not malfunction, Erica will not be injured.
    4) Rick orders Trip to run a rope test.

CONCLUSION: Erica does not file a lawsuit.

A. The conclusion is proved by Statements 1-4;
B. The conclusion is disproved by Statements 1-4;
C. The facts are not sufficient to prove or disprove the conclusion.

22. FACTUAL STATEMENTS:
    1) On Maple Street, which is four blocks long, Bill's shop is two blocks east of Ken's shop.
    2) Ken's shop is one block west of the only shop on Maple Street with an awning.
    3) Erma's shop is one block west of the easternmost block.
    4) Bill's shop is on the easternmost block.

    CONCLUSION: Bill's shop has an awning.

    A. The conclusion is proved by Statements 1-4;
    B. The conclusion is disproved by Statements 1-4;
    C. The facts are not sufficient to prove or disprove the conclusion.

23. FACTUAL STATEMENTS:
    1) Gear X rotates in a clockwise direction if Switch C is in the OFF position.
    2) Gear X will rotate in a counter-clockwise direction if Switch C is ON.
    3) If Gear X is rotating in a clockwise direction, then Gear Y will not be rotating at all.
    4) Gear Y is rotating.

    CONCLUSION: Gear X is rotating in a counter-clockwise direction.

    A. The conclusion is proved by Statements 1-4;
    B. The conclusion is disproved by Statements 1-4;
    C. The facts are not sufficient to prove or disprove the conclusion.

24. FACTUAL STATEMENTS:
    1) The Republic of Garbanzo's currency system has four basic denominations: the pastor, the noble, the donner, and the rojo.
    2) A pastor is worth 2 nobles.
    3) 2 donners can be exchanged for a rojo.
    4) 3 pastors are equal in value to 2 donners.

    CONCLUSION: The rojo is most valuable.

    A. The conclusion is proved by Statements 1-4;
    B. The conclusion is disproved by Statements 1-4;
    C. The facts are not sufficient to prove or disprove the conclusion.

25. FACTUAL STATEMENTS:
　1) At Prickett's Nursery, the only citrus trees left are either Meyer lemons or Valencia oranges, and every citrus tree left is either a dwarf or a semidwarf.
　2) Half of the semidwarf trees are Meyer lemons.
　3) There are more semidwarf trees left than dwarf trees.
　4) A quarter of the dwarf trees are Valencia oranges.

CONCLUSION: There are more Valencia oranges left at Prickett's Nursery than Meyer lemons.

　A. The conclusion is proved by Statements 1-4;
　B. The conclusion is disproved by Statements 1-4;
　C. The facts are not sufficient to prove or disprove the conclusion.

---

# KEY (CORRECT ANSWERS)

| | | | | |
|---|---|---|---|---|
| 1. | C | | 11. | B |
| 2. | B | | 12. | C |
| 3. | B | | 13. | A |
| 4. | A | | 14. | E |
| 5. | B | | 15. | D |
| 6. | C | | 16. | B |
| 7. | C | | 17. | B |
| 8. | A | | 18. | C |
| 9. | A | | 19. | C |
| 10. | E | | 20. | A |

| | |
|---|---|
| 21. | C |
| 22. | B |
| 23. | C |
| 24. | A |
| 25. | B |

# INTERPRETING STATISTICAL DATA
# GRAPHS, CHARTS AND TABLES
# EXAMINATION SECTION
# TEST 1

DIRECTIONS: Each questioner incomplete statement is followed by several suggested answers or completions. Select the one that BEST answers the question or completes the statement. *PRINT THE LETTER OF THE CORRECT ANSWER IN THE SPACE AT THE RIGHT.*

Questions 1-3.

DIRECTIONS: Questions 1 through 3 are to be answered SOLELY on the basis of the following table.

### QUARTERLY SALES REPORTED BY MAJOR INDUSTRY GROUPS

#### DECEMBER 2021 – FEBRUARY 2023
Reported Sales, Taxable & Non-Taxable (in Millions)

| Industry Groups | 12/21-2/22 | 3/22-5/22 | 6/22-8/22 | 9/22-11/22 | 12/22-2/23 |
|---|---|---|---|---|---|
| Retailers | 2,802 | 2,711 | 2,475 | 2,793 | 2,974 |
| Wholesalers | 2,404 | 2,237 | 2,269 | 2,485 | 2,974 |
| Manufacturers | 3,016 | 2,888 | 3,001 | 3,518 | 3,293 |
| Services | 1,034 | 1,065 | 984 | 1,132 | 1,092 |

1. The trend in total reported sales may be described as

   A. downward
   B. downward and upward
   C. horizontal
   D. upward

2. The two industry groups that reveal a similar seasonal pattern for the period December 2021 through November 2022 are

   A. retailers and manufacturers
   B. retailers and wholesalers
   C. wholesalers and manufacturers
   D. wholesalers and service

3. Reported sales were at a MINIMUM between

   A. December 2021 and February 2022
   B. March 2022 and May 2022
   C. June 2022 and August 2022
   D. September 2022 and November 2022

# TEST 2

DIRECTIONS: Each question or incomplete statement is followed by several suggested answers or completions. Select the one that BEST answers the question or completes the statement. *PRINT THE LETTER OF THE CORRECT ANSWER IN THE SPACE AT THE RIGHT*

Questions 1-4.

DIRECTIONS: Questions 1 through 4 are to be answered SOLELY on the basis of the following information.

The income elasticity of demand for selected items of consumer demand in the United States are:

| Item | Elasticity |
|---|---|
| Airline Travel | 5.66 |
| Alcohol | .62 |
| Dentist Fees | 1.00 |
| Electric Utilities | 3.00 |
| Gasoline | 1.29 |
| Intercity Bus | 1.89 |
| Local Bus | 1.41 |
| Restaurant Meals | .75 |

1. The demand for the item listed below that would be MOST adversely affected by a decrease in income is

   A. alcohol
   B. electric utilities
   C. gasoline
   D. restaurant meals

2. The item whose relative change in demand would be the same as the relative change in income would be

   A. dentist fees
   B. gasoline
   C. restaurant meals
   D. none of the above

3. If income increases by 12 percent, the demand for restaurant meals may be expected to increase by

   A. 9 percent
   B. 12 percent
   C. 16 percent
   D. none of the above

4. On the basis of the above information, the item whose demand would be MOST adversely affected by an increase in the sales tax from 7 percent to 8 percent to be passed on to the consumer in the form of higher prices

   A. would be airline travel
   B. would be alcohol
   C. would be gasoline
   D. cannot be determined

# TEST 3

DIRECTIONS: Each question or incomplete statement is followed by several suggested answers or completions. Select the one that BEST answers the question or completes the statement. *PRINT THE LETTER OF THE CORRECT ANSWER IN THE SPACE AT THE RIGHT.*

Questions 1-3.

DIRECTIONS: Questions 1 through 3 are to be answered SOLELY on the basis of the following graphs depicting various relationships in a single retail store.

### GRAPH 1
### RELATIONSHIP BETWEEN NUMBER OF CUSTOMERS STORE AND TIME OF DAY

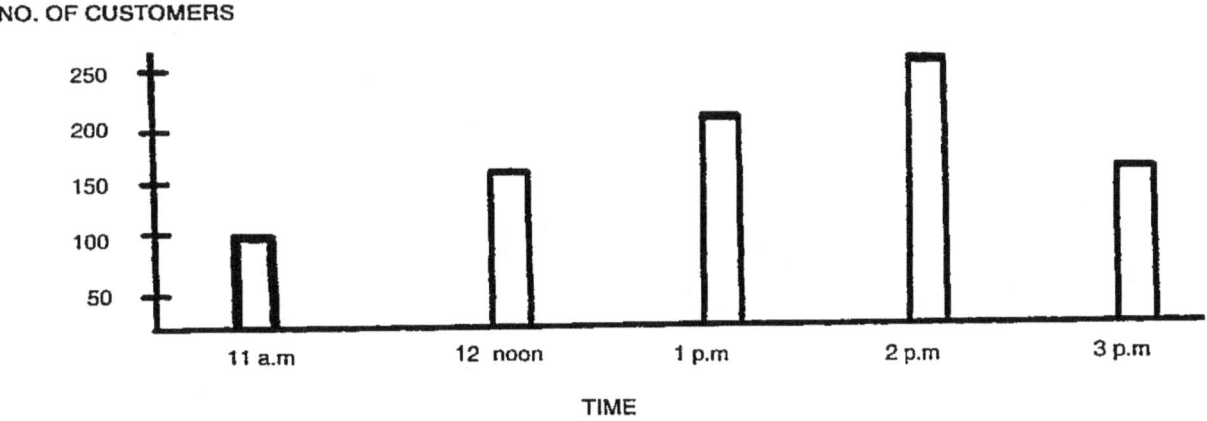

### GRAPH II
### RELATIONSHIP BETWEEN NUMBER OF CHECK-OUT LANES AVAILABLE IN STORE AND WAIT TIME FOR CHECK-OUT

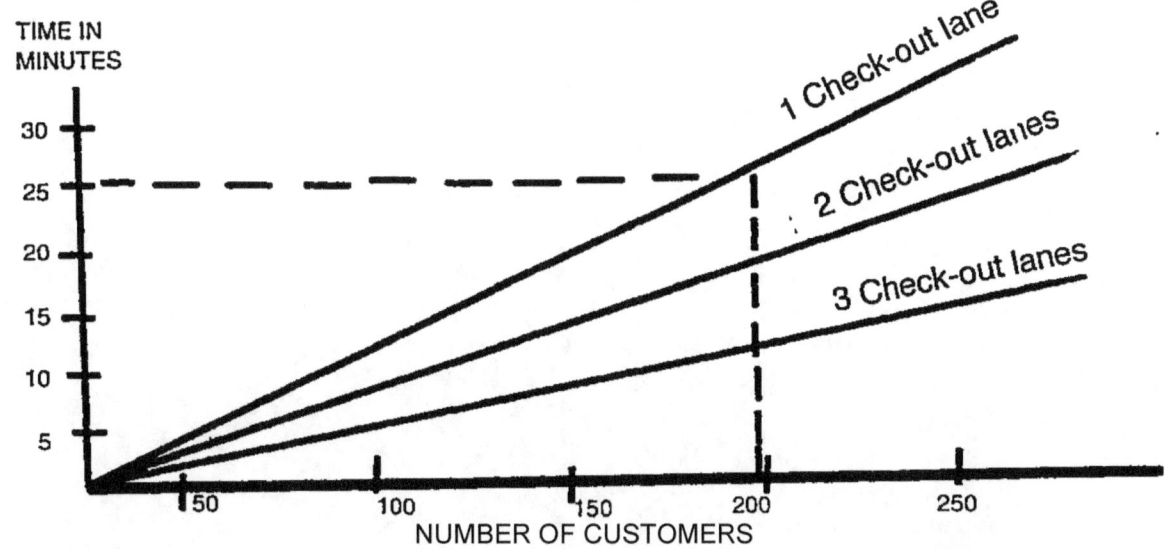

Note the dotted lines in Graph II. They demonstrate that, if there are 200 people in the store and only one check-out lane is open, the wait time will be 25 minutes.

1. At what time would a person be most likely NOT to have to wait more than 15 minutes if only one check-out lane is open?

    A. 11 A.M.　　　　B. 12 Noon　　　　C. 1 P.M.　　　　D. 3 P.M.

2. At what time of day would a person have to wait the LONGEST to check out if three check-out lanes are available?

    A. 11 A.M.　　　　B. 12 Noon　　　　C. 1 P.M.　　　　D. 2 P.M

3. The difference in wait times between 1 and 3 check-out lanes at 3 P.M. is MOST NEARLY

    A. 5　　　　　　　B. 10　　　　　　　C. 15　　　　　　　D. 20

# TEST 4

DIRECTIONS: Each question or incomplete statement is followed by several suggested answers or completions. Select the one that BEST answers the question or completes the statement. *PRINT THE LETTER OF THE CORRECT ANSWER IN THE SPACE AT THE RIGHT.*

Questions 1-4.

DIRECTIONS: Questions 1 through 4 are to be answered SOLELY on the basis of the graph below.

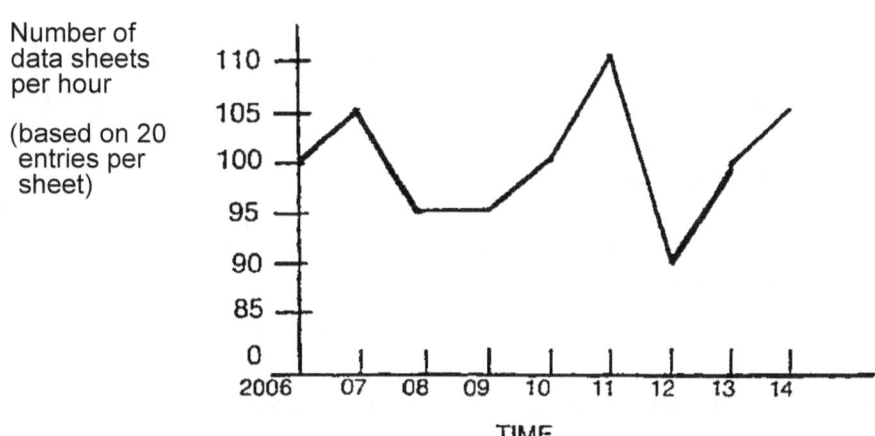

1. Of the following, during what four-year period did the average output of computer operators fall BELOW 100 sheets per hour?

    A. 2007-10    B. 2008-11    C. 2010-13    D. 2011-14

2. The average percentage change in output over the previous year's output for the years 2009 to 2012 is MOST NEARLY

    A. 2    B. 0    C. -5    D. -7

3. The difference between the actual output for 2012 and the projected figure based upon the average increase from 2006-2011 is MOST NEARLY

    A. 18    B. 20    C. 22    D. 24

4. Assume that after constructing the above graph you, an analyst, discovered that the average number of entries per sheet in 2012 was 25 (instead of 20) because of the complex nature of the work performed during that period.
    The average output in sheets per hour for the period 2010-13, expressed in terms of 20 items per sheet, would then be MOST NEARLY

    A. 95    B. 100    C. 105    D. 110

# TEST 6

DIRECTIONS: Each question or incomplete statement is followed by several suggested answers or completions. Select the one that BEST answers the question or completes the statement. *PRINT THE LETTER OF THE CORRECT ANSWER IN THE SPACE AT THE RIGHT.*

Questions 1-3.

DIRECTIONS: Questions 1 through 3 are to be answered on the basis of the following data assembled for a cost-benefit analysis.

|  | Cost | Benefit |
| --- | --- | --- |
| No program | 0 | 0 |
| Alternative W | $ 3,000 | $ 6,000 |
| Alternative X | $10,000 | $17,000 |
| Alternative Y | $17,000 | $25,000 |
| Alternative Z | $30,000 | $32,000 |

1. From the point of view of selecting the alternative with the best cost benefit ratio, the BEST alternative is Alternative

    A. W      B. X      C. Y      D. Z

2. From the point of view of selecting the alternative with the best measure of net benefit, the BEST alternative is Alternative

    A. W      B. X      C. Y      D. Z

3. From the point of view of pushing public expenditure to the point where marginal benefit equals or exceeds marginal cost, the BEST alternative is Alternative

    A. W      B. X      C. Y      D. Z

# TEST 6

DIRECTIONS: Each question or incomplete statement is followed by several suggested answers or completions. Select the one that BEST answers the question or completes the statement. *PRINT THE LETTER OF THE CORRECT ANSWER IN THE SPACE AT THE RIGHT.*

Questions 1-3.

DIRECTIONS: Questions 1 through 3 are to be answered SOLELY on the basis of the following data.

A series of cost-benefit studies of various alternative health programs yields the following results:

| Program | Benefit | Cost |
|---------|---------|------|
| K | 30 | 15 |
| L | 60 | 60 |
| M | 300 | 150 |
| N | 600 | 500 |

In answering Questions 1 and 2, assume that all programs can be increased or decreased in scale without affecting their individual benefit-to-cost ratios.

1. The benefit-to-cost ratio of Program M is

   A. 10:1  B. 5:1  C. 2:1  D. 1:2

2. The budget ceiling for one or more of the programs included in the study is set at 75 units. It may MOST logically be concluded that

   A. Programs K and L should be chosen to fit within the budget ceiling
   B. Program K would be the most desirable one that could be afforded
   C. Program M should be chosen rather than Program K
   D. the choice should be between Programs M and K

3. If no assumptions can be made regarding the effects of change of scale, the MOST logical conclusion, on the basis of the data available, is that

   A. more data are needed for a budget choice of program
   B. Program K is the most preferable because of its low cost and good benefit-to-cost ratio
   C. Program M is the most preferable because of its high benefits and good benefit-to-cost ratio
   D. there is no difference between Programs K and M, and either can be chosen for any purpose

# TEST 7

DIRECTIONS: Each question or incomplete statement is followed by several suggested answers or completions. Select the one that BEST answers the question or completes the statement. *PRINT THE LETTER OF THE CORRECT ANSWER IN THE SPACE AT THE RIGHT.*

Questions 1-6.

DIRECTIONS: Questions 1 through 6 are to be answered SOLELY on the basis of the information contained in the charts below which relate to the budget allocations of City X, a small suburban community. The charts depict the annual budget allocations by Department and by expenditures over a five-year period.

## CITY X BUDGET IN MILLIONS OF DOLLARS
### TABLE I. Budget Allocations by Department

| Department | 2017 | 2018 | 2019 | 2020 | 2021 |
|---|---|---|---|---|---|
| Public Safety | 30 | 45 | 50 | 40 | 50 |
| Health and Welfare | 50 | 75 | 90 | 60 | 70 |
| Engineering | 5 | 8 | 10 | 5 | 8 |
| Human Resources | 10 | 12 | 20 | 10 | 22 |
| Conservation & Environment | 10 | 15 | 20 | 20 | 15 |
| Education & Development | 15 | 25 | 35 | 15 | 15 |
| TOTAL BUDGET | 120 | 180 | 225 | 150 | 180 |

### TABLE II. Budget Allocations by Expenditures

| Category | 2017 | 2018 | 2019 | 2020 | 2021 |
|---|---|---|---|---|---|
| Raw Materials & Machinery | 36 | 63 | 68 | 30 | 98 |
| Capital Outlay | 12 | 27 | 56 | 15 | 18 |
| Personal Services | 72 | 90 | 101 | 105 | 64 |
| TOTAL BUDGET | 120 | 180 | 225 | 150 | 180 |

1. The year in which the SMALLEST percentage of the total annual budget was allocated to the Department of Education and Development is

   A. 2017  B. 2018  C. 2020  D. 2021

2. Assume that in 2020 the Department of Conservation and Environment divided its annual budget into the three categories of expenditures and in exactly the same proportion as the budget shown in Table II for the year 2020. The amount allocated for capital outlay in the Department of Conservation and Environment's 2020 budget was MOST NEARLY _____ million.

   A. $2  B. $4  C. $6  D. $10

3. From the year 2018 to the year 2020, the sum of the annual budgets for the Departments of Public Safety and Engineering showed an overall _____ million.

   A. decline; SB
   B. increase; $7
   C. decline; S15
   D. increase; S22

4. The LARGEST dollar increase in departmental budget allocations from one year to the next was in _____ from _____.

   A. Public Safety; 2017 to 2018
   B. Health and Welfare; 2017 to 2018
   C. Education and Development; 2019 to 2020
   D. Human Resources; 2019 to 2020

5. During the five-year period, the annual budget of the Department of Human Resources was GREATER than the annual budget for the Department of Conservation and Environment in _____ of the years.

   A. none   B. one   C. two   D. three

6. If the total City X budget increases at the same rate from 2021 to 2022 as it did from 2020 to 2021, the total City X budget for 2022 will be MOST NEARLY _____ million.

   A. $180   B. $200   C. $210   D. $215

# TEST 8

DIRECTIONS: Each question or incomplete statement is followed by several suggested answers or completions. Select the one that BEST answers the question or completes the statement. *PRINT THE LETTER OF THE CORRECT ANSWER IN THE SPACE AT THE RIGHT.*

Questions 1-3.

DIRECTIONS: Questions 1 through 3 are to be answered SOLELY on the basis of the following information.

Assume that in order to encourage Program A, the State and Federal governments have agreed to make the following reimbursements for money spent on Program A, provided the unreimbursed balance is paid from City funds.

During Fiscal Year 2021-2022 - For the first $2 million expended, 50% Federal reimbursement and 30% State reimbursement; for the next $3 million, 40% Federal reimbursement and 20% State reimbursement; for the next $5 million, 20% Federal reimbursement and 10% State reimbursement. Above $10 million expended, no Federal or State reimbursement.

During Fiscal Year 2022-2023 - For the first $1 million expended, 30% Federal reimbursement and 20% State reimbursement; for the next $4 million, 15% Federal reimbursement and 10% State reimbursement. Above $5 million expended, no Federal or State reimbursement.

1. Assume that the Program A expenditures are such that the State reimbursement for Fiscal Year 2021-2022 will be $1 million.
   Then, the Federal reimbursement for Fiscal Year 2021-2022 will be

   A. $1,600,000
   B. $1,800,000
   C. $2,000,000
   D. $2,600,000

2. Assume that $8 million were to be spent on Program A in Fiscal Year 2022-2023.
   The TOTAL amount of unreimbursed City funds required would be

   A. $3,500,000
   B. $4,500,000
   C. $5,500,000
   D. $6,500,000

3. Assume that the City desires to have a combined total of $6 million spent in Program A during both the Fiscal Year 2021-2022 and the Fiscal Year 2022-2023.
   Of the following expenditure combinations, the one which results in the GREATEST reimbursement of City funds is _____ in Fiscal Year 2021-2022 and _____ in Fiscal Year 2022-2023.

   A. $5 million; $1 million
   B. $4 million; $2 million
   C. $3 million; $3 million
   D. $2 million; $4 million

# KEY (CORRECT ANSWERS)

| TEST 1 | TEST 2 | TEST 3 | TEST 4 |
|---|---|---|---|
| 1. D | 1. B | 1. A | 1. A |
| 2. C | 2. A | 2. D | 2. B |
| 3. C | 3. A | 3. B | 3. C |
|      | 4. D |      | 4. C |

| TEST 5 | TEST 6 | TEST 7 | TEST 8 |
|---|---|---|---|
| 1. A | 1. C | 1. D | 1. B |
| 2. C | 2. D | 2. A | 2. D |
| 3. C | 3. A | 3. A | 3. A |
|      |      | 4. B |      |
|      |      | 5. B |      |
|      |      | 6. D |      |

# READING COMPREHENSION
## UNDERSTANDING AND INTERPRETING WRITTEN MATERIAL
# EXAMINATION SECTION
# TEST 1

DIRECTIONS: Each question or incomplete statement is followed by several suggested answers or completions. Select the one that BEST answers the question or completes the statement. *PRINT THE LETTER OF THE CORRECT ANSWER IN THE SPACE AT THE RIGHT.*

Questions 1-3.

DIRECTIONS: Questions 1 through 3 are to be answered SOLELY on the basis of the following passage.

    Every organization needs a systematic method of checking its operations as a means to increase efficiency and promote economy. Many successful private firms have instituted a system of audit or internal inspections to accomplish these ends. Law enforcement organizations, which have an extremely important service to *sell*, should be no less zealous in developing efficiency and economy in their operations. Periodic, organized, and systematic inspections are one means of promoting the achievement of these objectives. The necessity of an organized inspection system is perhaps greatest in those law enforcement groups which have grown to such a size that the principal officer can no longer personally supervise or be cognizant of every action taken. Smooth and effective operation demands that the head of the organization have at hand some tool with which he can study and enforce general policies and procedure and also direct compliance with day-to-day orders, most of which are put into execution outside his sight and hearing. A good inspection system can serve as that tool.

1. The central thought of the above passage is that a system of inspections within a police department
    A. is unnecessary for a department in which the principal officer can personally supervise all official actions taken
    B. should be instituted at the first indication that there is any deterioration in job performance by the force
    C. should be decentralized and administered by first-line supervisory officers
    D. is an important aid to the police administrator in the accomplishment of law enforcement objectives

1.____

2. The MOST accurate of the following statements concerning the need for an organized inspection system in a law enforcement organization is: It is
    A. never needed in an organization of small size where the principal officer can give personal supervision
    B. most needed where the size of the organization prevents direct supervision by the principal officer
    C. more needed in law enforcement organizations than in private firms
    D. especially needed in an organization about to embark upon a needed expansion of services

2.____

3. According to the above passage, the head of the police organization utilizes the internal inspection system
   A. as a tool which must be constantly re-examined in the light of changing demands for police service
   B. as an administrative technique to increase efficiency and promote economy
   C. by personally visiting those areas of police operation which are outside his sight and hearing
   D. to augment the control of local commanders over detailed field operations

Questions 4-10.

DIRECTIONS: Questions 4 through 10 are to be answered SOLELY on the basis of the following passage.

Job evaluation and job rating systems are intended to introduce scientific procedures. Any type of approach, when properly used, will give satisfactory results. The Point System, when properly validated by actual use, is more likely to be suitable for general use than the ranking system. In many aspects, the Factor Comparison Plan is a point system tied to money values. Of course, there may be another system that combines the ranking system with the point system, especially during the initial stages of the development of the program. After the program has been in use for some time, the tendency is to drop off the ranking phase and continue the use of the point system.

In the ranking system of rating of jobs, every job within the plant is arranged in some order, either from the one with the simplest qualifications to the one with maximum requirements, or in the reverse order. This system should be preceded by careful job analysis and the writing of accurate job descriptions before the rating process is undertaken. It is possible, of course, to take the jobs as they are found in the business enterprise and use the names as they are without any attempt at standardization, and merely rank them according to the general overall impression of the raters. Such a procedure is certain to fall short of what may reasonably be expected of job rating. Another procedure that is in reality merely a modification of the simple rating described above is to establish a series of grades or zones and arrange all he jobs in the plant into groups within these grades and zones. The practice in most common use is to arrange all the jobs in the plant according to their requirements by rating them and then to establish the classification or groups.

The actual ranking of jobs may be done by one individual, several individuals, or a committee. If several individuals are working independently on the task, it will usually be found that, in general, they agree but that their rankings vary in certain details. A conference between the individuals, with each person giving his reasons why he rated one way or another, usually produces agreement. The detailed job descriptions are particularly helpful when there is disagreement among raters as to the rating of certain jobs. It is not only possible but desirable to have workers participate in the construction of the job description and in rating the job.

4. The MAIN theme of this passage is
   A. the elimination of bias in job rating
   B. the rating of jobs by the ranking system
   C. the need or accuracy in allocating points in the point system
   D. pitfalls to avoid in selecting key jobs in the Factor Comparison Plan

5. The ranking system of rating jobs consists MAINLY of
   A. attaching a point value to each ratable factor of each job prior to establishing an equitable pay scale
   B. arranging every job in the organization in descending order and then following this up with a job analysis of the key jobs
   C. preparing accurate job descriptions after a job analysis and then arranging all jobs either in ascending or descending order based on job requirements
   D. arbitrarily establishing a hierarchy of job classes and grades and then fitting each job into a specific class and grade based on the opinions of unit supervisors

6. The above passage states that the system of classifying jobs MOST used in an organization is to
   A. organize all jobs in the organization in accordance with their requirements and then create categories or clusters of jobs
   B. classify all jobs in the organization according to the titles and rank by which they are currently known in the organization
   C. establish a pre-arranged series of grades or zones and then fit all jobs into one of the grades or zones
   D. determine the salary currently being paid for each job and then rank the jobs in order according to salary

7. According to the above passage, experience has shown that when a group of raters is assigned to the job evaluation task and each individual rates independently of the others, the raters GENERALLY
   A. *agree* with respect to all aspects of their rankings
   B. *disagree* with respect to all or nearly all aspects of the rankings
   C. *disagree* on overall ratings, but agree on specific rating factors
   D. *agree* on overall rankings, but have some variance in some details

8. The above passage states that the use of a detailed job description is of special value when
   A. employees of an organization have participated in the preliminary step involved in actual preparation of the job description
   B. labor representatives are not participating in ranking of the jobs
   C. an individual rater who is unsure of himself is ranking the jobs
   D. a group of raters is having difficulty reaching unanimity with respect to ranking a certain job

9. A comparison of the various rating systems as described in the above passage shows that
   A. the ranking system is not as appropriate for general use as a properly validated point system
   B. the point system is the same as the Factor Comparison Plan except that it places greater emphasis on money

4 (#1)

  C. no system is capable of combining the point system and the Factor Comparison Plan
  D. the point system will be discontinued last when used in combination with the Factor comparison System

10. The above passage implies that the PRINCIPAL reason for creating job evaluation and rating systems was to help      10._____
  A. overcome union opposition to existing salary plans
  B. base wage determination on a more objective and orderly foundation
  C. eliminate personal bias on the part of the trained scientific job evaluators
  D. management determine if it was overpricing the various jobs in the organizational hierarchy

Questions 11-13.

DIRECTIONS: Questions 11 through 13 are to be answered SOLELY on the basis of the following passage.

  The common sense character of the merit system seems so natural to most Americans that many people wonder why it should ever have been inoperative.  After all, the American economic system, the most phenomenal the world has ever known, is also founded on a rugged selective process which emphasizes the personal qualities of capacity, industriousness, and productivity.  The criteria may not have always been appropriate and competition has not always been fair, but competition there was, and the responsibilities and the rewards—with exceptions, of course—have gone to those who could measure up in terms of intelligence, knowledge, or perseverance.  This has been true not only in the economic area, in the money-making process, but also in achievement in the professions and other walks of life.

11. According to the above passage, economic rewards in the United State have      11._____
  A. always been based on appropriate, fair criteria
  B. only recently been based on a competitive system
  C. not going to people who compete too ruggedly
  D. usually gone to those people with intelligence, knowledge, and perseverance

12. According to the above passage, a merit system is      12._____
  A. an unfair criterion on which to base rewards
  B. unnatural to anyone who is not American
  C. based only on common sense
  D. based on the same principles as the American economic system

13. According to the above passage, it is MOST accurate to say that      13._____
  A. the United States has always had a civil service merit system
  B. civil service employees are very rugged
  C. the American economic system has always been based on a merit objective
  D. competition is unique to the American way of life

Questions 14-15.

DIRECTIONS: Questions 14 and 15 are to be answered SOLELY on the basis of the following passage.

In-basket tests are often used to assess managerial potential. The exercise consists of a set of papers that would be likely to be found in the in-basket of an administrator or manager at any given time, and requires the individuals participating in the examination to indicate how they would dispose of each item found in the in-basket. In order to handle the in-basket effectively, they must successfully manage their time, refer and assign some work to subordinates, juggle potentially conflicting appointments and meetings, and arrange for follow-up of problems generated by the items in the in-basket. In other words, the in-basket test is attempting to evaluate the participants' abilities to organize their work, set priorities, delegate, control, and make decisions.

14. According to the above passage, to succeed in an in-basket test, an administrator must
    A. be able to read very quickly
    B. have a great deal of technical knowledge
    C. know when to delegate work
    D. arrange a lot of appointments and meetings

14.____

15. According to the above passage, all of the following abilities are indications of managerial potential EXCEPT the ability to
    A. organize and control
    B. manage time
    C. write effective reports
    D. make appropriate decisions

15.____

Questions 16-19.

DIRECTIONS: Questions 16 through 19 are to be answered SOLELY on the basis of the following passage.

A personnel researcher has at his disposal various approaches for obtaining information, analyzing it, and arriving at conclusions that have value in predicting and affecting the behavior of people at work. The type of method to be used depends on such factors as the nature of the research problem, the available data, and the attitudes of those people being studied to the various kinds of approaches. While the experimental approach, with its use of control groups, is the most refined type of study, there are others that are often found useful in personnel research. Surveys, in which the researcher obtains facts on a problem from a variety of sources, are employed in research on wages, fringe benefits, and labor relations. Historical studies are used to trace the development of problems in order to understand them better and to isolate possible causative factors. Case studies are generally developed to explore all the details of a particular problem that is representative of other similar problems. A researcher chooses the most appropriate form of study for the problem he is investigating. He should recognize, however, that the experimental method, commonly referred to as the scientific method, if used validly and reliably, gives the most conclusive results.

16. The above passage discusses several approaches used to obtain information on particular problems.
    Which of the following may be MOST reasonably concluded from the passage?
    A(n)
    A. historical study cannot determine causative factors
    B. survey is often used in research on fringe benefits
    C. case study is usually used to explore a problem that is unique and unrelated to other problems
    D. experimental study is used when the scientific approach to a problem fails

17. According to the above passage, all of the following are factors that may determine the type of approach a researcher uses EXCEPT
    A. the attitudes of people toward being used in control groups
    B. the number of available sources
    C. his desire to isolate possible causative factors
    D. the degree of accuracy he requires

18. The words *scientific method*, as used in the last sentence of the above passage, refer to a type of study which, according to the above passage
    A. uses a variety of sources
    B. traces the development of problems
    C. uses control groups
    D. analyzes the details of a representative problem

19. Which of the following can be MOST reasonably concluded from the above passage?
    In obtaining and analyzing information on a particular problem, a researcher employs the method which is the
    A. most accurate
    B. most suitable
    C. least expensive
    D. least time-consuming

Questions 20-25.

DIRECTIONS: Questions 20 through 25 are to be answered SOLELY on the basis of the following passage.

　　The quality of the voice of a worker is an important factor in conveying to clients and co-workers his attitude and, to some degree, his character. The human voice, when not consciously disguised, may reflect a person's mood, temper, and personality. It has been shown in several experiments that certain character traits can be assessed with better than chance accuracy through listening to the voice of an unknown person who cannot be seen.
　　Since one of the objectives of the worker is to put clients at ease and to present an encouraging and comfortable atmosphere, a harsh, shrill, or loud voice could have a negative effect. A client who displays emotions of anger or resentment would probably be provoked even further by a caustic tone. In a face-to-face situation, an unpleasant voice may be compensated for, to some degree, by a concerned and kind facial expression. However, when one speaks on the telephone, the expression on one's face cannot be seen by the listener. A supervising clerk who wishes to represent himself effectively to clients should try to eliminate as many faults as possible in striving to develop desirable voice qualities.

7 (#1)

20. If a worker uses a sarcastic tone while interviewing a resentful client, the client, according to the above passage, would MOST likely
    A. avoid the face-to-face problem
    B. be ashamed of his behavior
    C. become more resentful
    D. be provoked to violence

    20._____

21. According to the passage, experiments comparing voice and character traits have demonstrated that
    A. prospects for improving an unpleasant voice through training are better than chance
    B. the voice can be altered to project many different psychological characteristics
    C. the quality of the human voice reveals more about the speaker than his words do
    D. the speaker's voice tells the hearer something about the speaker's personality

    21._____

22. Which of the following, according to the above passage, is a person's voice MOST likely to reveal?
    His
    A. prejudices
    B. intelligence
    C. social awareness
    D. temperament

    22._____

23. It may be MOST reasonably concluded from the above passage that an interested and sympathetic expression on the face of a worker
    A. may induce a client to feel certain he will receive welfare benefits
    B. will eliminate the need for pleasant vocal qualities in the interviewer
    C. may help to make up for an unpleasant voice in the interviewer
    D. is desirable as the interviewer speaks on the telephone to a client

    23._____

24. Of the following, the MOST reasonable implication of the above paragraph is that a worker should, when speaking to a client, control and use his voice to
    A. simulate a feeling of interest in the problems of the client
    B. express his emotions directly and adequately
    C. help produce in the client a sense of comfort and security
    D. reflect his own true personality

    24._____

25. It may be concluded from the above passage that the PARTICULAR reason for a worker to pay special attention to modulating her voice when talking on the phone to a client is that, during a telephone conversation
    A. there is a necessity to compensate for the way in which a telephone distorts the voice
    B. the voice of the worker is a reflection of her mood and character
    C. the client can react only on the basis of the voice and words she hears
    D. the client may have difficulty getting a clear understanding over the telephone

    25._____

# KEY (CORRECT ANSWERS)

| | | | | |
|---|---|---|---|---|
| 1. | D | | 11. | D |
| 2. | B | | 12. | D |
| 3. | B | | 13. | C |
| 4. | B | | 14. | C |
| 5. | C | | 15. | C |
| 6. | A | | 16. | B |
| 7. | D | | 17. | D |
| 8. | D | | 18. | C |
| 9. | A | | 19. | B |
| 10. | B | | 20. | C |

21. D
22. D
23. C
24. C
25. C

# TEST 2

DIRECTIONS: Each question or incomplete statement is followed by several suggested answers or completions. Select the one that BEST answers the question or completes the statement. *PRINT THE LETTER OF THE CORRECT ANSWER IN THE SPACE AT THE RIGHT.*

Questions 1-3.

DIRECTIONS: Questions 1 through 3 are to be answered SOLELY on the basis of the following paragraph.

Suppose you are given the job of printing, collating, and stapling 8,000 copies of a ten-page booklet as soon as possible. You have available one photo-offset machine, a collator with an automatic stapler, and the personnel to operate these machines. All will be available for however long the job takes to complete. The photo-offset machine prints 5,000 impressions an hour, and it takes about 15 minutes to set up a plate. The collator, including time for insertion of pages and stapling, can process about 2,000 booklets an hour. (Answers should be based on the assumption that there are no breakdowns or delays.)

1. Assuming that all the printing is finished before the collating is started, if the job is given to you late Monday and your section can begin work the next day and is able to devote seven hours a day, Monday through Friday, to the job until it is finished, what is the BEST estimate of when the job will be finished?
   A. Wednesday afternoon of the same week
   B. Thursday morning of the same week
   C. Friday morning of the same week
   D. Monday morning of the next week

1.____

2. An operator suggests to you that instead of completing all the printing and then beginning collating and stapling, you first print all the pages for 4,000 booklets, so that they can be collated and stapled while the last 4,000 pages are being printed.
   If you accepted this suggestion, the job would be completed
   A. sooner but would require more man-hours
   B at the same time using either method
   C. later and would require more man-hours
   D. sooner but there would be more wear and tear on the plates

2.____

3. Assume that you have the same assignment and equipment as described above, but 16,000 copies of the booklet are needed instead of 8,000.
   If you decided to print 8,000 complete booklets, then collate and staple them while you started printing the next 8,000 booklets, which of the following statements would MOST accurately describe the relationship between this new method and your original method of printing all the booklets at one time, and then collating and stapling them? The
   A. job would be completed at the same time regardless of the method used
   B. new method would result in the job's being completed 3½ hours earlier
   C. original method would result in the job's being completed an hour later
   D. new method would result in the job's being completed 1½ hours earlier

3.____

71

Questions 4-6.

DIRECTIONS: Questions 4 through 6 are to be answered SOLELY on the basis of the following passage.

When using words like company, association, council, committee, and board in place of the full official name, the writer should not capitalize these short forms unless he intends them to invoke the full force of the institution's authority. In legal contracts, in minutes, or in formal correspondence where one is speaking formally and officially on behalf of the company, the term Company is usually capitalized, but in ordinary usage, where it is not essential to load the short form with this significance, capitalization would be excessive. (Example: The company will have many good openings for graduates this June.)

The treatment recommended for short forms of place names is essentially the same as that recommended for short forms of organizational names. In general, we capitalize the full form but not the short form. If Park Avenue is referred to in one sentence, then the *avenue* is sufficient in subsequent references. The same is true with words like building, hotel, station, and airport, which are capitalized when part of a proper name changed (Pan Am Building, Hotel Plaza, Union Station, O'Hare Airport), but are simply lower-cased when replacing these specific names.

4. The above passage states that USUALLY the short forms of names of organizations
    A. and places should not be capitalized
    B. and places should be capitalized
    C. should not be capitalized, but the short forms of names of places should be capitalized
    D. should be capitalized, but the short forms of names of places should not be capitalized

5. The above passage states that in legal contracts, in minutes, and in formal correspondence, the short forms of names of organizations should
    A. usually not be capitalized      B. usually be capitalized
    C. usually not be used             D. never be used

6. It can be inferred from the above passage that decisions regarding when to capitalize certain words
    A. should be left to the discretion of the writer
    B. should be based on generally accepted rules
    C. depend on the total number of words capitalized
    D. are of minor importance

Questions 7-10.

DIRECTIONS: Questions 7 through 10 are to be answered SOLELY on the basis of the following passage.

Use of the systems and procedures approach to office management is revolutionizing the supervision of office work. This approach views an enterprise as an entity which seeks to fulfill definite objectives. Systems and procedures help to organize repetitive work into a routine, thus reducing the amount of decision making required for its accomplishment. As a result, employees are guided in their efforts and perform only necessary work. Supervisors are relieved of any details of execution and are free to attend to more important work. Establishing work guides which require that identical tasks be performed the same way each time permits standardization of forms, machine operations, work methods, and controls. This approach also reduces the probability of errors. Any error committed is usually discovered quickly because the incorrect work does not meet the requirement of the work guides. Errors are also reduced through work specialization, which allows each employee to become thoroughly proficient in a particular type of work. Such proficiency also tends to improve the morale of the employees.

7. The above passage states that the accuracy of an employee's work is INCREASED by
    A. using the work specialization approach
    B. employing a probability sample
    C. requiring him to shift at one time into different types of tasks
    D. having his supervisor check each detail of work execution

8. Of the following, which one BEST expresses the main theme of the above passage? The
    A. advantages and disadvantages of the systems and procedures approach to office management
    B. effectiveness of the systems and procedures approach to office management in developing skills
    C. systems and procedures approach to office management as it relates to office costs
    D. advantages of the systems and procedures approach to office management for supervisors and office workers

9. Work guides are LEAST likely to be used when
    A. standardized forms are used
    B. a particular office task is distinct and different from all others
    C. identical tasks are to be performed in identical ways
    D. similar work methods are expected from each employee

10. According to the above passage, when an employee makes a work error, it USUALLY
    A. is quickly corrected by the supervisor
    B. necessitates a change in the work guides
    C. can be detected quickly if work guides are in use
    D. increases the probability of further errors by that employee

Questions 11-12.

DIRECTIONS: Questions 11 and 12 are to be answered SOLELY on the basis of the following passage.

The coordination of the many activities of a large public agency is absolutely essential. Coordination, as an administrative principle, must be distinguished from and is independent of cooperation. Coordination can be of either the horizontal or the vertical type. In large organizations, the objectives of vertical coordination are achieved by the transmission of orders and statements of policy down through the various levels of authority. It is an accepted generalization that the more authoritarian the organization, the more easily may vertical coordination be accomplished. Horizontal coordination is arrived through staff work, administrative management, and conferences of administrators of equal rank. It is obvious that of the two types of coordination, the vertical kind is more important, for at best horizontal coordination only supplements the coordination effected up and down the line,

11. According to the above passage, the ease with which vertical coordination is achieved in a large agency depends upon  11._____
    A. the extent to which control is firmly exercised from above
    B. the objectives that have been established for the agency
    C. the importance attached by employees to the orders and statements of policy transmitted through the agency
    D. the cooperation obtained at the various levels of authority

12. According to the above passage,  12._____
    A. vertical coordination is dependent for its success upon horizontal coordination
    B. one type of coordination may work in opposition to the other
    C. similar methods may be used to achieve both types of coordination
    D. horizontal coordination is at most an addition to vertical coordination

Questions 13-17.

DIRECTIONS: Questions 13 through 17 are to be answered SOLELY on the basis of the following situation.

Assume that you are a newly appointed supervisor in the same unit in which you have been acting as a provisional for some time. You have in your unit the following workers:

WORKER I: He has always been an efficient worker. In a number of his cases, the clients have recently begun to complain that they cannot manage on the departmental budget.

WORKER II: He has been under selective supervision for some time as an experienced, competent worker. He now begins to be late for his supervisory conferences and to stress how much work he has to do.

WORKER III: He has been making considerable improvement in his ability to handle the details of his job. He now tells you, during an individual conference, that he does not need such close supervision and that he wants to operate more independently. He says that Worker II is always available when he needs a little information or help but, in general, he can manage very well by himself.

5 (#2)

WORKER IV: He brings you a complex case for decision as to eligibility. Discussion of the case brings out the fact that he has failed to consider all the available resources adequately but has stressed the family's needs to include every extra item in the budget. This is the third case of a similar nature that his worker has brought to you recently. This worker and Worker I work in adjacent territory and are rather friendly.

In the following questions, select the option that describes the method of dealing with these workers that illustrate BEST supervisory practice.

13. With respect to supervision of Worker I, the assistant supervisor should 13.____
    A. discuss with the worker, in an individual conference, any problems that he may be having due to the increase in the cost of living
    B. plan a group conference for the unit around budgeting, as both Workers I and IV seem to be having budgetary difficulties
    C. discuss with Workers I and IV together the meaning of money as acceptance or rejection to the clients
    D. discuss with Worker I the budgetary data in each case in relation to each client's situation

14. With respect to supervision of Worker II, the supervisory should 14.____
    A. move slowly with this worker and give him time to learn that the supervisor's official appointment has not changed his attitudes or methods of supervision
    B. discuss the worker's change of attitude and asks him to analyze the reasons for his change in behavior
    C. take time to show the worker how he is avoiding his responsibility in the supervisor-worker relationship and that he is resisting supervision
    D. hold an evaluatory conference with the worker and show him how he is taking over responsibilities that are not his by providing supervision for Worker III

15. With respect to supervision of Worker III, the supervisor should discuss with this worker 15.____
    A. why he would rather have supervision from Worker II than from the supervisor
    B. the necessity for further improvement before he can go on selective supervision
    C. an analysis of the improvement that has been made and the extent to which the worker is able to handle the total job for which he is responsible
    D. the responsibility of the supervisor to see that clients receive adequate service

16. With respect to supervision of Worker IV, the supervisor should 16.____
    A. show the worker that resources figures are incomplete but that even if they were complete, the family would probably be eligible for assistance
    B. ask the worker why he is so protective of these families since there are three cases so similar

C. discuss with the worker all three cases at the same time so that the worker may see his own role in the three situations
D. discuss with the worker the reasons for departmental policies and procedures around budgeting

17. With respect to supervision of Workers I and IV, since these two workers are friends and would seem to be influencing each other, the supervisor should

17.____

A. hold a joint conference with them both, pointing out how they should clear with the supervisor and not make their own rules together
B. handle the problems of each separately in individual conferences
C. separate them by transferring one to another territory or another unit
D. take up the problem of workers asking help of each other rather than from the supervisor in a group meeting

Questions 18-20.

DIRECTIONS: Questions 18 through 20 are to be answered SOLELY on the basis of the following passage.

One of the key supervisory problems in a large municipal recreation department is that many leaders are assigned to isolated playgrounds or small centers, where it is difficult to observe their work regularly. Often their facilities are extremely limited. In such settings, as well as in larger recreation centers, where many recreation leaders tend to have other jobs as well, there tends to be a low level of morale and incentive. Still, it is the supervisor's task to help recreation personnel to develop pride in their work and to maintain a high level of performance. With isolated leaders, the supervisor may give advice or assistance. Leaders may be assigned to different tasks or settings during the year to maximize their productivity and provide new challenges. When it is clear that leaders are no willing to make a real effort to contribute to the department, the possibility of penalties must be considered, within the scope of departmental policy and the union contract. However, the supervisor should be constructive, encourage and assist workers to take a greater interest in their work, be innovative, and try to raise morale and to improve performance in positive ways.

18. The one of the following that would the MOST appropriate title for the above passage is

18.____

A. Small Community Centers – Pro and Con
B. Planning Better Recreation Programs
C. The Supervisor's Task in Upgrading Personnel Performance
D. The Supervisor and the Municipal Union – Rights and Obligations

19. The above passage makes clear that recreation leadership performance in all recreation playgrounds and centers throughout a large city is

19.____

A. generally above average, with good morale on the part of most recreation leaders
B. beyond description since no one has ever observed or evaluated recreation leaders

C. a key test of the personnel department's effort to develop more effective hiring standards
D. of mixed quality, with many recreation leaders having poor morale and a low level of achievement

20. According to the above passage, the supervisor's role is to  20._____
    A. use disciplinary action as his major tool in upgrading performance
    B. tolerate the lack of effort of individual employees since they are assigned to isolated playgrounds or small centers
    C. employ encouragement, advice, and, when appropriate, disciplinary action to improve performance
    D. inform the county supervisor whenever malfeasance or idleness is detected

Questions 21-25.

DIRECTIONS: Questions 21 through 25 are to be answered SOLELY on the basis of the following passage.

### EMPLOYEE LEAVE REGULATIONS

Peter Smith, as a full-time permanent city employee under the Career and Salary Plan, earns an *annual leave allowance*. This consists of a certain number of days off a year with pay and may be used for vacation, personal business, and for observing religious holidays. As a newly appointed employee, during his first 8 years of city service, he will earn an annual leave allowance of 20 days off a year (an average of $1^2/_3$ days off a month). After he has finished 8 full years of working for the city, he will begin earning an additional 5 days off a year. His annual leave allowance, therefore, will then be 25 days a year and will remain at this amount for seven full years. He will begin earning an additional two days off a year at this amount for seven full years. He will begin earning an additional two days off a year after he has completed a total of 15 years of city employment. Therefore, in his sixteenth year of working for the city, Mr. Smith will be earning 27 days off a year as his annual leave allowance (an average of $2¼$ days off a month).

A *sick leave allowance* of one day a month is also given to Mr. Smith, but it can be used only in cases of actual illness. When Mr. Smith returns to work after using sick leave allowance, he must have a doctor's note if the absence is for a total of more than 3 days, but he may also be required to show a doctor's note for absences of 1, 2, or 3 days.

21. According to the above passage, Mr. Smith's annual leave allowance consists  21._____
    of a certain number of days off a year which he
    A. does not get paid for
    B. gets paid for at time and a half
    C. may use for personal business
    D. may not use for observing religious holidays

22. According to the above passage, after Mr. Smith has been working for the city  22._____
    for 9 years, his annual leave allowance will be _____ days a year.
    A. 20  B. 25  C. 27  D. 37

23. According to the above passage, Mr. Smith will begin earning an average of 2 days off a month as his annual leave allowance after he has worked for the city for _____ full years.
    A. 7   B. 8   C. 15   D. 17

    23._____

24. According to the above passage, Mr. Smith is given a sick leave allowance of
    A. 1 day every 2 months
    B. 1 day per month
    C. $1^2/_3$ days per month
    D. 2¼ days a month

    24._____

25. According to the above passage, when he uses sick leave allowance, Mr. Smith may be required to show a doctor's note
    A. even if his absence is for only 1 day
    B. only if his absence is for more than 2 days
    C. only if his absence is for more than 3 days
    D. only if his absence is for 3 days or more

    25._____

# KEY (CORRECT ANSWERS)

| | | | | |
|---|---|---|---|---|
| 1. | C | | 11. | A |
| 2. | C | | 12. | D |
| 3. | D | | 13. | D |
| 4. | A | | 14. | A |
| 5. | B | | 15. | C |
| 6. | B | | 16. | C |
| 7. | A | | 17. | B |
| 8. | D | | 18. | C |
| 9. | B | | 19. | D |
| 10. | C | | 20. | C |

| | |
|---|---|
| 21. | C |
| 22. | B |
| 23. | C |
| 24. | B |
| 25. | A |

# TEST 3

DIRECTIONS: Each question or incomplete statement is followed by several suggested answers or completions. Select the one that BEST answers the question or completes the statement. *PRINT THE LETTER OF THE CORRECT ANSWER IN THE SPACE AT THE RIGHT.*

Questions 1-6.

DIRECTIONS: Questions 1 through 6 are to be answered SOLELY on the basis of the following passage.

    A folder is made of a sheet of heavy paper (manila, kraft, pressboard, or red rope stock) that has been folded once so that the back is about one-half inch higher than the front. Folders are larger than the papers they contain in order to protect them. Two standard folder sizes are *letter size* for papers that are 8½" x 11" and *legal cap* for papers that are 8½" x 13".
    Folders are cut across the top in two ways: so that the back is straight (straight-cut) or so that the back has a tab that projects above the top of the folder. Such tabs bear captions that identify the contents of each folder. Tabs vary in width and position. The tabs of a set of folders that are *one-half cut* are half the width of the folder and have only two positions.
    *One-third cut* folders have three positions, each tab occupying a third of the width of the folder. Another standard tabbing is *one-fifth cut*, which has five positions. There are also folders with *two-fifths cut*, with the tabs in the third and fourth or fourth and fifth positions.

1. Of the following, the BEST title for the above passage is
   A. Filing Folders
   B. Standard Folder Sizes
   C. The Uses of the Folder
   D. The Use of Tabs

2. According to the above passage, one of the standard folder sizes is called
   A. Kraft cut
   B. legal cap
   C. one-half cut
   D. straight-cut

3. According to the above passage, tabs are GENERALLY placed along the _____ of the folder.
   A. back    B. front    C. left side    D. right side

4. According to the above passage, a tab is GENERALLY used to
   A. distinguish between standard folder sizes
   B. identify the contents of a folder
   C. increase the size of the folder
   D. protect the papers within the folder

5. According to the above passage, a folder that is two-fifths cut has _____ tabs.
   A. no    B. two    C. three    D. five

6. According to the above passage, one reason for making folders larger than the papers they contain is that
   A. only a certain size folder can be made from heavy paper
   B. they will protect the papers
   C. they will aid in setting up a tab system
   D. the back of the folder must be higher than the front

Questions 7-15.

DIRECTIONS: Questions 7 through 15 are to be answered SOLELY on the basis of the following passage.

The City University of New York traces its origins to 1847, when the Free Academy, which later became City College, was founded as the first tuition-free municipal college. City and Hunter Colleges were placed under the direction of the Board of Higher Education in 1926, and Brooklyn and Queens Colleges were subsequently added to the system of municipal colleges. In 1955, Staten Island Community College, the first of the two-year colleges sponsored by the Board of Higher Education under the program of the State University of New York, joined the system.

In 1961, the four senior colleges and three community colleges then under the jurisdiction of the Board of Higher Education became the City University of New York, and a University Graduate Division was organized to offer programs leading to the Ph.D. Since then, the university has undergone even more rapid growth. Today, it consists of nine senior colleges, an upper division college which admits students at the junior level, eight community colleges, a graduate division, and an affiliated medical center.

In the summer of 1969, the Board of Higher Education resolved that the time had come to commit the resources of the university to meeting an urgent social need—unrestricted access to higher education for all youths of the City. Determined to prevent the waste of human potential represented by the thousands of high school graduates whose limited educational opportunities left them unable to meet existing admission standards, the Board moved to adopt a policy of Open Admissions. It was their judgment that the best way of determining whether a potential student can benefit from college work is to admit him to college, provide him with the learning assistance he needs, and then evaluate his performance.

Beginning with the class of June 1970, every New York City resident who received a high school diploma from a public or private high school was guaranteed a place in one of the colleges of City University.

7. Of the following, the BEST title for the above passage is
   A. A Brief History of the City University
   B. High Schools and the City University
   C. The Components of the University
   D. Tuition-free Colleges

8. According to the above passage, which one of the following colleges of the City University was ORIGINALLY called the Free Academy?
   A. Brooklyn College        B. City College
   C. Hunter College          D. Queens College

9. According to the above passage, the system of municipal colleges became the City University of New York in
   A. 1926   B. 1955   C. 1961   D. 1969

10. According to the above passage, Staten Island Community College came under the jurisdiction of the Board of Higher Education
    A. 6 years after a Graduate Division was organized
    B. 8 years before the adoption of the Open Admissions Policy
    C. 29 years after Brooklyn and Queens Colleges
    D. 29 years after City and Hunter Colleges

11. According to the above passage, the Staten Island Community College is
    A. a graduate division center
    B. a senior college
    C. a two-year college
    D. an upper division college

12. According to the above passage, the TOTAL number of colleges, divisions, and affiliated branches of the City University is
    A. 18   B. 19   C. 20   D. 21

13. According to the above passage, the Open Admissions Policy is designed to determine whether a potential student will benefit from college by PRIMARILY
    A. discouraging competition for placement in the City University among high school students
    B. evaluating his performance after entry into college
    C. lowering admission standards
    D. providing learning assistance before entry into college

14. According to the above passage, the FIRST class to be affected by the Open Admissions Policy was the
    A. high school class which graduated in January 1970
    B. City University class which graduated in June 1970
    C. high school class when graduated in June 1970
    D. City University class when graduated in June 1970

15. According to the above passage, one of the reasons that the Board of Higher Education initiated the policy of Open Admission was to
    A. enable high school graduates with a background of limited educational opportunities to enter college
    B. expand the growth of the City University so as to increase the number and variety of degrees offered
    C. provide a social resource to the qualified youth of the City
    D. revise admission standards to meet the needs of the City

Questions 16-18.

DIRECTIONS: Questions 16 through 18 are to be answered SOLELY on the basis of the following passage.

Hereafter, all probationary students interested in transferring to community college career programs (associate degrees) from liberal arts programs in senior colleges (bachelor degrees) will be eligible for such transfers if they have completed no more than three semesters.

For students with averages 1.5 or above, transfer will be automatic. Those with 1.0 to 1.5 averages can transfer provisionally and will be required to make substantial progress during the first semester in the career program. Once transfer has taken place, only those courses in which passing grades were received will be computed in the community college grade-point average.

No request for transfer will be accepted from probationary students wishing to enter the liberal arts programs at the community college.

16. According to the above passage, the one of the following which is the BEST statement concerning the transfer of probationary students is that a probationary student
    A. may transfer to a career program at the end of one semester
    B. must complete three semester hours before he is eligible for transfer
    C. is not eligible to transfer to a career program
    D. is eligible to transfer to a liberal arts program

16.____

17. Which of the following is the BEST statement of academic evaluation for transfer purposes in the case of probationary students?
    A. No probationary student with an average under 1.5 may transfer.
    B. A probationary student with an average of 1.3 may not transfer.
    C. A probationary student with an average of 1.6 may transfer.
    D. A probationary student with an average of .8 may transfer on a provisional basis.

17.____

18. It is MOST likely that, of the following, the next degree sought by one who already holds the Associate in Science degree would be a(n) _____ degree.
    A. Assistantship in Science      B. Associate in Applied Science
    C. Bachelor of Science           D. Doctor of Philosophy

18.____

Questions 19-20.

DIRECTIONS: Questions 19 and 20 are to be answered SOLELY on the basis of the following passage.

Auto: Auto travel requires prior approval by the President and/or appropriate Dean and must be indicated in the *Request for Travel Authorization* form. Employees authorized to use personal autos on official College business will be reimbursed at the rate of 28¢ per mile for the first 500 miles driven and 18¢ per mile for mileage driven in excess of 500 mile. The Comptroller's Office may limit the amount of reimbursement to the expenditure that would have been made if a less expensive mode of transportation (railroad, airplane, bus, etc.) had been utilized. If this occurs, the traveler will have to pick up the excess expenditure as a personal expense.

Tolls, Parking Fees, and Parking Meter Fees are not reimbursable and many not be claimed.

19. Suppose that Professor T gives the office assistant the following memorandum: Used car for official trip to Albany, New York, and return. Distance from New York to Albany is 148 miles. Tolls were $3.50 each way. Parking garage cost $3.00. When preparing the Travel Expense Voucher for Professor T, the figure which should be claimed for transportation is
    A. $120.88      B. $113.88      C. $82.88      D. $51.44

    19._____

20. Suppose that Professor V gives the office assistant the following memorandum: Used car for official trip to Pittsburgh, Pennsylvania, and return. Distance from New York to Pittsburgh is 350 miles. Tolls were $3.30, $11.40 going, and $3.30, $2.00 returning.
    When preparing the Travel Expense Voucher for Professor V, the figure which should be claimed for transportation is
    A. $225.40      B. $176.00      C. $127.40      D. $98.00

    20._____

Questions 21-25.

DIRECTIONS:  Questions 21 through 25 are to be answered SOLELY on the basis of the following passage.

For a period of nearly fifteen years, beginning in the mid-1950's, higher education sustained a phenomenal rate of growth. The factor principally responsible were continuing improvement in the rate of college entrance by high school graduates, a 50 percent increase in the size of the college-age (eighteen to twenty-one) group and—until about 1967—a rapid expansion of university research activity supported by the Federal government.

Today, as one looks ahead to the year 2010, it is apparent that each of these favorable stimuli will either be abated or turn into a negative factor. The rate of growth of the college-age group has already diminished; and from 2000 to 2005, the size of the college-age group has shrunk annually almost as fast as it grew from 1965 to 1970. From 2005 to 2010, this annual decrease will slow down so that by 2010 the age group will be about the same size as it was in 2009. This substantial net decrease in the size of the college-age group (from 1995 to 2010) will dramatically affect college enrollments since, currently, 83 percent of undergraduates are twenty-one and under, and another 11 percent are twenty-to to twenty-four.

21. Which one of the following factors is NOT mentioned in the above passage as contributing to the high rate of growth of higher education?
    A. A large increase in the size of the eighteen to twenty-one age group
    B. The equalization of educational opportunities among socio-economic groups
    C. The Federal budget impact on research and development spending in the higher education sector
    D. The increasing rate at which high school graduates enter college

    21._____

22. Based on the information in the above passage, the size of the college-age group in 2010 will be
    A. larger than it was in 2009
    B. larger than it was in 1995
    C. smaller than it was in 2005
    D. about the same as it was in 2000

23. According to the above passage, the tremendous rate of growth of higher education started around
    A. 1950   B. 1955   C. 1960   D. 1965

24. The percentage of undergraduates who are over age 24 is MOST NEARLY
    A. 6%   B. 8%   C. 11%   D. 17%

25. Which one of the following conclusions can be substantiated by the information given in the above passage?
    A. The college-age group was about the same size in 2000 as it was in 1965.
    B. The annual decrease in the size of the college-age group from 2000 to 2005 is about the same as the annual increase from 1965 to 1970.
    C. The overall decrease in the size of the college-age group from 2000 to 2005 will be followed by an overall increase in its size from 2005 to 2010.
    D. The size of the college-age group is decreasing at a fairly constant rate from 1995 to 2010.

# KEY (CORRECT ANSWERS)

| | | | | |
|---|---|---|---|---|
| 1. | A | | 11. | C |
| 2. | B | | 12. | C |
| 3. | A | | 13. | B |
| 4. | B | | 14. | C |
| 5. | B | | 15. | A |
| 6. | B | | 16. | A |
| 7. | A | | 17. | C |
| 8. | B | | 18. | C |
| 9. | C | | 19. | C |
| 10. | D | | 20. | B |

21. B
22. C
23. B
24. A
25. B

# PREPARING WRITTEN MATERIAL

# PARAGRAPH REARRANGEMENT
# COMMENTARY

The sentences that follow are in scrambled order. You are to rearrange them in proper order and indicate the letter choice containing the correct answer at the space at the right.

Each group of sentences in this section is actually a paragraph presented in scrambled order. Each sentence in the group has a place in that paragraph; no sentence is to be left out. You are to read each group of sentences and decide upon the best order in which to put the sentences so as to form a well-organized paragraph.

The questions in this section measure the ability to solve a problem when all the facts relevant to its solution are not given.

More specifically, certain positions of responsibility and authority require the employee to discover connection between events sometimes, apparently, unrelated. In order to do this, the employee will find it necessary to correctly infer that unspecified events have probably occurred or are likely to occur. This ability becomes especially important when action must be taken on incomplete information.

Accordingly, these questions require competitors to choose among several suggested alternatives, each of which presents a different sequential arrangement of the events. Competitors must choose the MOST logical of the suggested sequences.

In order to do so, they may be required to draw on general knowledge to infer missing concepts or events that are essential to sequencing the given events. Competitors should be careful to infer only what is essential to the sequence. The plausibility of the wrong alternatives will always require the inclusion of unlikely events or of additional chains of events which are NOT essential to sequencing the given events.

It's very important to remember that you are looking for the best of the four possible choices, and that the best choice of all may not even be one of the answers you're given to choose from.

There is no one right way to solve these problems. Many people have found it helpful to first write out the order of the sentences, as they would have arranged them, on their scrap paper before looking at the possible answers. If their optimum answer is there, this can save them some time. If it isn't, this method can still give insight into solving the problem. Others find it most helpful to just go through each of the possible choices, contrasting each as they go along. You should use whatever method feels comfortable and works for you.

While most of these types of questions are not that difficult, we've added a higher percentage of the difficult type, just to give you more practice. Usually there are only one or two questions on this section that contain such subtle distinctions that you're unable to answer confidently. And you then may find yourself stuck deciding between two possible choices, neither of which you're sure about.

# EXAMINATION SECTION
# TEST 1

DIRECTIONS: Each group of sentences in this section is actually a paragraph presented in scrambled order. Each sentence in the group has a place in that paragraph; no sentence is to be left out. You are to read each group of sentences, so as to form a well-organized paragraph. Before trying to answer the questions which follow each group of sentences, jot down the correct order of the sentences. Then answer each of the questions by printing the letter of the correct answer in the space at the right. Remember that you will receive credit only for answers marked.

P. The infant only feels the positive stimulation of warmth and food and does not differentiate the warmth and food from their source, mother.
Q. The infant, at the moment of birth, would feel the fear of dying if gracious fate did not preserve it from any awareness of the anxiety involved in the separation from mother.
R. The infant's state, then, is what has been called narcissism.
S. Mother is warmth, mother is food, mother is the euphoric state of satisfaction and security.
T. Even after being born, the infant is not yet aware of itself, and of the world as being outside of itself.

1. Which sentence did you put before Sentence Q?    1.____
   A. P
   B. R
   C. S
   D. T
   E. None of the above. Sentence Q is first.

2. Which sentence did you put after Sentence S?    2.____
   A. P
   B. Q
   C. R
   D. T
   E. None of the above. Sentence S is last.

3. Which sentence did you put before Sentence P?    3.____
   A. Q
   B. R
   C. S
   D. T
   E. None of the above. Sentence P is first.

2 (#1)

4. Which sentence did you put after Sentence P?  4.____

    A. Q
    B. R
    C. S
    D. T
    E. None of the above. Sentence P is last.

5. Which sentence did you put after Sentence R?  5.____

    A. P
    B. Q
    C. S
    D. T
    E. None of the above. Sentence R is last.

## KEY (CORRECT ANSWERS)

1. E
2. C
3. D
4. C
5. E

# TEST 2

DIRECTIONS: Each group of sentences in this section is actually a paragraph presented in scrambled order. Each sentence in the group has a place in that paragraph; no sentence is to be left out. You are to read each group of sentences, so as to form a well-organized paragraph. Before trying to answer the questions which follow each group of sentences, jot down the correct order of the sentences. Then answer each of the questions by printing the letter of the correct answer in the space at the right. Remember that you will receive credit only for answers marked.

P. Then it requires knowledge and effort.
Q. The former is my view.
R. Or is love a pleasant sensation, something one *falls into* if one is lucky?
S. The majority of people today, however, believe in the latter.
T. Is love an art?

1. Which sentence did you put second?

   A. P   B. Q   C. R   D. S   E. T

2. Which sentence did you put after Sentence S?

   A. P
   B. Q
   C. R
   D. T
   E. None of the above. Sentence S is last.

3. Which sentence did you put before Sentence Q?

   A. P
   B. R
   C. S
   D. T
   E. None of the above. Sentence Q is first.

4. Which sentence did you put before Sentence P?

   A. Q
   B. R
   C. S
   D. T
   E. None of the above. Sentence P is first.

5. Which sentence did you put after Sentence Q?

   A. P
   B. R
   C. S
   D. T
   E. None of the above. Sentence Q is last.

## 2 (#2)
# KEY (CORRECT ANSWERS)

1. A
2. E
3. B
4. D
5. C

# TEST 3

DIRECTIONS: Each group of sentences in this section is actually a paragraph presented in scrambled order. Each sentence in the group has a place in that paragraph; no sentence is to be left out. You are to read each group of sentences, so as to form a well-organized paragraph. Before trying to answer the questions which follow each group of sentences, jot down the correct order of the sentences. Then answer each of the questions by printing the letter of the correct answer in the space at the right. Remember that you will receive credit only for answers marked.

P. Indeed, in his time, Freud's theories of sex had a challenging and revolutionary character.
Q. Sexual mores have changed so much that Freud's theories no longer are shocking to the middle classes.
R. Freud has been criticized for his overevaluation of sex.
S. But what was true sixty years ago is no longer true.
T. This criticism resulted from a wish to remove an element from Freud's system which might arouse criticism among conventionally-minded people.

1. Which sentence did you put last?
   A. P   B. Q   C. R   D. S   E. T

2. Which sentence did you put before Sentence Q?
   A. P
   B. R
   C. S
   D. T
   E. None of the above. Sentence Q is first.

3. Which sentence did you put after Sentence T?
   A. P
   B. Q
   C. R
   D. S
   E. None of the above. Sentence T is last.

4. Which sentence did you put before Sentence R?
   A. P
   B. Q
   C. S
   D. T
   E. None of the above. Sentence R is first.

5. Which sentence did you put after Sentence R?
   A. P
   B. Q
   C. S
   D. T
   E. None of the above. Sentence R is last.

# KEY (CORRECT ANSWERS)

1. B
2. C
3. A
4. E
5. D

# TEST 4

DIRECTIONS: Each group of sentences in this section is actually a paragraph presented in scrambled order. Each sentence in the group has a place in that paragraph; no sentence is to be left out. You are to read each group of sentences, so as to form a well-organized paragraph. Before trying to answer the questions which follow each group of sentences, jot down the correct order of the sentences. Then answer each of the questions by printing the letter of the correct answer in the space at the right. Remember that you will receive credit only for answers marked.

P. Early Scandanavian accounts, as well, are too mythological and legendary to serve as history.
Q. The first trustworthy written evidence of a kingdom of Denmark belongs to the beginning of the Viking period.
R. Ancient Roman knowledge of this remote country was fragmentary and unreliable.
S. Archaeology and the study of place names, however, provide a certain amount of information about the earliest settlements.
T. Everything before that is prehistory.

1. Which sentence did you put fourth?
   A. P   B. B. Q   C. C. R   D. D. S   E. E. T

2. Which sentence did you put after Sentence T?
   A. Q
   B. R
   C. S
   D. None of the above. Sentence T is last.

3. Which sentence did you put after Sentence Q?
   A. P
   B. R
   C. S
   D. T
   E. None of the above. Sentence Q is last.

4. Which sentence did you put before Sentence Q?
   A. P
   B. R
   C. S
   D. T
   E. None of the above. Sentence Q is first.

5. Which sentence did you put after Sentence P?
   A. Q
   B. R
   C. S
   D. T
   E. None of the above. Sentence P is last.

# KEY (CORRECT ANSWERS)

1. A
2. C
3. D
4. E
5. C

# TEST 5

DIRECTIONS: Each group of sentences in this section is actually a paragraph presented in scrambled order. Each sentence in the group has a place in that paragraph; no sentence is to be left out. You are to read each group of sentences, so as to form a well-organized paragraph. Before trying to answer the questions which follow each group of sentences, jot down the correct order of the sentences. Then answer each of the questions by printing the letter of the correct answer in the space at the right. Remember that you will receive credit only for answers marked.

P. In 1268, ambassadors were required to surrender all gifts they had received on their missions.
Q. In the 13th century, the Venetian republic began to lay down rules of conduct for its ambassadors.
R. In 1288, it was decreed that ambassadors were to report in writing on the results of their missions.
S. Such reports are a mine of historical material.
T. It is in Venice that the origins of modern diplomacy are to be sought.

1. Which sentence did you put second? 1._____
   A. P   B. Q   C. R   D. S   E. T

2. Which sentence did you put after Sentence R? 2._____
   A. P
   B. Q
   C. S
   D. T
   E. None of the above. Sentence R is last.

3. Which sentence did you put before Sentence P? 3._____
   A. Q
   B. R
   C. S
   D. T
   E. None of the above. Sentence P is first.

4. Which sentence did you put before Sentence T? 4._____
   A. P
   B. Q
   C. R
   D. S
   E. None of the above. Sentence T is first.

5. Which sentence did you put last? 5._____
   A. P   B. B. Q   C. C. R   D. D. S   E. E. T

2 (#5)

# KEY (CORRECT ANSWERS)

1. B
2. C
3. A
4. E
5. D

---

# PREPARING WRITTEN MATERIALS
## EXAMINATION SECTION
## TEST 1

DIRECTIONS: Each question consists of a sentence which may be classified appropriately under one of the following four categories:
- A. Incorrect because of faulty grammar or sentence structure;
- B. Incorrect because of faulty punctuation;
- C. Incorrect because of faulty capitalization;
- D. Correct

Examine each sentence carefully. Then, in the space at the right, indicate the letter preceding the category which is the BEST of the four suggested above. Each incorrect sentence contains only one type of error. Consider a sentence correct if it contains no errors, although there may be other correct ways of expressing the same thought.

1. All the employees, in this office, are over twenty-one years old.  1._____

2. Neither the clerk nor the stenographer was able to explain what had happened.  2._____

3. Mr. Johnson did not know who he would assign to type the order.  3._____

4. Mr. Marshall called her to report for work on Saturday.  4._____

5. He might of arrived on time if the train has not been delayed.  5._____

6. Some employees on the other hand, are required to fill out these forms every month.  6._____

7. The supervisor issued special instructions to his subordinates to prevent their making errors.  7._____

8. Our supervisor Mr. Williams, expects to be promoted in about two weeks.  8._____

9. We were informed that prof. Morgan would attend the conference.  9._____

10. The clerks were assigned to the old building; the stenographers, to the new building.  10._____

11. The supervisor asked Mr. Smith and I to complete the work as quickly as possible.  11._____

12. He said, that before an employee can be permitted to leave, the report must be finished.  12._____

13. A calculator, in addition to the three computers, are needed in the new office.  13._____

14. Having made many errs in her work, the supervisor asked the typist to be more careful.  14._____

15. "If you are given an assignment," he said, "you should begin work on it as quickly as possible."  15._____

16. All the clerks, including those who have been appointed recently are required to work on the new assignment.  16._____

17. The office manager asked each employee to work one Saturday a month.  17._____

18. Neither Mr. Smith nor Mr. Jones was able to finish his assignment on time.  18._____

19. The task of filing these cards is to be divided equally between you and he.  19._____

20. He is an employee whom we consider to be efficient.  20._____

21. I believe that the new employees are not as punctual as us.  21._____

22. The employees, working in this office, are to be congratulated for their work.  22._____

23. The delay in preparing the report was caused, in his opinion, by the lack of proper supervision and coordination.  23._____

24. John Jones accidentally pushed the wrong button and then all the lights went out.  24._____

25. The investigator ought to of had the witness sign the statement.  25._____

## KEY (CORRECT ANSWERS)

| | | | |
|---|---|---|---|
| 1. | B | 11. | A |
| 2. | D | 12. | B |
| 3. | A | 13. | A |
| 4. | C | 14. | A |
| 5. | A | 15. | D |
| | | | |
| 6. | B | 16. | B |
| 7. | D | 17. | C |
| 8. | B | 18. | D |
| 9. | C | 19. | A |
| 10. | D | 20. | D |

| | |
|---|---|
| 21. | A |
| 22. | B |
| 23. | D |
| 24. | D |
| 25. | A |

# TEST 2

Questions 1-10.

DIRECTIONS: Each of the following sentences may be classified under one of the following four options:
A. Faulty; contains an error in grammar only
B. Faulty; contains an error in spelling only
C. Faulty; contains an error in grammar and an error in spelling
D. Correct; contains no error in grammar or in spelling

Examine each sentence carefully to determine under which of the above four options it is BEST classified. Then, in the space at the right, write the letter preceding the option which is the best of the four listed above.

1. A recognized principle of good management is that an assignment should be given to whomever is best qualified to carry it out. 1.____

2. He considered it a privilege to be allowed to review and summarize the technical reports issued annually by your agency. 2.____

3. Because the warehouse was in an inaccessible location, deliveries of electric fixtures from the warehouse were made only in large lots. 3.____

4. Having requisitioned the office supplies, Miss Brown returned to her desk and resumed the computation of petty cash disbursements. 4.____

5. One of the advantages of this chemical solution is that records treated with it are not inflamable. 5.____

6. The complaint of this employee, in addition to the complaints of the other employees, were submitted to the grievance committee. 6.____

7. A study of the duties and responsibilities of each of the various categories of employees was conducted by an unprejudiced classification analyst. 7.____

8. Ties of friendship with this subordinate compels him to withold the censure that the subordinate deserves. 8.____

9. Neither of the agencies are affected by the decision to institute a program for rehabilitating physically handi-caped men and women. 9.____

10. The chairman stated that the argument between you and he was creating an intolerable situation. 10.____

Questions 11-25.

DIRECTIONS: Each of the following sentences may be classified under one of the following four options:
    A. Correct
    B. Sentence contains an error in spelling
    C. Sentence contains an error in grammar
    D. Sentence contains errors in both grammar and spelling.

11. He reported that he had had a really good time during his vacation although the farm was located in a very inaccessible portion of the country.   11.____

12. It looks to me like he has been fasinated by that beautiful painting.   12.____

13. We have permitted these kind of pencils to accumulate on our shelves, knowing we can sell them at a profit of five cents apiece any time we choose.   13.____

14. Believing that you will want an unexagerated estimate of the amount of business we can expect, I have made every effort to secure accurate figures.   14.____

15. Each and every man, woman and child in that untrammeled wilderness carry guns for protection against the wild animals.   15.____

16. Although this process is different than the one to which he is accustomed, a good chemist will have no trouble.   16.____

17. Insensible to the fuming and fretting going on about him, the engineer continued to drive the mammoth dynamo to its utmost capacity.   17.____

18. Everyone had studied his lesson carefully and was consequently well prepared when the instructor began to discuss the fourth dimention.   18.____

19. I learned Johnny six new arithmetic problems this afternoon.   19.____

20. Athletics is urged by our most prominent citizens as the pursuit which will enable the younger generation to achieve that ideal of education, a sound mind in a sound body.   20.____

21. He did not see whoever was at the door very clearly but thinks it was the city tax appraiser.   21.____

22. He could not scarsely believe that his theories had been substantiated in this convincing fashion.   22.____

23. Although you have displayed great ingenuity in carrying out your assignments, the choice for the position still lies among Brown and Smith.   23.____

24. If they had have pleaded at the time that Smith was an accessory to the crime, it would have lessened the punishment.   24.____

25. It has proven indispensible in his compilation of the facts in the matter.   25.____

## KEY (CORRECT ANSWERS)

| | | | | |
|---|---|---|---|---|
| 1. | A | | 11. | A |
| 2. | D | | 12. | D |
| 3. | B | | 13. | C |
| 4. | D | | 14. | B |
| 5. | B | | 15. | D |
| 6. | A | | 16. | C |
| 7. | D | | 17. | A |
| 8. | C | | 18. | B |
| 9. | C | | 19. | C |
| 10. | A | | 20. | A |

| | |
|---|---|
| 21. | B |
| 22. | D |
| 23. | C |
| 24. | D |
| 25. | B |

# TEST 3

Questions 1-5.

DIRECTIONS: Questions 1 through 5 consist of sentences which may or may not contain errors in grammar or spelling or both. Sentences which do not contain errors in grammar or spelling or both are to be considered correct, even though there may be other correct ways of expressing the same thought. Examine each sentence carefully. Then, in the space at the right, write the letter of the answer which is the BEST of those suggested below.
    A. If the sentence is correct
    B. If the sentence contains an error in spelling
    C. If the sentence contains an error in grammar
    D. If the sentence contains errors in both grammar and spelling.

1. Brown is doing fine although the work is irrevelant to his training.     1._____

2. The conference of sales managers voted to set its adjournment at one o'clock in order to give those present an opportunity to get rid of all merchandise.     2._____

3. He decided that in view of what had taken place at the hotel that he ought to stay and thank the benificent stranger who had rescued him from an embarassing situation.     3._____

4. Since you object to me criticizing your letter, I have no alternative but to consider you a mercenary scoundrel.     4._____

5. I rushed home ahead of schedule so that you will leave me go to the picnic with Mary.     5._____

Questions 6-15.

DIRECTIONS: Some of the following sentences contain an error in spelling, word usage, or sentence structure, or punctuation. Some sentences are correct as they stand although there may be other correct ways of expressing the same thought. All incorrect sentences contain only one error. Mark your answer to each question in the space at the right as follows:
    A. If the sentence has an error in spelling
    B. If the sentence has an error in punctuation or capitalization
    C. If the sentence has an error in word usage or sentence structure
    D. If the sentence is correct

6. Because the chairman failed to keep the participants from wandering off into irrelevant discussions, it was impossible to reach a consensus before the meeting was adjourned.     6._____

7. Certain employers have an unwritten rule that any applicant, who is over 55 years of age, is automatically excluded from consideration for any position whatsoever.     7._____

8. If the proposal to build schools in some new apartment buildings were to be accepted by the builders, one of the advantages that could be expected to result would be better communication between teachers and parents of schoolchildren.  8.____

9. In this instance, the manufacturer's violation of the law against deseptive packaging was discernible only to an experienced inspector.  9.____

10. The tenants' anger stemmed from the president's going to Washington to testify without consulting them first.  10.____

11. Did the president of this eminent banking company say; "We intend to hire and train a number of these disadvantaged youths?"  11.____

12. In addition, today's confidential secretary must be knowledgable in many different areas: for example, she must know modern techniques for making travel arrangements for the executive.  12.____

13. To avoid further disruption of work in the offices, the protesters were forbidden from entering the building unless they had special passes.  13.____

14. A valuable secondary result of our training conferences is the opportunities afforded for management to observe the reactions of the participants.  14.____

15. Of the two proposals submitted by the committee, the first one is the best.  15.____

Questions 16-25.

DIRECTIONS: Each of the following sentences may be classified MOST appropriately under one of the following three categories:
- A. Faulty because of incorrect grammar
- B. Faulty because of incorrect punctuation
- C. Correct

Examine each sentence. Then, print the capital letter preceding the BEST choice of the three suggested above. All incorrect sentences contain only one type of error. Consider a sentence correct if it contains none of the types of errors mentioned, even though there may be other ways of expressing the same thought.

16. He sent the notice to the clerk who you hired yesterday.  16.____

17. It must be admitted, however that you were not informed of this change.  17.____

18. Only the employees who have served in this grade for at least two years are eligible for promotion.  18.____

19. The work was divided equally between she and Mary.  19.____

3 (#3)

20. He thought that you were not available at that time. 20._____

21. When the messenger returns; please give him this package. 21._____

22. The new secretary prepared, typed, addressed, and delivered, the notices. 22._____

23. Walking into the room, his desk can be seen at the rear. 23._____

24. Although John has worked here longer than she, he produces a smaller amount of work. 24._____

25. She said she could of typed this report yesterday. 25._____

## KEY (CORRECT ANSWERS)

| | | | | |
|---|---|---|---|---|
| 1. | D | | 11. | B |
| 2. | A | | 12. | A |
| 3. | D | | 13. | C |
| 4. | C | | 14. | D |
| 5. | C | | 15. | C |
| 6. | A | | 16. | A |
| 7. | B | | 17. | B |
| 8. | D | | 18. | C |
| 9. | A | | 19. | A |
| 10. | D | | 20. | C |

21. B
22. B
23. A
24. C
25. A

# TEST 4

Questions 1-5.

DIRECTIONS: Each of the following sentences may be classified MOST appropriately under one of the following three categories:
- A. Faulty because of incorrect grammar
- B. Faulty because of incorrect punctuation
- C. Correct

Examine each sentence. Then, print the capital letter preceding the BEST choice of the three suggested above. All incorrect sentences contain only one type of error. Consider a sentence correct if it contains none of the types of errors mentioned, even though there may be other ways of expressing the same thought.

1. Neither one of these procedures are adequate for the efficient performance of this task.   1._____

2. The keyboard is the tool of the typist; the cash register, the tool of the cashier.   2._____

3. "The assignment must be completed as soon as possible" said the supervisor.   3._____

4. As you know, office handbooks are issued to all new employees.   4._____

5. Writing a speech is sometimes easier than to deliver it before an audience.   5._____

Questions 6-15.

DIRECTIONS: Each statement given in Questions 6 through 15 contains one of the faults of English usage listed below. For each, choose from the options listed the MAJOR fault contained.
- A. The statement is not a complete sentence.
- B. The statement contains a word or phrase that is redundant.
- C. The statement contains a long, less commonly used word when a shorter, more direct word would be acceptable.
- D. The statement contains a colloquial expression that normally is avoided in business writing.

6. The fact that this activity will afford an opportunity to meet your group.   6._____

7. Do you think that the two groups can join together for next month's meeting?   7._____

8. This is one of the most exciting new innovations to be introduced into our college.   8._____

106

2 (#4)

9. We expect to consummate the agenda before the meeting ends tomorrow at noon. 9._____

10. While this seminar room is small in size, we think we can use it. 10._____

11. Do you think you can make a modification in the date of the Budget Committee meeting? 11._____

12. We are cognizant of the problem but we think we can ameliorate the situation. 12._____

13. Shall I call you around three on the day I arrive in the City? 13._____

14. Until such time that we know precisely that the students will be present. 14._____

15. The consensus of opinion of all the members present is reported in the minutes. 15._____

Questions 16-25.

DIRECTIONS: For each of Questions 16 through 25, select from the options given below the MOST applicable choice.
  A. The sentence is correct.
  B. The sentence contains a spelling error only.
  C. The sentence contains an English grammar error only.
  D. The sentence contains both a spelling error and an English grammar error.

16. Every person in the group is going to do his share. 16._____

17. The man who we selected is new to this University. 17._____

18. She is the older of the four secretaries on the two staffs that are to be combined. 18._____

19. The decision has to be made between him and I. 19._____

20. One of the volunteers are too young for his complicated task, don't you think? 20._____

21. I think your idea is splindid and it will improve this report considerably. 21._____

22. Do you think this is an exagerated account of the behavior you and me observed this morning? 22._____

23. Our supervisor has a clear idea of excelence. 23._____

24. How many occurences were verified by the observers? 24._____

25. We must complete the typing of the draft of the questionaire by noon tomorrow.  25._____

## KEY (CORRECT ANSWERS)

1. A
2. C
3. B
4. C
5. A

6. A
7. B
8. B
9. C
10. B

11. C
12. C
13. D
14. A
15. B

16. A
17. C
18. C
19. C
20. D

21. B
22. D
23. B
24. B
25. B

# WRITTEN ENGLISH EXPRESSION
## EXAMINATION SECTION
## TEST 1

DIRECTIONS: In each of the sentences below, four portions are underlined and lettered. Read each sentence and decide whether any of the UNDERLINED parts contains an error in spelling, punctuation, or capitalization, or employs grammatical usage which would be inappropriate for carefully written English. If so, note the letter printed under the unacceptable form and indicate this choice in the space at the right. If all four of the underlined portions are acceptable as they stand, select the answer E. (No sentence contains more than ONE unacceptable form.)

1. The revised <u>procedure</u> was <u>quite</u> different <u>than</u> the one which <u>was</u> employed up to that time. <u>No error</u>
       A             B             C                  D     E

1.____

2. <u>Blinded</u> by the storm that <u>surrounded</u> him, his plane <u>kept going</u> in <u>circles</u>. <u>No error</u>
    A                  B                    C     D    E

2.____

3. They <u>should</u> give the book to <u>whoever</u> <u>they</u> think deserves <u>it</u>. <u>No error</u>
        A                    B   C            D  E

3.____

4. The <u>government</u> will not consent to your <u>firm</u> <u>sending</u> that package as <u>second class</u> matter. <u>No error</u>
        A                       B    C         D     E

4.____

5. She <u>would have</u> avoided all the trouble <u>that</u> followed if she <u>would have</u> waited ten minutes <u>longer</u>. <u>No error</u>
      A                   B            C       D   E

5.____

6. <u>His</u> poetry, <u>when</u> it was carefully examined, showed <u>characteristics</u> not unlike <u>Wordsworth</u>. <u>No error</u>
 A         B                           C          D   E

6.____

7. <u>In my opinion</u>, based upon long years of research, <u>I think</u> the plan offered by my opponent is <u>unsound</u>, because it is not <u>founded</u> on true facts. <u>No error</u>
    A                                  B              C               D       E

7.____

8. The soldiers of <u>Washington's</u> army at Valley Forge <u>were</u> men ragged in
        A                                                B
<u>appearance</u> but <u>who were</u> noble in character.  <u>No error</u>
        C              D                                      E

9. Rabbits <u>have a distrust</u> of man <u>due to</u> the fact <u>that</u> they are <u>so often</u> shot.
                    A                       B                C                     D
<u>No error</u>
      E

10. <u>This</u> is the man <u>who</u> I believe <u>is</u> best <u>qualified</u> for the position.  <u>No error</u>
         A                      B                 C               D                                              E

11. Her voice was <u>not only</u> <u>good</u>, but <u>she</u> also very clearly <u>enunciated</u>.
                             A              B             C                                    D
<u>No error</u>
      E

12. <u>Today he</u> is wearing a <u>different</u> suit <u>than</u> the <u>one</u> he wore yesterday.  <u>No error</u>
          A                                B                 C              D                                              E

13. Our work <u>is</u> to improve the club; if anybody <u>must</u> resign, let it <u>not</u> be you or <u>I</u>.
                     A                                             B                          C                     D
<u>No error</u>
      E

14. There was so much talking <u>in back of</u> me <u>as</u> I <u>could</u> not <u>enjoy</u> the music.
                                                A                  B             C                  D
<u>No error</u>
      E

15. <u>Being that</u> he is that <u>kind of</u> <u>boy</u>, he cannot be blamed <u>for</u> the mistake.
           A                            B              C                                            D
<u>No error</u>
      E

16. <u>The king, having read</u> the speech, <u>he</u> and the <u>queen</u> <u>departed</u>.  <u>No error</u>
                   A                                       B                       C                D                E

17. I <u>am</u> <u>so tired</u> I <u>can't</u> <u>scarcely</u> stand.  <u>No error</u>
        A         B              C               D                           E

18. We are <u>mailing bills</u> to our customers <u>in Canada</u>, and, <u>being</u> eager to
                       A                                             B                        C
clear our books before the new season opens, it is <u>to be hoped</u> they will
                                                                                    D
send their remittances promptly.  <u>No error</u>
                                                           E

3 (#1)

19. I reluctantly acquiesced to the proposal. No error      19._____
    A    B          C              D          E

20. It had lain out in the rain all night. No error      20._____
    A  B   C          D        E

21. If he would have gone there, he would have seen a marvelous sight.      21._____
         A              B          C                   D
    No error
    E

22. The climate of Asia Minor is somewhat like Utah. No error      22._____
                 A            B     C          D     E

23. If everybody did unto others as they would wish others to do unto them, this      23._____
          A      B    C                 D
    world would be a paradise. No error
                               E

24. This was the jockey whom I saw was most likely to win the race. No error      24._____
    A                  B        C              D               E

25. The only food the general demanded was potatoes. No error      25._____
        A                     B       C    D         E

---

# KEY (CORRECT ANSWERS)

| | | | | |
|---|---|---|---|---|
| 1. | C | | 11. | C |
| 2. | A | | 12. | C |
| 3. | B | | 13. | D |
| 4. | B | | 14. | B |
| 5. | C | | 15. | A |
| 6. | D | | 16. | A |
| 7. | B | | 17. | C |
| 8. | D | | 18. | C |
| 9. | B | | 19. | E |
| 10. | E | | 20. | E |

21. A
22. D
23. D
24. B
25. E

# TEST 2

DIRECTIONS: In each of the sentences below, four portions are underlined and lettered. Read each sentence and decide whether any of the UNDERLINED parts contains an error in spelling, punctuation, or capitalization, or employs grammatical usage which would be inappropriate for carefully written English. If so, note the letter printed under the unacceptable form and indicate this choice in the space at the right. If all four of the underlined portions are acceptable as they stand, select the answer E. (No sentence contains more than ONE unacceptable form.)

1. A party <u>like</u> <u>that</u> <u>only</u> <u>comes</u> once a year. <u>No error</u>
           A     B    C     D                      E

2. <u>Our's</u> <u>is</u> <u>a</u> <u>swift moving</u> age. <u>No error</u>
   A    B C     D              E

3. The <u>healthy</u> climate soon <u>restored</u> him <u>to</u> his <u>accustomed</u> vigor. <u>No error</u>
      A                  B         C        D              E

4. <u>They</u> needed six typists and hoped that <u>only</u> that <u>many</u> <u>would</u> apply for the position. <u>No error</u>
   A                                        B         C    D
   E

5. He <u>interviewed</u> people <u>whom</u> he thought had <u>something</u> <u>to impart</u>. <u>No error</u>
        A                B                    C       D      E

6. <u>Neither</u> of his three sisters <u>is</u> older <u>than</u> <u>he</u>. <u>No error</u>
    A                      B        C D   E

7. <u>Since</u> he is <u>that</u> <u>kind</u> of <u>a</u> boy, he cannot be expected to cooperate with us. <u>No error</u>
   A         B   C    D
   E

8. <u>When passing</u> <u>through</u> the tunnel, the air pressure <u>affected</u> <u>our</u> years. <u>No error</u>
     A             B                                 C    D          E

9. <u>The story having</u> a sad ending, <u>it</u> never <u>achieved</u> popularity <u>among</u> the students. <u>No error</u>
     A                            B        C                 D
   E

10. <u>Since</u> we are both hungry, <u>shall</u> we go <u>somewhere</u> for lunch<u>?</u> <u>No error</u>
    A                       B          C              D  E

11. Will you please bring this book down to the library and give it to my friend, 11.____
    A         B              C                                              D
    who is waiting for it?  No error
                            E

12. You may have the book; I am finished with it.  No error              12.____
        A    B             C           D          E

13. I don't know if I should mention it to her or not.  No error         13.____
       A       B    C            D                      E

14. Philosophy is not a subject which has to do with philosophers and    14.____
                       A        B      C
    mathematics only.  No error
                D       E

15. The thoughts of the scholar in his library are little different than the old woman  15.____
                                A                                    B
    who first said, "It's no use crying over spilt milk."  No error
                     C                                D    E

16. A complete system of philosophical ideas are implied in many simple   16.____
                A                           B    C
    utterances.  No error
        D         E

17. Even if one has never put them into words, his ideas compose a kind of a  17.____
         A                 B              C         D
    philosophy.  No error
                 E

18. Perhaps it is well enough that most people do not attempt this formulation.  18.____
              A   B                 C                              D
    No error
    E

19. Leading their ordered lives, this confused body of ideas and feelings is  19.____
        A                              B       C                         D
    sufficient.  No error
                 E

20. Why should we insist upon them formulating it?  No error             20.____
        A         B     C    D                      E

21. Since it includes something of the wisdom of the ages, it is adequate for the  21.____
      A              B                                          C
    purposes of ordinary life.  No error
        D                       E

22. Therefore, I <u>have sought</u> to make a pattern <u>of mine,</u> <u>and so</u> there were, early
                  A                                  B      C
    moments of <u>my trying</u> to find out what were the elements with which I had to
                     D
    deal. <u>No error</u>
            E

    22.____

23. I <u>wanted</u> <u>to get</u> <u>what</u> knowledge I <u>could</u> about the general structure of the
        A      B     C            D
    universe. <u>No error</u>
               E

    23.____

24. I wanted to <u>know</u> <u>if</u> life <u>per se</u> had any meaning or <u>whether</u> I must strive to give
                 A  B       C                     D
    it one. <u>No error</u>
            E

    24.____

25. <u>So,</u> in a <u>desultory</u> way, I <u>began</u> <u>to read</u>. <u>No error</u>
     A         B             C    D      E

    25.____

## KEY (CORRECT ANSWERS)

| | | | | |
|---|---|---|---|---|
| 1. | C | | 11. | B |
| 2. | A | | 12. | C |
| 3. | A | | 13. | B |
| 4. | C | | 14. | D |
| 5. | B | | 15. | B |
| 6. | A | | 16. | B |
| 7. | D | | 17. | A |
| 8. | A | | 18. | C |
| 9. | A | | 19. | A |
| 10. | E | | 20. | D |

| | |
|---|---|
| 21. | E |
| 22. | C |
| 23. | C |
| 24. | B |
| 25. | E |

# WRITTEN ENGLISH EXPRESSION
# EXAMINATION SECTION
# TEST 1

DIRECTIONS: The following questions are designed to test your knowledge of grammar, sentence structure, correct usage, and punctuation. In each group there is one sentence that contains no errors. Select the letter of the CORRECT sentence. *PRINT THE LETTER OF THE CORRECT ANSWER IN THE SPACE AT THE RIGHT.*

1. A. A low ceiling is when the atmospheric conditions make flying inadvisable.
   B. They couldn't tell who the card was from.
   C. No one but you and I are to help him.
   D. What kind of a teacher would you like to be?
   E. To him fall the duties of foster parent.

   1.____

2. A. They couldn't tell whom the cable was from.
   B. We like these better than those kind.
   C. It is a test of you more than I.
   D. The person in charge being him, there can be no change in policy.
   E. Chicago is larger than any city in Illinois.

   2.____

3. A. Do as we do for the celebration.
   B. Do either of you care to join us?
   C. A child's food requirements differ from the adult.
   D. A large family including two uncles and four grandparents live at the hotel.
   E. Due to bad weather, the game was postponed.

   3.____

4. A. If they would have done that they might have succeeded.
   B. Neither the hot days or the humid nights annoy our Southern visitor.
   C. Some people do not gain favor because they are kind of tactless.
   D. No sooner had the turning point come than a new issue arose.
   E. I wish that I was in Florida now.

   4.____

5. A. We haven't hardly enough tine.
   B. Immigration is when people come into a foreign country to live.
   C. After each side gave their version, the affair was over with.
   D. Every one of the cars were tagged by the police.
   E. He either will fail in his attempt or will seek other employment.

   5.____

6. A. They can't seem to see it when I explain the theory.
   B. It is difficult to find the genuine signature between all those submitted.
   C. She can't understand why they don't remember who to give the letter to
   D. Every man and woman in America is interested in his tax bill.
   E. Honor as well as profit are to be gained by these studies.

   6.____

7.  A. He arrived safe.
    B. I do not have any faith in John running for office.
    C. The musicians began to play tunefully and keeping the proper tempo indicated for the selection.
    D. Mary's maid of honor bought the kind of an outfit suitable for an afternoon wedding.
    E. If you would have studied the problem carefully you would have found the solution more quickly.

8.  A. The new plant is to be electric lighted.
    B. The reason the speaker was offended was that the audience was inattentive.
    C. There appears to be conditions that govern his behavior.
    D. Either of the men are influential enough to control the situation.
    E. The gallery with all its pictures were destroyed.

9.  A. If you would have listened more carefully, you would have heard your name called.
    B. Did you inquire if your brother were returning soon?
    C. We are likely to have rain before nightfall.
    D. Let's you and I plan next summer's vacation together.
    E. The man whom I thought was my friend deceived me.

10. A. There's a man and his wife waiting for the doctor since early this morning.
    B. The owner of the market with his assistants is applying the most modern principles of merchandise display.
    C. Every one of the players on both of the competing teams were awarded a gold watch.
    D. The records of the trial indicated that, even before attaining manhood, the murderer's parents were both dead.
    E. We had no sooner entered the room when the bell rang.

11. A. Why don't you start the play like I told you?
    B. I didn't find the construction of the second house much different from that of the first one I saw.
    C. "When", inquired the child, "Will we begin celebrating my birthday?"
    D. There isn't nothing left to do but not to see him anymore.
    E. There goes the last piece of cake and the last spoonful of ice cream.

12. A. The child could find neither the shoe or the stocking.
    B. The musicians began to play tunefully and keeping the proper tempo indicated for the selection.
    C. The amount of curious people who turned out for Opening Night was beyond calculation.
    D. I fully expected that the children would be at their desks and to find them ready to begin work,
    E. "Indeed," mused the poll-taker, "the winning candidate is much happier than I."

13. A. Just as you said, I find myself gaining weight.
    B. A teacher should leave the capable pupils engage in creative activities.
    C. The teacher spoke continually during the entire lesson, which, of course, was poor procedure.
    D. We saw him steal into the room, pick up the letter, and tear it's contents to shreds.
    E. It is so dark that I can't hardly see.

13.____

14. A. The new schedule of working hours and rates was satis factory to both employees and employer.
    B. Many common people feel keenly about the injustices of Power Politics.
    C. Mr. and Mrs. Burns felt that their grandchild was awfully cute when he waved good-bye.
    D. The tallest of the twins was also the most intelligent,
    E. Please come here and try and help me finish this piece of work.

14.____

15. A. My younger brother insists that he is as tall as me.
    B. Suffering from a severe headache all day, one dose of the prescribed medicine relieved me,
    C. "Please let my brothers and I help you with your packages," said Frank to Mrs. Powers.
    D. Every one of the rooms we visited had displays of pupils' work in them.
    E. Do you intend bringing most of the refreshments yourself?

15.____

16. A. The telephone linesmen, working steadily at their task during the severe storm, the telephones soon began to ring again.
    B. Meat, as well as fruits and vegetables, is considered essential to a proper diet.
    C. He looked like a real good boxer that night in the ring.
    D. The man has worked steadily for fifteen years before he decided to open his own business.
    E. The winters were hard and dreary, nothing could live without shelter.

16.____

17. A. No one can foretell when I will have another opportunity like that one again.
    B. The last group of paintings shown appear really to have captured the most modern techniques,
    C. We searched high and low, both in the attic and cellar, but were unsuccessful in locating mementos.
    D. None of the guests was able to give the rules of the game accurately.
    E. When you go to the library tomorrow, please bring this book to the librarian in the reference room.

17.____

18. A. After the debate, every one of the speakers realized that, given another chance, he could have done better.
    B. The reason given by the physician for the patient's trouble was because of his poor eating habits.
    C. The fog was so thick that the driver couldn't hardly see more than ten feet ahead.
    D. I suggest that you present the medal to who you think best.
    E. I don't approve of him going along.

18.____

19. A. A decision made by a man without much deliberation is sometimes no different than a slow one.
    B. By the time Mr. Brown's son will graduate Dental School, he will be twenty-six years of age.
    C. Who did you predict would win the election?
    D. The auctioneer had less stamps to sell this year than last year.
    E. Being that he is occupied, I shall not disturb him.

20. A. Having pranced into the arena with little grace and unsteady hoof for the jumps ahead, the driver reined his horse.
    B. Once the dog wagged it's tail, you knew it was a friendly animal.
    C. Like a great many artists, his life was a tragedy.
    D. When asked to choose corn, cabbage, or potatoes, the diner selected the latter.
    E. The record of the winning team was among the most noteworthy of the season.

21. A. The maid wasn't so small that she couldn't reach the top window for cleaning.
    B. Many people feel that powdered coffee produces a really good flavor.
    C. Would you mind me trying that coat on for size?
    D. This chair looks much different than the chair we selected in the store.
    E. I wish that he would have talked to me about the lesson before he presented it.

22. A. After trying unsuccessfully to land a job in the city, Will located in the country on a farm.
    B. On the last attempt, the pole-vaulter came nearly to getting hurt.
    C. The observance of Armistice Day throughout the world offers an opportunity to reflect on the horrors of war.
    D. Outside of the mistakes in spelling, the child's letter was a very good one.
    E. The annual income of New York is far greater than Florida.

23. A. Scissors is always dangerous for a child to handle.
    B. I assure you that I will not yield to pressure to sell my interest.
    C. Ask him if he has recall of the incident which took place at our first meeting.
    D. The manager felt like as not to order his usher-captain to surrender his uniform.
    E. Everyone on the boat said their prayers when the storm grew worse.

24. A. The mother of the bride climaxed the occasion by exclaiming, "I want my children should be happy forever."
    B. We read in the papers where the prospects for peace are improving.
    C. "Can I share the cab with you?" was frequently heard during the period of gas rationing.
    D. The man was enamored with his friend"s sister.
    E. Had the police suspected the ruse, they would have taken proper precautions.

25. A. The teacher admonished the other students neither to speak to John, nor should they annoy him.
    B. Fortunately we had been told that there was but one service station in that area.
    C. An usher seldom rises above a theatre manager.
    D. The epic, "Gone With the Wind," is supposed to have taken place during the Civil War Era.
    E. Now that she has been graduated she should be encouraged to make her own choice as to the career she is to follow.

## KEY (CORRECT ANSWERS)

1. E
2. A
3. A
4. D
5. E

6. D
7. A
8. B
9. C
10. B

11. B
12. E
13. A
14. A
15. E

16. B
17. D
18. A
19. C
20. E

21. B
22. C
23. B
24. E
25. B

---

# TEST 2

DIRECTIONS: The following questions are designed to test your knowledge of grammar, sentence structure, correct usage, and punctuation. In each group, there is one sentence that contains no errors. Select the letter of the CORRECT sentence. *PRINT THE LETTER OF THE CORRECT ANSWER IN THE SPACE AT THE RIGHT.*

1. 
   A. Shall you be at home, let us say, on Sunday at two o'clock?
   B. We see Mr. Lewis take his car out of the garage daily, newly polished always.
   C. We have no place to keep our rubbers, only in the hall closet.
   D. Isn't it true what you told me about the best way to prepare for an examination?
   E. Mathematics is among my favorite subjects.

   1._____

2. 
   A. The host thought the guests were of the hungry kinds so he prepared much food.
   B. The museum is often visited by students who are fond of early inventions, and especially patent attorneys.
   C. I rose to nominate the man who most of us felt was the most diligent worker in the group.
   D. The child was sent to the store to purchase a bottle of milk, and brought home fresh rolls, too.
   E. Hidden away in the closet, I found the long-lost purse.

   2._____

3. 
   A. The garden tool was sent to be sharpened, and a new handle to be put on.
   B. At the end of her vacation, Joan came home with little money, but which systematic thrift soon overcame.
   C. We people have opportunities to show the rest of the world how real democracy functions.
   D. The guide paddled along, then fell in a reverie which he related the history of the region.
   E. No sooner had the curtain dropped when the audience shouted its approval in chorus.

   3._____

4. 
   A. The data you need is to be made available shortly.
   B. The first few strokes of the brush were enough to convince me that Tom could paint much better than me.
   C. We inquired if we could see the owner of the store, after we waited for one hour.
   D. The highly-strung parent was aggravated by the slightest noise that the baby made.
   E. We should have investigated the cause of the noise by bringing the car to a halt.

   4._____

5. 
   A. The police, investigating the crime, were successful in discovering only one possibly valuable clue.
   B. Due to an unexpected change in plans, the violin soloist did not perform.
   C. Besides being awarded a Bachelor's degree at college, the scientist has since received many honorary degrees.
   D. The data offered in advance of the recent Presidential election seems to have possessed elements of inaccuracy.
   E. I don't believe your the only one who has been asked to come here.

   5._____

6.  A. I don't quite see that I will be able to completely finish the job in time.
    B. By my statement, I infer that you are guilty of the offense as charged.
    C. Wasn't it strange that they wouldn't let no one see the body?
    D. I hope that this is the kind of rolls you requested me to buy.
    E. The storekeeper distributed cigars as bonuses between his many customers.

    6._____

7.  A. He said he preferred the climate of Florida to California.
    B. Because of the excessive heat, a great amount of fruit juice was drunk by the guests.
    C. This week's dramatic presentation was neither as lively nor as entertaining as last week.
    D. The fashion expert believed that no one could develop new creations more successfully than him.
    E. A collection of Dicken's works is a "must" for every library.

    7._____

8.  A. There was such a large amount of books on the floor that I couldn't find a place for my rocking chair.
    B. Walking up the rickety stairs, the bottle slipped from his hands and smashed.
    C. The reason they granted his request was because he had a good record.
    D. Little Tommy was proud that the teacher always asked him to bring messages to the office.
    E. That kind of orange is grown only in Florida.

    8._____

9.  A. The new mayor is a resident of this city for thirty years.
    B. Do you mean to imply that had he not missed that shot he would have won?
    C. Next term I shall be studying French and history.
    D. I read in last night's paper where the sales tax is going to be abolished.
    E. In order to prevent breakage, she placed a sheet of paper between each of the plates when she packed them.

    9._____

10. A. To have children vie against one another is psychologically unsound.
    B. Would anyone else care to discuss his baby?
    C. He was interested and aware of the problem.
    D. I sure would like to discover if he is motivating the lesson properly.
    E. The cloth was first lain on a flat surface; then it was pressed with a hot iron.

    10._____

11. A. She graduated Barnard College twenty-five years ago.
    B. He studied the violin since he was seven.
    C. She is not so diligent a researcher as her classmate.
    D. He discovered that the new data corresponds with the facts disclosed by Werner.
    E. How could he enjoy the television program; the dog was barking and the baby was crying.

    11._____

12. A. You have three alternatives: law, dentistry, or teaching.
    B. If I would have worked harder, I would have accomplished my purpose.
    C. He affected a rapid change of pace and his opponents were outdistanced.
    D. He looked prosperous, although he had been unemployed for a year.
    E. The engine not only furnishes power but light and heat as well.

    12._____

13. A. The children shared one anothers toys and seemed quite happy.
    B. They lay in the sun for many hours, getting tanned.
    C. The reproduction arrived, and had been hung in the living room.
    D. First begin by calling the roll.
    E. Tell me where you hid it; no one shall ever find it.

14. A. Deliver these things to whomever arrives first.
    B. Everybody but she and me is going to the conference.
    C. If the number of patrons is small, we can serve them.
    D. When each of the contestants find their book, the debate may begin.
    E. Some people, farmers in particular, lament the substitution of butter by margarine.

15. A. After his illness, he stood in the country three weeks.
    B. If you wish to effect a change, submit your suggestions.
    C. It is silly to leave children play with knives.
    D. Play a trick on her by spilling water down her neck.
    E. There was such a crowd of people at the crossing we couldn't hardly get on the bus.

16. A. This is a time when all of us must show our faith and devotion to our country.
    B. Either you or I are certain to be elected president of the new club.
    C. The interpellation of the Minister of Finance forced him to explain his policies.
    D. After hoisting the anchor and removing the binnacle, the ship was ready to set sail.
    E. Please bring me a drink of cold water from the refrigerator.

17. A. Mistakes in English, when due to carelessness or haste, can easily be rectified.
    B. Mr. Jones is one of those persons who will try to keep a promise and usually does.
    C. Being very disturbed by what he had heard, Fred decided to postpone his decision.
    D. There is a telephone at the other end of the corridor which is constantly in use.
    E. In his teaching, he always kept the childrens' interests and needs in mind.

18. A. The lazy pupil, of course, will tend to write the minimum amount of words acceptable.
    B. His success as a political leader consisted mainly of his ability to utter platitudes in a firm and convincing manner.
    C. To be cognizant of current affairs, a person must not only read newspapers and magazines but also recent books by recognized authorities.
    D. Although we intended to have gone fishing, the sudden outbreak of a storm caused us to change our plans.
    E. It is the colleges that must take the responsibility for encouraging greater flexibility in the high-school curriculum.

19.  A. "I am sorry," he said, "but John's answer was 'No'."
     B. A spirited argument followed between those who favored and opposed Marie's expulsion from the club.
     C. Whether a forward child should be humored or punished often depends upon the circumstances.
     D. Excessive alcoholism is certainly not conducive with efficient performance of one's work.
     E. Stroking his beard thoughtfully, an idea suddenly came to him.

     19._____

20.  A. "Take care, my children," he said sadly, "lest you not be deceived."
     B. Those continuous telephone calls are preventing Betty from completing her homework.
     C. They dug deep into the earth at the spot indicated on the map, but they found nothing.
     D. We petted and cozened the little girl until she finally stopped weeping.
     E. There was, in the mail, an inquiry for a house by a young couple with two or three bedrooms.

     20._____

21.  A. Please fill in the required information on the application form and return same by April 15.
     B. Tom was sitting there idly, watching the clouds scud across the sky.
     C. We started for home so that our parents would not suspect that anything out of the ordinary took place.
     D. The sudden abatement from the storm enabled the ladies to resume their journey.
     E. Each of the twelve members were agreed that the accused man was innocent.

     21._____

22.  A. The number of gifted students not continuing their education beyond secondary school present a nationwide problem.
     B. A man's animadversions against those he considers his enemies are usually reflections of his own inadequacies.
     C. The alembic of his fevered imagination produced some of the greatest romantic poetry of his era.
     D. The first case of smallpox dates back more than 3000 years and has gone unchecked until recently.
     E. He promised to go irregardless of the rain or snow.

     22._____

23.  A. The child picked up several of the coracles, which he had seen glittering in the sand, and brought them to his mother.
     B. He muttered in dejected tones – and no one contradicted him – "We have failed."
     C. A girl whom I believed to be she waved cheerily to me from a passing automobile.
     D. We discovered that she was a former resident of our own neighborhood who eloped some years ago with a milkman.
     E. It looks now like he will not be promoted after all.

     23._____

24. A. Mary is the kind of a person on whom you can depend in any emergency. 24.____
    B. I am sure that either applicant can fill the job you offer competently and efficiently.
    C. Although we searched the entire room, the scissors was not to be found.
    D. Being that you are here, we can proceed with the discussion.
    E. In spite of our warning whistle, the huge ship continued to sail athwart our course.

25. A. The salaries earned by college graduates vary as much if not more than those 25.____
       earned by high school graduates.
    B. The apothegms that he felt to be so witty were all too often either trite or platitudinous.
    C. She read the letter carefully, took out one of the pages, and tore it into small pieces.
    D. A young man, who hopes to succeed, must be diligent in his work and alert to his opportunities.
    E. No one should plan a long journey for pleasure in these days.

# KEY (CORRECT ANSWERS)

1. A
2. C
3. C
4. E
5. A

6. D
7. B
8. E
9. B
10. B

11. C
12. D
13. E
14. C
15. B

16. C
17. A
18. E
19. C
20. C

21. B
22. C
23. B
24. E
25. B

# ENGLISH EXPRESSION
# EXAMINATION SECTION
## TEST 1

DIRECTIONS: In each of the following groups, ONE sentence contains an underlined word which makes the sentence INCORRECT. Select this incorrect sentence. *PRINT THE LETTER OF THE CORRECT ANSWER IN THE SPACE AT THE RIGHT.*

1.  A. It is easier to overlook a man's faults when one is fully cognizant of his virtues.
    B. Federal aid to education is still a moot question.
    C. The acrid odor made the passengers glad to leave the stalled bus.
    D. We understand people of other historical periods better if we can extemporize the characteristics of men of all ages.
    E. The tourists found it difficult to balance themselves atop the ambling dromedaries.

    1.____

2.  A. An organization will not succeed if fractious persons are allowed to disrupt the meetings.
    B. Playwrights must avoid anachronisms, for such errors may be distracting or wrongly humorous to an audience.
    C. Some legislators object to leaving their home towns twice a year to attend the biennial sessions of the legislature.
    D. Few would argue that vicarious experience is a satisfactory substitute for personal participation.
    E. The missionaries did not realize the futility of trying to trace the tributaries of the Amazon.

    2.____

3.  A. Cognate words come from the same root, but they often develop different meanings.
    B. An effete civilization tends to produce little or nothing that is new.
    C. In a tribal society, numerous subtribes or diatribes develop as new leaders arise.
    D. The man is so maladroit in his relations with other people that he makes everybody angry.
    E. A person as gauche as he is must find social gatherings difficult.

    3.____

4.  A. The drug took effect quickly, and the patient was soon quiescent.
    B. India has in the last two years taken steps to defend her own territory from encroachments by Communist China.
    C. The governor dismissed the condemned man's plea in cavalier fashion.
    D. No financial institution would ever consider hiring a cashier guilty of such duplicity.
    E. The sedimentary habits of the penguin make it an unusually easy creature to capture.

    4.____

2 (#1)

5.  A. The chieftains relied upon necromancy to guide them in making their decisions.
    B. The meat glowed as it was brought into the dining room on ewers.
    C. His heart remained obdurate to the many cries for help.
    D. The community was shocked to find that the child had been accused of parricide.
    E. No person with so raucous a voice should be a teacher.

5.____

6.  A. Acids have a deleterious effect on the skin and should be handled with care.
    B. The index of the encyclopedia brings all subjects together in one weighty tone.
    C. He was sorry to find that his dissidence made him one of a very small minority.
    D. This television set is so light that even a child finds it easily potable.
    E. Men like Abraham Lincoln educated themselves only by remitting effort

6.____

7.  A. George's long-standing interest in insect life has led him to make entomology his career.
    B. The Russian trochee is a vehicle admirably suited for traversing the rugged countryside.
    C. Although he was unemployed and penniless, Barton's fierce pride precluded his becoming a mendicant.
    D. The magazine rejected the manuscript with the comment that it was a banal attempt at satire.
    E. Some pupils find mnemonic devices helpful when they take tests.

7.____

8.  A. Cranshaw is considered a perfect gentleman because of his neat appearance and implacable manner.
    B. "You tend to exaggerate," the teacher responded euphemistically, knowing full well the student had lied.
    C. Who would dare question the rectitude of Sir Winston Churchill?
    D. The tractable puppy was trained quite easily.
    E. The audience's sincere applause was an auspicious beginning for the new opera company.

8.____

9.  A. His prevarication upon the witness stand may lead to his being indicted for perjury.
    B. She has so volatile temperament that we never know just what reaction to expect.
    C. A parsimonious person is hardly likely to make liberal donations to charity.
    D. Unless additional facts are disclosed, the evidence militates against acquittal.
    E. Most golfers agree that an enervating massage gives them the stamina for an additional nine holes.

9.____

10. A. We felt the seriousness of his offense was somewhat mitigated when he explained the circumstances fully.
    B. The folk singers were accused of violating the city's anti-noise ordnance.

10.____

C. The acrimony of the campaign was very much in evidence in bitter exchanges in the last debate.
D. The writer's quixotic approach to the problems of life indicates a lack of maturity.
E. Although Mr. Jones disavowed his agent's acts, the court found him guilty.

11. A. The speaker's message was lost, for the audience was distracted by his raucous voice.
    B. He found his low-lying property to be of little value because an overflowing stream had turned it into a fen.
    C. Mundane affairs keep some people so busy that they have no time for intellectual or spiritual pursuits.
    D. The typical hermit, living simply and frugally, hoped to become a model of sybaritic existence.
    E. Certain foods are perennial favorites.

11._____

12. A. Careful study of synonyms makes it possible to bring out nuances of meaning.
    B. One way to change the terms of a will is to add a codicil.
    C. Excessive development of fatuous tissue puts a strain on the heart.
    D. The politician tried to flay his opponent in a series of scathing speeches.
    E. It is a sobering thought that all man builds seems to be transitory.

12._____

13. A. The team's winning the pennant so pleased the mayor that he declared a day of holocaust for the entire city.
    B. Most people would enjoy a covert spot in which they could escape the annoyances of daily life.
    C. To a stupid person, cerebration is neither easy nor interesting.
    D. False advertising often is intended to conceal the fact that the merchandise offered is mere trumpery.
    E. Her manner was so effusive upon being introduced that we doubted her sincerity.

13._____

14. A. When the defending chess champion lost his queen, he knew that the outcome of the game was inevitable, regardless of the dilatory tactics he might employ.
    B. False cures are dangerous because they merely palliate a disease.
    C. The audience relished hearing the speaker's euphonious statements.
    D. One needs an agile mind and a glib tongue to cope with such persiflage.
    E. The judge noted that it would have taxed the court's credibility to the utmost to believe so untrustworthy a witness.

14._____

15. A. We must consider orthography to be a basic element of the language arts program.
    B. The prolixity of the oration caused many in the audience to become restless.
    C. The guns were quickly dissembled so that they could be packed for shipment.

15._____

D. The besieged potentate was informed that he was not to be considered the quondam king.
E. In a democratic society, one who tries to arrogate to himself too much power may find himself rejected by the voters.

16. A. Although the final surface has not been laid, the contractor believes that the road is viable for light traffic.
    B. The judge ordered the attorney's rude remark expunged from the record.
    C. Can you trust a man whose philosophy is the very antithesis of your own?
    D. He can supply rabbits to a large market because he maintains a warren on his farm.
    E. Not wishing to make a new will, he added a codicil to the old one.

16.____

17. A. The ichthyologist was interested in deep-sea diving, because he wanted to study the kinds of life found in the ocean.
    B. Numbed by the cold of the Arctic regions, the explorer realized that he had become torpid.
    C. In the vernacular days of March, weather is likely to be very changeable.
    D. Since he preferred the company of his books, the author eschewed the parties given by his friends.
    E. The unwilling convert is almost sure to recant when persuasion has stopped.

17.____

18. A. The strange combination of the speaker's handsome appearance and his uncouth language caused ambivalent reactions among the audience.
    B. City people often are surprised to find farmers in an indigenous condition, for food is easily available on a farm.
    C. Some weeds are so prolific that they will overrun a lawn in one season.
    D. To contravene a law without following usual legal procedures tends to disrupt normal governmental action.
    E. A prolific composer does not necessarily produce masterpieces.

18.____

19. A. To avoid detection by enemy agents, the spies arranged a clandestine meeting.
    B. The emolument for any position should be commensurate with its responsibility.
    C. The theater's proscenium arch should be painted at once.
    D. The reviewer's cursory examination of the book gave him little on which to base a valid judgment.
    E. Sir Thomas Beecham entered the theater, mounted the pediment, and tapped for attention of the orchestra.

19.____

20. A. Garibaldi led the brigantines over the mountains for a surprise attack on Rome.
    B. Fettered by financial obligations, he became more and more discouraged.
    C. The execrable manner in which she behaved brought great distress to her family.
    D. The strikers gathered in front of the colliery, loudly voicing their demands.
    E. The crudity of her behavior was noted by the interviewer.

20.____

5 (#1)

21. A. Florida has been stressing its <u>salubrious</u> climate in an attempt to attract new residents.
    B. We were astonished to learn that the senior partner of a prominent law firm had died <u>intestate</u>.
    C. The call to active duty of members of the army reserve is <u>contiguous</u> upon the declaration of a national emergency.
    D. The choir decided to meet weekly in the <u>transept</u> of the cathedral.
    E. We were glad that the criminal's confession resulted in the <u>exoneration</u> of our friend.

    21.____

22. A. The bulldog, clamping his strong jaws on the other dog's leg, could not be induced to relax his <u>tenuous</u> hold.
    B. The untrained players produced a kind of <u>cacophony</u> that upset the orchestra leader.
    C. Numerous American writers became <u>expatriates</u> and lived abroad after World War I.
    D. Satirists delight in attacking the <u>foibles</u> of the society in which they live.
    E. Some avoid teaching as a profession because they find other fields more <u>lucrative</u>.

    22.____

23. A. One essential for success in ballet dancing is a <u>lithe</u> body.
    B. It is easier to <u>deride</u> the plans of others than to offer a better alternative.
    C. <u>Occlusion</u> of a blood vessel, perhaps by a clot, can result in a stroke or even death.
    D. Persistent irritation of the flesh, as when one uses a pair of shears, may result in a <u>callow</u> spot.
    E. Although the food was <u>palatable</u>, the poor service made the restaurant unpopular.

    23.____

24. A. Gold is considered to be a <u>malleable</u> metal.
    B. The social worker was loved for his helpfulness and <u>mendacity</u>
    C. The scuffle left him with a <u>protuberant</u> eye.
    D. The <u>somnolent</u> students did not contribute very much to the discussion.
    E. An <u>equestrian</u> statue may have the unfortunate effect of making the horse appear more important than the rider.

    24.____

25. A. Being engaged in fierce political battles, he found it necessary to maintain a <u>polemical</u> tone in all his speeches.
    B. <u>Shards</u> of broken earthenware are evidence that man has lived in the area where these objects are found.
    C. Severe fright can be a <u>traumatic</u> experience to a young child.
    D. Since neither management nor labor would compromise, their deliberations had reached an <u>impasse</u>.
    E. Having crashed into the windshield of the car, he had suffered <u>forensic</u> injuries.

    25.____

## KEY (CORRECT ANSWERS)

| | | | | |
|---|---|---|---|---|
| 1. | D | | 11. | D |
| 2. | C | | 12. | C |
| 3. | C | | 13. | A |
| 4. | E | | 14. | E |
| 5. | B | | 15. | C |
| 6. | D | | 16. | A |
| 7. | B | | 17. | C |
| 8. | A | | 18. | B |
| 9. | E | | 19. | E |
| 10. | B | | 20. | A |

21. C
22. A
23. D
24. B
25. E

# TEST 2

DIRECTIONS: In each of the following groups, ONE sentence contains an underlined word which makes the sentence INCORRECT. Select this incorrect sentence. *PRINT THE LETTER OF THE CORRECT ANSWER IN THE SPACE AT THE RIGHT.*

1.  A. Having been reared in a farming community, he tended to write about <u>pastoral</u> scenes.
    B. Once bitten, the victim needs immediate attention, for this snake's venom is unusually <u>virulent</u>.
    C. Spices, used moderately in the preparation of food, will usually <u>enhance</u> its savory qualities.
    D. In spite of the speaker's eloquence, we felt that his arguments were weak, <u>redoubtable</u>, and illogical.
    E. While most people are <u>gregarious</u> by nature, hermits prefer to live in isolation.

2.  A. The object of the experiment was to <u>liquefy</u> the solid.
    B. We made no <u>illusion</u> to his exalted opinion of himself
    C. His <u>scurrilous</u> language showed his lack of good manners.
    D. The water began to <u>permeate</u> every part of the cloth.
    E. He learned little, for his mind seemed <u>impervious</u> to new ideas.

3.  A. As we hiked up the mountain trail, we saw <u>conifers</u> growing all around us.
    B. Peace cannot be attained when nations adopt <u>belligerent</u> attitudes toward one another.
    C. The gourmet eagerly awaited the <u>vapid</u> food, a feature of this fine restaurant.
    D. I recently read a book which attempts to excuse Benedict Arnold for his <u>perfidy</u>.
    E. People are not really convinced if they have been <u>coerced</u> into expressing agreement.

4.  A. <u>Perusal</u> of the fine print in a contract may reveal unexpected restrictions.
    B. The <u>recantation</u> of popular music by the chorus delighted the audience.
    C. Indicate with a <u>caret</u> the place were a word is omitted.
    D. Mozart was <u>precocious</u>, for he composed music at the age of four.
    E. He is a true <u>hedonist</u>, for he devotes his life to a search for pleasure.

5.  A. He tried to soften the sodden mass by <u>calcifying</u> it slowly.
    B. The effects of pouring the <u>corrosive</u> liquid on the varnished table were soon apparent.
    C. The tyrant hurled <u>imprecations</u> at his hapless subjects.
    D. Under the <u>regimen</u> of military life, some gain weight; others lose it.
    E. The children learning to swim were told to place themselves <u>prone</u> on the benches to practice strokes.

6.  A. One who speaks vauntingly of his own accomplishments may be very annoying to others.
    B. The hand is well adapted to its prehensile functions.
    C. Such an insult was bound to rankle and cause the victim to seek redress.
    D. Bricks were baked in the kiln and shipped by truck to the city.
    E. The novice wore his new tussock to the ceremony.

7.  A. Many persons obtain vicariously through books experiences that they cannot have in real life.
    B. I decided to rescind my subscription for the magazine because it cost so little for an additional year.
    C. In spite of the confusion, the chairman's stentorian voice could be heard throughout the hall.
    D. The presence of paupers in the midst of plenty is a paradoxical situation.
    E. The alchemists were interested in finding one all important elixir.

8.  A. She was given the part of the sobriquet in Sheridan's THE SCHOOL FOR SCANDAL.
    B. The congressman set for himself the invidious task of opposing the pork-barrel legislation which would have given his state a goodly share of political assets.
    C. Watching TV has a soporific effect on many people.
    D. A venial indiscretion during his college days was seized upon by his opponents and magnified to the point where it cost him the election.
    E. The gamesome spirits of the younger campers tended to make it rather difficult for the older ones to study.

9.  A. When the knight swung his mace, all opposition fled.
    B. Stalin was an insidious foe, continually offering terms he had no intention of fulfilling.
    C. Good medical care soon made the patient ambivalent for a few hours daily.
    D. A labial injury might prevent one's saying "proboscis" correctly.
    E. The hibiscus was so colorful it attracted everyone's attention.

10. A. I thought the candidate far too intelligent to be guilty of the fatuous remarks attributed to him.
    B. The condiments included such savory items as curry, sage, and Worcestershire sauce.
    C. The unctuous Uriah Heep deserves our scorn.
    D. The doctor prescribed an anodyne to soothe the pain caused by the burn.
    E. Knowing your integrity, I shall be happy to attest to the complete voracity of your deposition.

11. A. Sam's arm is in a sling because he fractured his tibia.
    B. Henry was loath to accept a fee for his services.
    C. When the hot sun of July beats down, our town is affected with such lassitude that nobody gets anything done.

D. Reporters at the great man's funeral were impressed by the sincerity of the <u>eulogies</u> delivered by all the speakers.
E. His works are characterized by <u>hyperbole</u> for he greatly exaggerates all of his descriptions.

12. A. If one is too <u>complacent</u>, he is likely to appear conceited to others.       12._____
    B. The teacher found that few of his pupils could construct a regular <u>polyglot</u>.
    C. Too many people <u>prophesy</u> coming events on the basis of inadequate data.
    D. Water lilies are often so <u>prolific</u> that they cover a pond completely.
    E. The pupil who breaks rules again and again cannot expect to do so with <u>impunity</u>.

13. A. The druggist advised the man to use a new <u>emolument</u> on his sore shoulder.   13._____
    B. The detective admitted that the man's presence at the scene of the crime could have been <u>fortuitous</u>.
    C. A civilization cannot be <u>effete</u> if it still produces great leaders in various fields.
    D. The <u>cadaverous</u> appearance of the sick man was shocking to his relatives.
    E. In many high schools, we find <u>heterogeneous</u> grouping in the gymnasium classes.

14. A. Politicians often <u>inveigh</u> against the alleged faults of their opponents.    14._____
    B. The grand jury issued a <u>presentiment</u> attacking inadequate police protection.
    C. She was reprimanded for having been <u>remiss</u> in her duties.
    D. Strangely enough, he felt no <u>rancor</u> against those who attacked him.
    E. The slight <u>declivity</u> made it easy for us to push the cart to the road.

15. A. Modern journalism lacks the <u>vitriolic</u> criticism that characterized political   15._____
       articles before the close of the century.
    B. The jewels glittered so brightly that only an expert could tell that they were <u>spurious</u>.
    C. <u>Exuberant</u> praise irritates me as much as the other extreme—no recognition at all.
    D. The dictator <u>abrogated</u> to himself powers which even an absolute monarch would not have claimed.
    E. Music affords an excellent medium for the <u>sublimation</u> of the emotions.

16. A. Critics who <u>decry</u> the social and ethical goals of modern educators forget    16._____
       that man does not live by intellect alone.
    B. After the murder of Lincoln, John Wilkes Booth became a <u>pariah</u> to Americans.
    C. The American continent has been blessed with a <u>plethora</u> of natural gifts.
    D. It <u>devolves</u> upon every American teacher worthy of the profession to support the cause of academic freedom.
    E. In Pope's poetry are found many <u>illusions</u> to the Roman writer named Horace.

4 (#2)

17.
- A. The boy's <u>egregious</u> cheating left the principal no choice but to suspend him.
- B. The <u>façade</u> of Notre Dame appeared in the photograph.
- C. The <u>ephemeral</u> of Hollywood stardom has led many an actor to forsake the more lasting fame of the legitimate theatre.
- D. A person wearing dark glasses may wish to travel <u>incognito</u>.
- E. He was habitually <u>negligible</u> about reporting his income.

17._____

18.
- A. His quiet manner of speaking is inconsistent with his <u>bellicose</u> actions.
- B. Failure to build <u>transitory</u> roads from one side of the city to the other will cause serious traffic problems.
- C. Authors should avoid <u>anachronisms</u> such as a reference to an automobile in a book on the Civil War period.
- D. What soldier would be so <u>pusillanimous</u> as to desert his post under fire?
- E. He is not likely to be a good chairman, for his habit of <u>procrastination</u> will prevent him from bringing projects to a conclusion.

18._____

19.
- A. It is very difficult to do business if your methods or machines are <u>obsolete</u>.
- B. Pupils should ask questions, but they must learn that a teacher cannot be <u>omniscient</u>.
- C. Few men, if any, are satisfied to be concerned with <u>mundane</u> matters only.
- D. Having escaped from his cage, the monkey was so <u>captious</u> and quick in his movements that it proved very hard to catch him.
- E. His <u>nascent</u> interest in literature caused him to read omnivorously.

19._____

20.
- A. In times of prosperity, the number of <u>indigent</u> persons tends to decline.
- B. Numerous fires in a community may indicate an <u>incipient</u> breakdown in the organization for fire prevention.
- C. The <u>penultimate</u> day of a month has a special significance for some people, because they think that the next day, bringing a new month, will also bring a new beginning for them.
- D. She was not selected for a part in the play, for she really has no <u>histrionic</u> ability.
- E. Finding the area of the <u>octagonal</u> figure was a challenge to the young student.

20._____

21.
- A. A neatly kept room is characteristic of a <u>meticulous</u> person.
- B. The <u>scurrilous</u> sound of mice seeking safety in the walls of the old house did not surprise us.
- C. Hymns sung slowly and lifelessly make a <u>lugubrious</u> impression upon the listeners.
- D. The <u>inference</u> drawn by the speaker did not follow from the evidence he had offered.
- E. Arthur's <u>perception</u> of the implications of the situation helped him to reach a wise decision.

21._____

22.
- A. The <u>arc</u> of a great circle is important in the study of navigation.
- B. The tourists, with a limited time to spend in the city, were dismayed to see the length of the queue at the famous showplace.

22._____

C. It was quite a casting feat to have mild-mannered George play the pompous old bore.
D. The party members tried to bring the recalcitrant senator around to the majority opinion on the civil rights issue.
E. The gay, querulous young man asked when the next plane would leave for Dallas.

23. A. With great bravado, the bully dominated his awe-stricken followers.      23.____
    B. The good news made the old man quite lissome.
    C. The dictator regarded as a traitor any citizen having even a tangential connection with the revolutionists.
    D. The subcutaneous tissue quickly healed.
    E. Engineers who plan concert halls must know something about acoustics.

24. A. An expletive does not influence the number of the verb.      24.____
    B. The candidate's campaign speeches were enlivened by squibs and jests that made his opponent look ridiculous.
    C. After the two attorneys had met several times, the litigation was finally settled out of court.
    D. The increased study of etymology has made scientists more aware of the need for effective pest control.
    E. Debaters frequently try to confuse their adversaries by using false analogies.

25. A. The author's discussion of esoteric, esthetic, and stylistic theories insured      25.____
    popular acceptance of his book.
    B. The ebullient enthusiasm of the crowd reached a peak when they tore down the goal posts.
    C. The perfunctory manner in which Charles performed his tasks caused him to lose his job.
    D. One does not have to be clairvoyant to see that man will eventually travel to the moon.
    E. Upon reaching the age of twenty, Baxter abandoned all of his father's precepts of behavior.

## KEY (CORRECT ANSWERS)

| | | | | |
|---|---|---|---|---|
| 1. | D | | 11. | A |
| 2. | B | | 12. | B |
| 3. | C | | 13. | A |
| 4. | B | | 14. | B |
| 5. | A | | 15. | D |
| 6. | E | | 16. | E |
| 7. | B | | 17. | E |
| 8. | A | | 18. | B |
| 9. | C | | 19. | D |
| 10. | E | | 20. | C |

21. B
22. E
23. B
24. D
25. A

# WRITTEN ENGLISH EXPRESSION
# EXAMINATION SECTION
# TEST 1

DIRECTIONS: The questions that follow the paragraph below are designed to test your appreciation of correctness and effectiveness of expression in English. The paragraph is presented first in full so that you may read it through for sense. Disregard the errors you find, as you will be asked to correct them in the questions that follow. The paragraph is then presented sentence by sentence with portions underlined and numbered. At the end of this material, you will find numbers corresponding to those below the underlined portions, each followed by five alternatives lettered A to E. In every case, the usage in the alternative lettered A is the same as that in the original paragraph and is followed by four possible usages. Choose the usage you consider BEST in each case. *PRINT THE LETTER OF THE CORRECT ANSWER IN THE SPACE AT THE RIGHT.*

    When this war is over, no nation will either be isolated in war or peace. Each will be within trading distance of all the others and will be able to strike them. Every nation will be most as dependent on the rest for the maintainance of peace as is any of our own American states on all the others. The world that we have known was a world made up of individual nations, each of which has the priviledge of doing about as they pleased without being embarassed by outside interference. The world has dissolved before the impact of an invention, the airplane has done to our world what gunpowder did to the feudal world. Whether the coming century will be a period of further tragedy or one of peace and progress depend very largely on the wisdom and skill with which the present generation adjusts their thinking to the problems immediately at hand. Examining the principal movements sweeping through the world, it can be seen that they are being accelerated by the war. There is undoubtedly many of these whose courses will be affected for good or ill by the settlement that will follow the war. The United States will share the responsibility of these settlements with Russia, England and China. The influence of the United States, however, will be great. This country is likely to emerge from the war stronger than any other nation. Having benefitted by the absence of actual hostilities on our own soil, we shall probably be less exhausted than our allies and better able to help restore the devastated areas. However many mistakes have been made in our past, the tradition of America, not only the champion of freedom but also fair play, still lives among millions who can see light and hope scarcely nowhere else.

1. When this war is over, no nation will <u>either be isolated in war or peace</u>.     1._____
   A. either be isolated in war or peace
   B. be either isolated in war or peace
   C. be isolated in neither war nor peace
   D. be isolated either in war or in peace
   E. be isolated neither in war or peace

2. <u>Each</u>     2._____
   A. Each    B. It    C. Some    D. They    E. A nation

3. within trading distance of all the others and will be able to strike them.
   A. within trading distance of all the others and will be able to strike them.
   B. near enough to trade with and strike all the others.
   C. trading and striking the others.
   D. within trading and striking distance of all the others.
   E. able to strike and trade with all the others,

4. Every nation will be most as dependent on
   A. most   B. wholly   C. much   D. mostly   E. almost

5. the rest for the maintainance of peace as is
   A. maintainance   B. maintainence   C. maintenence
   D. maintenance   E. maintanence

6. any of our own American states on all the others. The world that we have known was a world made up of individual nations, each
   A. nations, each   B. nations. Each   C. nations: each
   D. nations; each   E. nations each

7. of which had the priviledge of doing about as
   A. priviledge   B. priveledge   C. privelege
   D. privalege   E. privilege

8. they pleased without being
   A. they   B. it   C. they individually
   D. he   E. the nations

9. embarassed by outside interference. That
   A. embarassed   B. embarrassed   C. embaressed
   D. embarrased   E. embarressed

10. world has dissolved before the impact of an invention, the airplane has done to our world what gunpowder did to the feudal world. Whether the coming century will be a period of further tragedy or one of peace and
    A. invention, the   B. invention but the   C. invention: the
    D. invention. The   E. invention and the

11. progress depend very largely on the wisdom and skill with which the present generation
    A. depend   B. will have depended   C. depends
    D. depended   E. shall depend

12. adjusts their thinking to the problems immediately at hand.
    A. adjusts their   B. adjusts there   C. adjusts its
    D. adjust our   E. adjust it's

13. Examining the principal movements sweeping through the world, it can be seen
    A. Examining the principal movements sweeping through the world, it can be seen
    B. Having examined the principal movements sweeping through the world, it can be seen
    C. Examining the principal movements sweeping through the world can be seen
    D. Examining the principal movements sweeping through the world, we can see
    E. It can be seen examining the principal movements sweeping through the world

13.____

14. that they are being accelerated by the war.
    A. accelerated     B. acelerated     C. accelerated
    D. acellerated     E. acelerrated

14.____

15. There is undoubtedly many of these whose courses will be affected for good or ill by the settlements that will follow the war. The United States will share the responsibility of these settlements with Russia, England and China. The influence of the United
    A. is     B. were     C. was     D. are     E. might be

15.____

16. States, however, will be great. This country is likely to emerge from the war stronger than any other nation.
    A. , however,     B. however,     C. , however
    D. however        E. ; however

16.____

17. Having benefitted by the absence of actual hostilities on our own soil, we shall probably be less exhausted
    A. benefitted     B. benifitted     C. benefited
    D. benifited      E. benafitted

17.____

18. than our allies and better able than them to help restore the devastated areas. However many mistakes have been made in our past, the tradition of American,
    A. them           B. themselves     C. they
    D. the world      E. the nations

18.____

19. not only the champion of freedom but also fair play, still lives among millions who can
    A. not only the champion of freedom but also fair play,
    B. the champion of not only freedom but also of fair play,
    C. the champion not only of freedom but also of fair play,
    D. not only the champion but also freedom and fair play,
    E. not the champion of freedom only, but also fair play,

19.____

20. see light and hope <u>scarcely nowhere else.</u>  20._____
   A. scarcely nowhere else
   B. elsewhere
   C. nowhere
   D. scarcely anywhere else
   E. anywhere

## KEY (CORRECT ANSWERS)

1. D    11. C
2. A    12. C
3. D    13. D
4. E    14. A
5. D    15. D

6. A    16. A
7. E    17. C
8. B    18. C
9. B    19. C
10. D   20. D

# TEST 2

DIRECTIONS: The questions that follow the paragraph below are designed to test your appreciation of correctness and effectiveness of expression in English. The paragraph is presented first in full so that you may read it through for sense. Disregard the errors you find, as you will be asked to correct them in the questions that follow. The paragraph is then presented sentence by sentence with portions underlined and numbered. At the end of this material, you will find numbers corresponding to those below the underlined portions, each followed by five alternatives lettered A to E. In every case, the usage in the alternative lettered A is the same as that in the original paragraph and is followed by four possible usages. Choose the usage you consider BEST in each case. *PRINT THE LETTER OF THE CORRECT ANSWER IN THE SPACE AT THE RIGHT.*

    The use of the machine produced up to the present time outstanding changes in our modern world. One of the most significant of these changes have been the marked decreases in the length of the working day and the working week. The fourteen-hour day not only has been reduced to one of ten hours but also, in some lines of work, to one of eight or even six. The trend toward a decrease is further evidenced in the longer weekend already given to employees in many business establishments. There seems also to be a trend toward shorter working weeks and longer summer vacations. An important feature of this development is that leisure is no longer the privilege of the wealthy few,—it has become the common right of most people. Using it wisely, leisure promotes health, efficiency, and happiness, for there is time for each individual to live their own "more abundant life" and having opportunities for needed recreation.
    Recreation, like the name implies, is a process of revitalization. In giving expression to the play instincts of the human race, new vigor and effectiveness are afforded by recreation to the body and to the mind. Of course not all forms of amusement, by no means, constitute recreation. Furthermore, an activity that provides recreation for one person may prove exhausting for another. Today, however, play among adults, as well as children, is regarded as a vital necessity of modern life. Play being recognized as an important factor in improving mental and physical health and thereby reducing human misery and poverty,
    Among the most important forms of amusement available at the present time are the automobile, the moving picture, the radio, television, and organized sports. The automobile, especially, has been a boon to the American people, since it has been the chief means of them getting out into the open. The motion picture, the radio and television have tremendous opportunities to supply wholesome recreation and to promote cultural advancement. A criticism often leveled against organized sports as a means of recreation is because they make passive spectators of too many people. It has been said "that the American public is afflicted with "spectatoritis," but there is some recreational advantages to be gained even from being a spectator at organized games. Such sports afford a release from the monotony of daily toil, get people outdoors and also provide an exhilaration that is tonic in its effect.
    The chief concern, of course, should be to eliminate those forms of amusement that are socially undesirable. There are, however, far too many people who, we know, do not use their leisure to the best advantage. Sometimes leisure leads to idleness, and idleness may lead to demoralization. The value of leisure both to the individual and to society will depend on the uses made of it.

2 (#2)

1. The use of the machine produced up to the
   A. produced     B. produces     C. has produced
   D. had produced  E. will have produced

2. present time many outstanding changes in our modern world. One of the most significant of these changes have been the marked
   A. have been    B. was          C. were
   D. has been     E. will be

3. decreases in the length of the working day and the working week. The fourteen-hour day not only has been reduced to one of ten hour but also, in some line of work, to one of eight or even six.
   A. The fourteen-hour day not only has been reduced
   B. Not only the fourteen-hour day has been reduced
   C. Not the fourteen-hour day only has been reduced
   D. The fourteen-hour day has not only been reduced
   E. The fourteen-hour day has been reduced not only

4. The trend toward a decrease is further evidenced in the longer week end already given
   A. already   B. all ready   C. allready   D. ready   E. all in all

5. to employees in many business establishments. There seems also to be a trend toward shorter working weeks and longer summer vacations. An important feature of this development is that leisure is no longer the privilege of the wealthy few,—it has become the common right of people.
   A. ,—it         B. : it         C. ; it
   D. …it          E. omit punctuation

6. Using it wisely, leisure promotes health, efficiency, and happiness, for there is time for
   A. Using it wisely          B. If used wisely
   C. Having used it widely    D. Because of its wise use
   E. Because of usefulness

7. each individual to live their own "more abundant life"
   A. their   B. his   C. its   D. our   E. your

8. and having opportunities for needed recreation.
   A. having       B. having had     C. to have
   D. to have had  E. had

9. Recreation, like the name implies, is a
   A. like   B. since   C. through   D. for   E. as

3 (#2)

10. process of revitalization. In giving expression to the play instincts of the human race, <u>new vigor and effectiveness are afforded by recreation to the body and to the mind.</u>
    A. new vigor and effectiveness are afforded by recreation to the body and to the mind.
    B. recreation affords new vigor and effectiveness to the body and to the mind.
    C. there are afforded new vigor and effectiveness to the body and to the mind.
    D. by recreation the body and mind are afforded new vigor and effectiveness.
    E. the body and the mind afford new vigor and effectiveness to themselves by recreation.

10.____

11. Of course not all forms of amusement, <u>by no means,</u> constitute recreation. Furthermore, an activity that provides recreation for one person may prove exhausting for another. Today, however, play among adults, as well as children, is regarded as a vital necessity of modern life.
    A. by no means   B. by those means   C. by some means
    D. by every means   E. by any means

11.____

12. <u>Play being recognized</u> as an important factor in improving mental and physical health and thereby reducing human misery and poverty.
    A. . Play being recognized as   B. . by their recognizing play as
    C. . They recognizing play as   D. . Recognition of it being
    E. , for play is recognized as

12.____

13. Among the most important forms of amusement available at the present time are the automobile, the moving picture, the radio, television, and organized sports. The automobile, especially, has been a boon to the American people, since it has been the chief means of <u>them</u> getting out into the open. The motion picture, the radio, and television have tremendous opportunities to supply wholesome recreation and to promote cultural advancement. A criticism often leveled against organized
    A. them   B. their   C. his   D. our   E. the people

13.____

14. sports as a means of recreation is <u>because</u> they make passive spectators of too many people
    A. because   B. since   C. as   D. that   E. why

14.____

15. It has been said "<u>that</u> the American public is afflicted with "spectatoritis,"
    A. "that   B. "that"   C. that"   D. 'that   E. that

15.____

16. but there <u>is</u> some recreational advantages to be gained even from being a spectator at organized games
    A. is   B. was   C. are   D. were   E. will be

16.____

145

17. Such sports afford a release from the monotony of daily toil, get people outdoors and also provide an exhilaration that is tonic in its effect. The chief concern, of course, should be to eliminate those forms of amusement that are socially undesirable. There are, however, far too many people who, we know, do not use their leisure to the best advantage. Sometimes leisure leads to idleness, and idleness may lead to demoralization. The value of leisure both to the individual and to society will depend on the uses made of it.

   A. who   B. whom   C. which   D. such as   E. that which

## KEY (CORRECT ANSWERS)

| | | | |
|---|---|---|---|
| 1. | C | 11. | E |
| 2. | D | 12. | E |
| 3. | E | 13. | B |
| 4. | A | 14. | D |
| 5. | C | 15. | E |
| 6. | B | 16. | C |
| 7. | B | 17. | A |
| 8. | C | | |
| 9. | E | | |
| 10. | B | | |

# TEST 3

DIRECTIONS: The questions that follow the paragraph below are designed to test your appreciation of correctness and effectiveness of expression in English. The paragraph is presented first in full so that you may read it through for sense. Disregard the errors you find, as you will be asked to correct them in the questions that follow. The paragraph is then presented sentence by sentence with portions underlined and numbered. At the end of this material, you will find numbers corresponding to those below the underlined portions, each followed by five alternatives lettered A to E. In every case, the usage in the alternative lettered A is the same as that in the original paragraph and is followed by four possible usages. Choose the usage you consider BEST in each case. *PRINT THE LETTER OF THE CORRECT ANSWER IN THE SPACE AT THE RIGHT.*

    The process by which the community influence the actions of its members is known as social control. Imitation which takes place when the action of one individual awakens the impulse in each other to attempt the same thing, is one of the means by which society gains this control. When the child acts as other members of his group acts, he receives their approval. There is also adults who seem almost equally imitative. Advertisers of luxuries are careful to convey the idea that important persons use and indorse the merchandise concerned, for most folk will do their utmost to follow the example of those whom they think are the best people.

    Akin to imitation as a means of social control is suggestion. The child is taught to think and feel as do the adults of his community. He is neither encouraged to be critical or to examine all the evidence for his opinion. To be sure, there would be scarcely no time left for other things if school children would have been expected to have considered all sides of every matter on which they hold opinions. It is possible, however and probably very desirable, for pupils of high school age to learn that the point of view accepted in their community is not the only one, and that many widely held opinions may be mistaken. The way in which suggestion operates is illustrated by advertising methods. Depending on skillful suggestion, argument is seldom used in advertising. The words accompanying the picture do not seek to convince the reason but only to intensify the suggestion.

    Some persons are more susceptible to suggestion than others. The ignorant person is more easily moved to action by suggestion than he who is well educated, education developing the habit of criticizing what is read and heard. Whoever would think clearly, freeing himself from emotion and prejudice, must beware of the influence of the crowd or mob. A crowd is a group of people in a highly suggestible condition, each stimulating the feelings of the others until an intense uniform emotion has control of the group. Such a crowd may become irresponsible and anonymous, and whose activity may lead in any direction. The educated person ought to be beyond reach of this kind of appeal, no one may be said to have a real individuality who, at the mercy of the suggestions of others, allow themselves to succumb to "crowd-mindedness."

1. The process by which the community <u>influence the action of its members</u> is known as social control.
    A. influence the actions of its members
    B. influences the actions of its members
    C. had influenced the actions of its members
    D. influences the actions of their members
    E. will influence the actions of its members

1.\_\_\_\_

2. Imitation which takes place when the action
   A. which   B. , which   C. —which   D. that   E. what

3. of one individual awakens the impulse in each other to attempt the same thing, is one of the means by which society gains this control.
   A. each other   B. some other   C. one other
   D. another   E. one another

4. When the child acts as other members of his group acts, he receives their approval
   A. acts   B. act   C. has acted
   D. will act   E. will have acted

5. There is also adults who seem almost equally imitative.
   A. is   B. are   C. was   D. were   E. will be

6. Advertisers of luxuries are careful to convey the idea that important persons use and indorse the merchandise concerned, for most folk will do their utmost to follow the example of those whom they think are the best people.
   A. whom   B. what   C. which
   D. who   E. that which

7. Akin to imitation as a means of social control is suggestion. The child is taught to think and feel as do the adults of his community.
   A. do   B. does   C. had   D. may   E. might

8. He is neither encouraged to be critical or to examine all the evidence for his opinions.
   A. neither encouraged to be critical or to examine
   B. neither encouraged to be critical nor to examine
   C. either encouraged to be critical or to examine
   D. encouraged either to be critical nor to examine
   E. not encouraged either to be critical or to examine

9. To be sure, there would be scarcely no time left for other things.
   A. scarcely no   B. hardly no   C. scarcely any
   D. enough   E. but only

10. if school children would have been expected
    A. would have been   B. should have been   C. would have
    D. were   E. will be

11. to have considered all sides of every matter on which they hold opinions
    A. to have considered   B. to be considered
    C. to consider   D. to have been considered
    E. and have considered

12. It is possible, however and probably very desirable, for pupils of high school age to learn that the point of view accepted in their community is not the only one, and that many widely held opinions may be mistaken. The way in which suggestion operates is illustrated by advertising methods.  12.____
    A. , however
    B. however,
    C. ; however,
    D. however
    E. , however,

13. Depending on skillful suggestion, argument is seldom used in advertising. The words accompanying the picture do not seek to convince the reason but only to intensify the suggestion.  13.____
    A. Depending on skillful suggestion, argument is seldom used in advertising.
    B. Argument is seldom used by advertisers, who depend instead on skillful suggestion.
    C. Skillful suggestion is depended on by advertisers instead of argument.
    D. Suggestion, which is more skillful, is used in place of argument by advertisers.
    E. Instead of suggestion, depending on argument is used by skillful advertisers.

14. Some persons are more susceptible to suggestion than others. The ignorant person is more easily moved to action by suggestion than he who is well educated, education developing the habit of criticizing what is read and heard. Whoever would think clearly, freeing himself from emotion and prejudice, must beware of the influence of the crowd or mob.  14.____
    A. , education developing
    B. , education developed by
    C. , for education develops
    D. . Education will develop
    E. . Education developing

15. A crowd is a group of people in a highly suggestible condition, each stimulating the feelings of the others until an intense uniform emotion has control of the group. Such a crowd may become irresponsible and anonymous, and whose activity may lead in any direction. The educated person ought to be beyond reach of this kind of appeal,  15.____
    A. and whose
    B. whose
    C. and its
    D. and the
    E. and the crowd's

16. no one may be said to have a real individuality who,  16.____
    A. , no
    B. : no
    C. —no
    D. . No
    E. omit punctuation

17. at the mercy of the suggestions of others, allow themselves to succumb to "crowd-mindedness."  17.____
    A. allow themselves
    B. allows themselves
    C. allow himself
    D. allows himself
    E. allow ourselves

# KEY (CORRECT ANSWERS)

| | | | |
|---|---|---|---|
| 1. | B | 11. | C |
| 2. | B | 12. | E |
| 3. | D | 13. | B |
| 4. | B | 14. | C |
| 5. | B | 15. | C |
| | | | |
| 6. | D | 16. | D |
| 7. | A | 17. | D |
| 8. | E | | |
| 9. | C | | |
| 10. | D | | |

# TEST 4

DIRECTIONS: The questions that follow are designed to test your appreciation of correctness and effectiveness of expression in English. In each statement, you will find underlined portions. In some cases, the usage in the underlined portion is correct. In other cases, it requires correction. Five (5) alternatives lettered A to E are presented. In every case, the usage in the alternative lettered A (No Change) is the same as that in the original statement and is followed by four (4) other possible usages. Choose the usage you consider BEST in each case. *PRINT THE LETTER OF THE CORRECT ANSWER IN THE SPACE AT THE RIGHT.*

### Sample Questions and Answers

Questions
1. John ran home.
    - A. No change
    - B. run
    - C. runned
    - D. runed
    - E. None right

2. John aint here.
    - A. No change
    - B. ain't
    - C. am not
    - D. arre'nt
    - E. None right

Answers
1. A
   (The sentence is obviously correctly written. Therefore, the correct answer is A. No change.)

2. E
   (word aint is unacceptable in usage today. The correct answer should be is not or isn't. Since the alternatives offered in A, B, C, and D are all incorrect, the correct answer is, therefore, E. None right.)

---

1. It takes study to become a lawyer.
    - A. No change
    - B. before you can become
    - C. in becoming
    - D. for becoming
    - E. None right

2. His novels never concern old people who wished to be young.
    - A. No change
    - B. concerned old people who wish
    - C. concerned old people who had wished
    - D. concern old people who wish
    - E. None right

3. You people like we boys as much as we. boys like you.
    - A. No change
    - B. we boys as much as us
    - C. us boys as much as us
    - D. us boys as much as we
    - E. None right

151

4. Jane and Mary are more poised than he, but Bill is the brighter of all three.  4._____
   A. No change
   B. more poised than he, but Bill is the brightest
   C. more poised than him, but Bill is the brightest
   D. more poised than him, but Bill is the brighter
   E. None right

5. It is a thing of joy, beauty, and containing terror.  5._____
   A. No change    B. and abounding in    C. and of
   D. and contains    E. None right

6. If he was able, he would demand that she return home.  6._____
   A. No change
   B. were able, he would demand that she return
   C. was able, he would demand that she returns
   D. were able, he would demand that she returns
   E. None right

7. He use to visit when he was supposed to.  7._____
   A. No change
   B. use to visit when he was suppose to.
   C. used to visit when he was suppose to.
   D. used to visit when he was supposed to.
   E. None right

8. I saw the seamstress and asked her for a needle, hook and eye, and thimble.  8._____
   A. No change
   B. seamstress, and asked her for a needle, hook and eye
   C. seamstress and asked her for a needle, hook and eye
   D. seamstress, and asked her for a needle, hook and eye
   E. None right

9. A tall, young, man threw the heavy, soggy, ball.  9._____
   A. No change
   B. , young man threw the heavy, soggy
   C. young man threw the heavy, soggy
   D. , young man threw the heavy soggy
   E. None right

10. The week before my sister, thinking of other matters, thrust her hand into the fire.  10._____
    A. No change
    B. before, my sister thinking of other matters
    C. before my sister thinking of other matters
    D. before my sister, thinking of other matters
    E. None right

11. We seldom eat a roast at our house. My wife being a vegetarian.  11._____
    A. No change    B. my    C. , my
    D. ; my    E. None right

3 (#4)

12. I have only one request. That you leave at once. 12.____
    A. No change  B. that  C. ; that
    D. : that  E. None right

13. I admire stimulating conversation and appreciative listening, therefore I talk 13.____
    to myself.
    A. No change  B. , therefore,  C. therefore
    D. therefore,  E. None right

14. The battle-scarred veteran was as bald as a newlaid egg. 14.____
    A. No change
    B. battlescarred veteran was as bald as a new-laid egg.
    C. battle-scarred veteran was as bald as a new-laid egg.
    D. battle scarred veteran was as bald as a new laid egg.
    E. None right

15. The President's proclamation opened with the following statement: "The 15.____
    intention of the government is, to make the people aware of one of the greatest
    dangers to the safety of the country."
    A. No change
    B. , "The intention of the government is
    C. : "The intention of the government is:
    D. : "The intention of the government is
    E. None right

16. I get only a week vacation after two years work. 16.____
    A. No change
    B. week's vacation after two years work.
    C. week's vacation after two years' work.
    D. weeks vacation after two years work.
    E. None right

17. You first wash your brush in turpentine. Then hang it up to dry. 17.____
    A. No change  B. First you  C. First you should
    D. First  E. None right

18. The teacher insisted that you and he were responsible for the mistakes of 18.____
    Joe and me.
    A. No change
    B. him were responsible for the mistakes of Joe and me.
    C. he were responsible for the mistakes of Joe and I.
    D. him were responsible for the mistakes of Joe and I.
    E. None right

19. He sometimes in a generous mood gave the flowers to others that he had grown 19.____
    in his garden.
    A. No change
    B. He in a generous mood sometimes gave to others the flowers
    C. In a generous mood he sometimes gave the flowers to others

D. Sometimes in a generous mood he gave to others the flowers
E. None right

20. He is attending college since September.
    A. No change
    B. has attended
    C. was attending
    D. attended
    E. None right

21. He enjoys me hearing him singing.
    A. No change
    B. my hearing him sing
    C. me hearing him sing
    D. me hearing his singing
    E. None right

22. Even patients of anxious temperament occasionally feel an element of primitive pleasure.
    A. No change
    B. temperament occassionally feel an element of primitive
    C. temperment occasionally feel an element of primitive
    D. temperament occasionally feel an element of primitive
    E. None right

23. Undoubtedly even the loneliest patient feels tranquill.
    A. No change
    B. Undoubtably even the loneliest patient feels tranquill.
    C. Undoubtedly even the loneliest patient feels tranquil.
    D. Undouvtably even the loneliest patient feels tranquil.
    E. None right

24. Sophmores taking behavioral psychology must pay a labratory fee.
    A. No change
    B. Sophmores taking behavioral psychology must pay a laboratory
    C. Sophmores taking behavioral psychology must pay a laboratory
    D. Sophomores taking behavioral psychology must pay a labratory
    E. None right

25. Atheletic heroes often find their studies an unnecessary hinderance.
    A. No change
    B. Athletic heroes often find their studies an unnecessary hinderance.
    C. Athletic heros often find their studies an unnecessary hindrance.
    D. Athletic heroes often find their studies an unnecessary hindrance.
    E. None right

## KEY (CORRECT ANSWERS)

| | | | |
|---|---|---|---|
| 1. | A | 11. | C |
| 2. | D | 12. | D |
| 3. | D | 13. | E |
| 4. | B | 14. | C |
| 5. | E | 15. | D |
| | | | |
| 6. | B | 16. | C |
| 7. | D | 17. | D |
| 8. | D | 18. | A |
| 9. | C | 19. | D |
| 10. | E | 20. | B |

21. B
22. A
23. E
24. C
25. D

# TEST 5

DIRECTIONS: The questions that follow are designed to test your appreciation of correctness and effectiveness of expression in English. In each statement, you will find underlined portions. In some cases, the usage in the underlined portion is correct. In other cases, it requires correction. Five (5) alternatives lettered A to E are presented. In every case, the usage in the alternative lettered A (No Change) is the same as that in the original statement and is followed by four (4) other possible usages. Choose the usage you consider BEST in each case. *PRINT THE LETTER OF THE CORRECT ANSWER IN THE SPACE AT THE RIGHT.*

1. Many of the <u>childrens' games were supervised by students who's</u> interests lay in teaching.
   A. No change
   B. children's games were supervised by students who's
   C. childrens' games were supervised by students whose
   D. children's games were supervised by students whose
   E. None right

   1.____

2. I told <u>father that a college president</u> was invited to speak.
   A. No change
   B. Father that a college president
   C. father that a College President
   D. Father that a College president
   E. None right

   2.____

3. One should either <u>be able to read</u> German or French.
   A. No change
   B. be able either to read
   C. be able to either read
   D. be able to read either
   E. None right

   3.____

4. <u>Twirling around on my piano stool, my head begins to swim.</u>
   A. No change
   B. My head begins to swim, twirling around on my piano stool.
   C. Twirling around on my piano stool, a dizzy spell ensues.
   D. Twirling around on my piano stool, I begin to feel dizzy.
   E. None right

   4.____

5. As the reverberations of my deep bass voice <u>increase, one of my dogs starts</u> to howl.
   A. No change
   B. increase, one of my dogs start
   C. increases, one of my dogs start
   D. increases, one of my dogs starts
   E. None right

   5.____

6. Roy bellows at Eve that it is <u>her, not he</u> who shouts.
   A. No change
   B. her, not him
   C. she, not him
   D. she, not he
   E. None right

   6.____

7. The only man who I think will knock out whoever he fights is Roy.  7.____
   A. No change
   B. who I think will knock out whomever
   C. whom I think will knock out whomever
   D. whom I think will knock out whoever
   E. None right

8. The more prettier of my eyes is the glass one.  8.____
   A. No change    B. most pretty    C. prettier
   D. prettiest    E. None right

9. When a good actress cries, she feels real sad.  9.____
   A. No change              B. feels real sadly
   C. feels really sadly     D. really feels sad
   E. None right

10. I asked the instructor what I should do with this examina-paper. Can you imagine what he said?  10.____
    A. No change                              B. ? Can you imagine what he said.
    C. ? Can you imagine what he said?        D. . Can you imagine what he said.
    E. None right

11. Not wishing to hurt my friend's feeling, I tell him that I am leaving, because I have a previous engagement.  11.____
    A. No change                          B. I tell him that I am leaving
    C. , I tell him that I am leaving     D. I tell him that I am leaving,
    E. None right

12. I remember Utopia College where I studied, while I lived abroad, when the world was at peace.  12.____
    A. No change
    B. College where I studied, while I lived abroad
    C. College, where I studied while I lived abroad
    D. College, where I studied, while I lived abroad
    E. None right

13. Would Robinson Crusoe have survived if he was less unimaginative?  13.____
    A. No change       B. were         C. had been
    D. would have been E. None right

14. Neither time nor tide delay either the traveler or the stay-at-home from his pastime.  14.____
    A. No change
    B. delays either the traveler or the stay-at-home from his
    C. delay either the traveler or the stay-at-home from their
    D. delays either the traveler or the stay-at-home from their
    E. None right

15. When the committee reports its findings somebody will lose their composure.    15._____
    A. No change
    B. their findings somebody will lose their
    C. their findings somebody will lose his
    D. its findings somebody will lose his
    E. None right

16. The worst one of the problems which is confronting me concern money.    16._____
    A. No change                     B. are confronting me concern
    C. is confronting me concerns    D. are confronting me concerns
    E. None right

17. Far in the distance rumble the motors of the convoy, but there's no signs of    17._____
    it yet.
    A. No change
    B. rumbles the motors of the convoy, but there is
    C. rumbles the motors of the convoy, but there are
    D. rumble the motors of the convoy, but there are
    E. None right

18. Neither of the patients believe that Hansel or Gretel are alive.    18._____
    A. No change                          B. believes that Hansel or Gretel are
    C. believe that Hansel or Gretel is   D. believes that Hansel or Gretel is
    E. None right

19. Its in untried emergencies that a man's native metal receives its ultimate test.    19._____
    A. No change
    B. It's in untried emergencies that a man's native metal receives its
    C. It's in untried emergencies that a man's native metal receives its
    D. It's in untried emergencies that a man's native metal receives its'
    E. None right

20. Expecting my friends to be on time, their tardiness seemed almost an insult.    20._____
    A. No change
    B. it seemed that their tardiness was almost an insult.
    C. resentment at their tardiness grew in my mind.
    D. only an accident on the way could account for their tardiness.
    E. None right

21. On first reading "The Wasteland" seems obscure.    21._____
    A. No change
    B. On first reading it, "The Wasteland" seems obscure.
    C. "The Wasteland" seems an obscure poem on first reading it.
    D. On first reading "The Wasteland," it seems an obscure poem.
    E. None right

22. A special light will be required to inspect the engine.                                22.____
    A. No change
    B. To inspect the engine, a special light will be required.
    C. To inspect the engine, you will require a special light.
    D. To inspect the engine, your light must be special.
    E. None right

23. When mixing it, the cake batter must be thoroughly beaten.                              23.____
    A. No change         B. mixing              C. being mixed
    D. being mix         E. None right

24. What you say may be different from me.                                                  24.____
    A. No change         B. from what I say     C. than me
    D. than mine         E. None right

25. Trumping is playing a trump when another suit has been led.                             25.____
    A. No change         B. to play             C. if you play
    D. where one plays   E. None right

---

# KEY (CORRECT ANSWERS)

| | | | | |
|---|---|---|---|---|
| 1. | D | | 11. | C |
| 2. | A | | 12. | C |
| 3. | D | | 13. | C |
| 4. | D | | 14. | B |
| 5. | A | | 15. | D |
| 6. | D | | 16. | D |
| 7. | B | | 17. | D |
| 8. | C | | 18. | D |
| 9. | D | | 19. | B |
| 10. | A | | 20. | E |

21. B
22. B
23. C
24. B
25. A

# BASIC FUNDAMENTALS OF ORAL COMMUNICATION

## TABLE OF CONTENTS

| | Page |
|---|---|
| Instructional Objectives | 1 |
| Content | 1 |
|     Introduction | 1 |
|     General Principles | 1 |
|     Principles Affecting Delivery | 2 |
|     Physical Delivery | 2 |
|     Verbal Delivery | 5 |
| Principles Affecting Human Relations | 7 |
|     Respect the Dignity of Others | 7 |
|     Develop an Honest Interest in Other People | 8 |
|     Recognize Individual Uniqueness and Worth | 8 |
|     Cooperate With the Wants of Others | 9 |
| Person-to-Person Communications | 9 |
|     Informal Conversation | 10 |
|     Interviewing | 10 |
|     Group Discussion | 11 |
| Speaking Before Groups | 13 |
|     Speaking to Inform | 13 |
|     Speaking to Instruct | 14 |
|     Speaking to Persuade | 14 |
|     Speaking to Motivate | 15 |
|     Speaking to Entertain | 15 |
| Student Learning Activities | 15 |
| Teacher Management Activities | 16 |
| Evaluation Questions | 16 |
|     Answer Key | 18 |

# BASIC FUNDAMENTALS OF ORAL COMMUNICATION

**Instructional Objectives**

1. Ability to speak fluently, with correct articulation and pronunciation;
2. Ability to group words into meaningful phrases;
3. Ability to stress words and phrases to enhance communication;
4. Ability to control voice volume and tone according to needs;
5. Ability to use speech forms appropriate for the audience;
6. Ability to use body control and visual aids to enhance communication;
7. Ability to participate effectively in informal conversation and group discussion;
8. Ability to speak effectively and confidently before a group;
9. Ability to persuade or convince listeners; and
10. Ability to value the importance of oral communication as an essential skill for working in public service occupations.

**Content**

*Introduction*

Oral communication is one of the more basic processes underlying human relationships. The use of speech to transmit ideas, to probe the ideas of others, to teach, to persuade, to entertain, to motivate, and to otherwise influence and affect others is a uniquely human activity. Speech is used in the most casual and informal of human interactions, as well as in formal settings involving many persons. Through the mass media, the sounds and forms of speech may reach millions of persons simultaneously. Thus the ability to speak effectively in a variety of settings is an essential skill in all activities in which human beings interact with one another.

A basis is provided herein for the development of the student's ability to communicate effectively through speech for a variety of purposes and in a variety of settings, particularly those common to public-service occupational settings. Whatever the particular purpose or setting, however, effective speech will require the speaker to have a clear idea of his purpose and his audience, to organize his thoughts and information in an orderly way, to express himself effectively through his delivery and his knowledge of human relations, to report relevant facts, to explain and summarize clearly, and to evaluate the effectiveness of his communication.

This unit provides a framework for organizing instruction in basic speech skills, while providing practice in speaking for several purposes in several settings.

*General Principles*

Whatever the particular purpose or setting for oral communication, the speaker can add to his effectiveness by applying certain general principles. In general, these principles can be considered under two broad categories:
- principles affecting delivery, and
- principles affecting human relations.

These two categories are perhaps the most important aspects of oral communication. The principles of delivery and human relations must be applied in a variety of speaking situations.

*Principles Affecting Delivery*

The delivery of oral communications may be considered under two general categories of:
- *physical delivery,* which includes voice control, articulation, pronunciation, body control, and visual aids; and
- *verbal delivery,* including choice of words and style of delivery.

*Physical Delivery*

*Voice Control:* The effectiveness of oral communication depends in large measure upon the physical delivery of speech symbols, one major aspect which is voice control. Voice control has several distinguishing characteristics: pitch, volume, duration, and quality:
- *Pitch* is the characteristic of sound as it relates to the musical scale. Each person's voice has a certain pitch level that may be considered as high, low, or medium. Certain conditions of pitch can cause communication to suffer:
    - when the voice is pitched too high
    - when it is pitched too low
    - when it lacks variety of pitch and is monotonous

- *Volume,* or loudness, is another characteristic of voice. Speakers may be troubled when the voice volume is:
    - too great
    - too weak, or
    - lacking variety, or monotonous.

- *Duration* refers to the length of time a sound lasts, particularly the vowel sounds. There are two chief problems related to this control:
    - over-lengthening of vowels, resulting in a drawl
    - eliminating or clipping of vowels, resulting in erratic and staccato speech patterns.

- *Quality of voice* refers to that characteristic which distinguishes one person's voice from another's, the voice's "fingerprint," so to speak. The student should strive to achieve a pleasing and harmonious quality. Common quality faults include:
    - nasality (too much nasal resonance)
    - denasality (too little nasal resonance)
    - harshness, hoarseness and breathiness.

*Articulation:* To make himself understood, the speaker must produce speech in such a way that the audience is able to recognize the individual words he speaks. This is dependent upon the elements of:
- *Articulation,* or the joining together of consonants and vowels that go to make up the word, and

- *pronunciation,* or the fitting together of these sounds according to commonly accepted standards.

These concepts are often confused. *Articulation has to do with the clarity or distinctness of utterance,* while *pronunciation has to do with regional or dictionary standards.* It may be said, "We mispronounce words when we don't know how to pronounce them; we misarticulate words when we know how to pronounce them but fail to do so." Through habit, carelessness, and indifference, individuals may acquire such articulation problems as:
- *substitution of one sound for another,* in such words as:
  - "dat" for that
  - "winduh" for window
  - "git" for get
  - "yur" for your
  - "liddle" for little

- *insertion of extra sounds,* as:
  - ath-uh-lete for athlete
  - ekscape for escape
  - acrosst for across
  - fil-um for film.

- *omission of certain sounds,* such as:
  - at for that
  - probly for probably
  - em for them
  - slep for slept
  - pitcher for picture

- *misplacement of accent,* for example:
  - com-PAIR-a-ble for COM-par-a-ble
  - pre-FER-a-ble for PREF-er-a-ble
  - the-A-ter for THE-a-ter

*Pronunciation:* A person may be able to form all the speech sounds in a word accurately without saying the word correctly. The letters of words do not always represent the same sounds. When the person can form the sounds of a word correctly but does not know the acceptable way to form them, he has a pronunciation problem. The way to achieve acceptable pronunciation is to check new words in the dictionary and to be sensitive to the pronunciations heard in the speech of others. If others pronounce a word differently, the word should be looked up at the very next opportunity before using it again. The teacher must play a central role in identifying words misarticulated and mispronounced by students.

*Body Language as Communication:* In addition to voice and articulation-pronunciation controls, a speaker's whole body acts as an important tool in the physical delivery of speech. Through the judicious use of eye contact, facial expression, and body activity the speaker can supplement and reinforce his spoken communication by means of visual symbols.

*Eye Contact:* It is important for effective oral communication that the listeners feel that the speaker is speaking directly to them. No matter if the speaker is addressing one person or many, each listener should gain a feeling that the speaker is addressing him. Thus, *eye contact* between the speaker and his audience is essential in virtually every speaking situation. No matter what the setting, therefore, the speaker should make every attempt to meet the eyes of all members of the audience to achieve a feeling of directness and all-inclusiveness. The eyes of the speaker should meet those of members of the audience, not look past them or avoid them, nor over their heads, out of the window, down at the floor, or up at the ceiling. Eye contact with members of the audience will also help the speaker watch for audience reactions, for signs of misunderstanding, doubt, or question which may help him modify his communication in response to audience reactions.

*Facial Expression:* Another form of body control is the use of *facial expression* to clarify and enliven oral communication. The speaker's face, used effectively, can reflect his interest in his own message, the intensity of his feelings, his sincerity and purposefulness. Hiding behind a mask of blankness and composure can deny the speaker an important tool in the communication of his ideas. To develop this facility with facial expression, the learner should try always to communicate ideas in which he has a high interest and in which he has a sense of competence and concern. It is difficult to generate facial liveliness when speaking on a topic of little personal concern.

*Body Activity:* The use of gestures and general *body activity* provides another means for supplementing speech. The use of motor activity involving the head, torso, arms, hands, or gross body movement to emphasize the spoken word is a skill that may be cultivated. A shrug of the shoulders, a nod of the head, a straightening of the torso, a lift of the chin, or a step toward the audience can indicate indifference, emphasis, firmness of purpose, a questioning attitude, or determination.

Body activity can, however, be overdone to the point where too much activity may distract from the message. The use of body activity must be judicious if it is to have a controlled and desired effect on the listeners.

Another fault in this area involves the unconscious use of distracting mannerisms that may result from habit, nervousness, or preoccupation. Such mannerisms usually are unrelated to the content of the message, such as shifting weight from foot to foot, finger or foot tapping, nose or head fiddling, generalized arm waving, lint picking, and the like. The student should learn to normally use body movement only for specific purposes, while trying to eliminate all mannerisms and overuses that distract from the message.

*Visual Aids Help Oral Communication:* The physical delivery of speech may be enhanced also through the use of visual aids. Visual aids may be useful for several purposes:

- *for getting attention and interest.* Well-chosen and relevant aids command attention through their shape, color, texture, or movement. A speaker can capture attention by using materials that appeal directly to the senses.
- *for clarifying.* When words are insufficient to communicate an idea, a visual aid may help make an idea clearer. A sketch or drawing, a photograph or model, often can clarify in an instant what may be impossible to describe verbally.

- *for impressing on memory.* Aside from getting attention and clarifying an idea, the speaker may wish to affect the listener's memory. A well-chosen visual aid may help etch an idea on the memory far more effectively than a well-turned phrase.
- *for increasing poise.* The use of visual aids may provide a framework for the speaker's activity, giving him something to do that may serve to increase confidence. The use of visual aids as a "crutch" should not be encouraged in the long run; however, their use in this way may serve to aid the self-confidence of the learner in the initial stages of speech training.

Many types of visual aids may be found useful to supplement oral communications. These include charts, graphs, maps, globes, chalkboard sketches, flip charts, models, moving pictures, projected slides and illustrations, photographs, or television enlargements. In using visual aids, the speaker should follow several basic guidelines:
- He should use the visual material purposefully;
- He should be certain that the entire audience can see the aid;
- He should maintain eye contact while using the aid; and
- He should avoid dividing attention with the aid when it is not in use.

**Verbal Delivery**

The effectiveness of oral communication depends also upon the speaker's choice of language and his style of delivery. The words he uses, the phrasing by which he assembles them, and the manner in which he delivers them, are the elements of *verbal delivery.*

*Choice of Language:* Good language in oral communication is language adapted to the audience and to the occasion. In choosing language, the speaker must consider himself, the ideas he wants to express, the characteristics of the audience, and the nature of the setting. Thus he must ask himself, "Is this expression suitable for me to use in communicating this thought to this audience on this occasion?"

*Use clear language:* To accomplish this, the speaker should use language that clarifies his thoughts. Language should be simple and not pompous. Unnecessarily complex expressions or technical terms should be avoided. Too many words, too ornate words, too pretentious words, can hamper communication. The criteria of clarity in speaking are directness, economy, and aptness. For example,
- Instead of "prevarication", say "lie";
- Instead of "domicile", say "home";
- Instead of "this moment is one of great joy to my heart," say "I'm glad to be here."

*Seek precise words:* It is also a good idea to use precise language. Words and expressions which are specific to the intended meaning are more likely to communicate that meaning than more general and abstract words. In this vein:
- Instead of "car," try hardtop, sedan, Ford, or 1973 hatch-back Pinto;
- Instead of "said," try replied, stated, cried, commented, uttered.

*Avoid imprecise wording:* Avoid roundabout expressions, or *euphemisms,* which create special problems in lack of precision. "Soft-pedaling" an idea now and then may be justified if the speaker does not sacrifice his overall credibility. But care must be taken that the use of euphemisms does not act to call into question the speaker's ideas or intent. Therefore,
- Instead of "he passed to his just reward," try → "he died"
- "he received his termination notice" → "he was fired"
- "the effects were not inconsiderable" → "the effects were great"

*Use appealing language:* The speaker should also seek to use language that will enliven his thoughts. One way to achieve this is to use language that appeals to the senses. Thus language that appeals to movement, color, light, texture, form, taste, smell, sound, and the like will tend to put life in the speaking. Thus,
- Instead of "a difficult peace", try → "a hard and bitter peace"
- "an old ship" → "a splintery, creaking old ship"

*Animate abstract ideas:* Figurative language, too, can enliven speech by animating an abstract idea. The use of simile, metaphor, personification, and irony (look up the meanings in your dictionary) are especially useful. For example,
- Instead of "her arrival silenced everyone", try → "her arrival was like a chill winter wind"
- "he paced to and fro" → "he was like a caged lion"
- "the winds rustled the trees" → "the trees whispered in the winds"
- "we worked a lot of overtime" → "oh, we twiddled away our time and often left early!"

*Use varied techniques:* The speaker should develop ways to vary his choice of language. Variety in expression can help to sustain interest and attention, while often clarifying meaning. Students should practice changing their language by use of techniques such as:
- varying the shaping of sentences (use of questions, use of imperatives, varying order of phrases, etc.);
- building climax within passages;
- using parallelisms (recurring similarities of phrase or word arrangements);
- using alliteration (repeating first syllables, or consonants in consecutive words)
- using repetition of phraseology;
- using fresh language, i.e. avoiding the ordinary and the hackneyed, or shopworn, cliché-type phrases.

*Use appropriate language:* The speaker should always take special pains to use language appropriate to the occasion, and language which is standard. The speaker can be too formal or too informal, either of which will reduce, for particular occasions, the effectiveness of his communication. While the formality of language may be adjusted to the occasion, rarely will it be appropriate to use common slang or the language of the streets in any formal communication setting. Similarly, the use of standard speech will usually be appropriate and aid in communicating ideas, whereas the use of substandard language forms may inhibit understanding and reduce the speaker's credibility among many segments of his audience.

*Use natural language:* Further, it is important on all occasions that the speaker use language that is his own, language that is familiar and comfortable. Each student should work toward developing broader vocabulary and a greater variety of language skills, but should be discouraged from trying to achieve these in large steps. Language skills are developed over long periods of time, and at any given stage of development the student should use the language with which he is most comfortable and natural. In this way each student, over time, may develop uniqueness and effectiveness of style – that characteristic of one's speech which brands it distinctly as his own.

*Develop a Good Style of Delivery:* Finally, *control of delivery rate, rhythm* and *phrasing* will be essential to achieving clarity and effectiveness in oral communication. *Rate* may be controlled by the number and duration of the silent spaces between words and phrases, as well as by the time taken in the production of individual sounds, particularly the vowel sounds. Faster rates may be called for at times; at other times, slower rates. Variations in rate can affect the clarity of communication as well as the mood. A slow and ponderous rate may create a mood of solemnity; a rapid rate, one of lightness and joyfulness. One should vary his rate within speech to achieve variety as he varies other aspects of verbal delivery.

These variations, together with the individual's use of pauses and techniques of sound production act to generate a *rhythm of speech* that is part of the individual's style. Care should be taken that the use of pauses aids rather than hinders meaning – that pauses occur in appropriate places.

Also, special care should be taken that irrelevant sounds, such as "ah," "uh," and "um" do not creep into the individual's speech to fill up the spaces and to break up the flow of ideas. The rate and rhythm of speaking should compare favorably to a musical composition in which the breaks, accelerations, slow-downs, and repetitions add interest and clarity to the composer's purpose.

## Principles Affecting Human Relations

In addition to those principles of oral communication which affect delivery, a number of principles of oral communication affect the relationship between the speaker and his audience. It should be self-evident that a listener will be more receptive to a speaker's ideas if a positive relationship exists between them. The speaker can apply certain principles which will tend to create and to maintain this type of positive relationship.

*Respect the Dignity of Others*

Every human being desires self-respect, a sense of personal worth, and dignity. In dealing with others it is basic to honestly nourish this desire. If we do or say anything which will injure another's dignity, if we humiliate or demean him in any way, we create resentment and antagonism which can obstruct effective communication. To implement this principle, try the following techniques in both formal and informal communications:

- *Make the other person right in something.* Even though you may disagree with him, start your search for agreement by pinpointing something in which he is right and go on from there.
- *Avoid complaining or finding fault.* The complainer and the faultfinder destroy all reasonable relations with others. Follow the maxim, "fix the error, not the blame." Protect the dignity of others by showing your respect for them personally, even while you may disagree with their ideas or criticize their work.

- *Avoid arguments.* Arguing with another implies that he is ignorant or mistaken and thereby diminishes his dignity. Antagonism can easily form around argument and obstruct effective communication. By being modest in advancing ideas and by avoiding telling others they are wrong, a speaker can reduce the possibility of damaging arguments. Rather than saying, "It is obvious that.. ..," or "Any right-thinking person can see that.. ..," try saying, "It appears to me that ....," or "Let us consider the possibility that ...."
- *Admit personal mistakes.* If one is willing to admit that he is human enough to make an error, others find their own self-image taking on increased stature.

*Develop An Honest Interest in Other People*

This second principle challenges us to develop an attitude of curiosity about others and to pursue this curiosity rather than to tell others about ourselves. Rather than a "Here I am" attitude, develop a "There you are" attitude. Such an attitude creates respect in others, and enables one to know those with whom he deals, to understand them, and to treat them as individuals. To cultivate an attitude of interest in others, try the following techniques:

- *Be an interested listener.* One cannot possibly respect another's point of view unless he hears it out.
- *Smile honestly and often.* A person need not agree with, approve of, or like another's point of view; understanding, recognition, and interest are sufficient to stimulate an honest smile which will reflect one's appreciation and respect for the other's point of view.
- *Ask questions frequently to understand others.* Questions are valuable because they require people to take specific actions in the direction of others. A good question reveals that one has really been listening and further, that he has an interest in what was said. And it gives another an opportunity to further reveal himself, thus providing a mechanism for getting better acquainted.

*Recognize Individual Uniqueness and Worth*

This third principle asks us to see people as individuals, to respond positively to their better qualities, and to understand their weaknesses. To develop ability in this area, try such methods as:

- *Get names right and use them often.* One's use of it reveals recognition of his uniqueness. Using names correctly and frequently not only satisfies the natural desire of another for recognition, but also aids a person to identify another as an individual.
- *Be appreciative and quick to give approval.* Being ready and generous with appreciation builds good human relations in two ways. It nourishes the receiver's feeling of self-esteem and worth, and it trains the giver to be observant of the strong or desirable traits and behavior of others.
- *Assume that people will behave in a good manner.* If we ascribe the best of motives and intentions to others, they will be inclined to live up to them. Assume the best of every person and you will rarely be disappointed. Assuming the best of them gives implied recognition to their worth as individuals.
- *Respect the rights and opinions of others.* A person need not always agree with the opinions of others, but he must respect the right of others to hold opinions different from his own and refrain from belittling or contradicting them.

The opinions of others are very much a part of their psychological and intellectual makeup, and to refuse respect for an opinion is to deny respect to the person himself. *Effective communication cannot occur between persons without mutual respect for their rights and opinions.*

*Cooperate With the Wants of Others*

This fourth principle emphasizes that behavior is directed from within a person as he attempts to satisfy his own wants or to solve his own problems. If a person seeks to communicate with others and to direct their behavior in a particular direction, he must cooperate with the wants which motivate them. That is, he must align his purposes with their wants and avoid the appearance of denying or frustrating those wants. Nevertheless, there is a difference between cooperating with the wants of others and giving in to them. Cooperation simply implies that one should present his case in a way which will reveal how the listener will benefit. Some techniques for implementing this principle follow:

- *Encourage initiative.* Great energy can be released by encouraging and tactfully guiding the initiative of others. Challenging the creative imagination of others in proposing solutions to problems; in developing plans, in organizing for action, and the like reveals the speaker's respect for the ideas of others, and can go a long way to assure their cooperation and participation in the final activity. When one's own initiative and imagination has been challenged, he is more likely to align himself with the decisions that are finally reached.
- *Help the other person get what he wants.* When another sees a person willing to help him satisfy his wants, an atmosphere conducive to effective communication and cooperation has been established. Try to recognize what others want and address the issues from their point of view.
- *Present problems and ask for solutions.* When one must ask another for help, when he must assign work, or when he wants to enlist cooperation, then he will often find it more productive to present the problem and ask for help in its solution than to make a direct demand. Instead of saying, "George, move those boxes out of the aisle," try saying, "George, these boxes are dangerous where they are; someone may injure themselves. Is there some other handy place for them where they will be out of the way?" By involving George in solving the problem you show respect for his ideas, and he will likely WANT to help solve the problem.
- *Present doubts, opinions or objections in question form.* Sometimes we must necessarily disagree with another. When it is necessary, we can make our disagreement more objective and more acceptable to others if we avoid over-positive or challenging statements. One technique for achieving this is to voice our concerns in the form of questions, which may minimize the possibility of arousing resentment or starting an argument.

**Person-to-Person Communications**

Not only in the public-service occupations, but also in business, industry, and everyday life, the form of communication most often used is *person-to-person speaking*. Any human activity which requires the interaction of two or more persons will rely heavily on person-to-person speaking to establish and maintain social relationships, to plan, coordinate, and carry out cooperative tasks. *Effectiveness in person-to-person communication is essential for effectiveness in most jobs.*

*Informal Conversation:* The major difference between conversation and public speaking is that in conversation there is give-and-take, while in public speaking the speaker does all the talking. Yet even this difference may be more apparent than actual, for in real life conversants may hold the floor for long periods of time, and public speakers may be seeking two-way communication with their audiences.

There are few firm rules of conversation that will hold true in all situations because conversational situations may vary so widely. Not only do topics vary, but the makeup of the conversants in age, occupation, interest, education may also vary. So may the time, place, and purpose of the gathering. So many situations are possible that the conversationalist who tries to meet them all in the same manner is doomed to failure. *The good conversationalist will try to develop a wise adaptability.* Some guidelines that may prove helpful are:

- Pursue only those subjects of interest to all the conversants;
- Avoid saying about another what you might resent being said about yourself;
- Avoid statements which you would be embarrassed to have repeated with your name cited as the source;
- Maintain a conversational tone: good-humored, alert, and vigorous, without being rancorous;
- Express opinions, but avoid being opinionated; contend without being contentious;
- In general, adhere to the principles of good human relations discussed in the previous section.

*Interviewing:* Most persons, at one time or another, have been interviewed. Public service employees, at one time or another, may be expected to conduct interviews. While interviews have many characteristics in common with conversation, there are important differences. An interview is a planned conversation – it is arranged in advance by the parties and is intended to accomplish some purpose. Interviews may be *structured* (directive) or *unstructured* (non-directive) in form. The former is likely to be task- or subject-centered and is most common in work situations. The latter are likely to be person-centered and are used for counseling, analysis, and therapy. Thus, they usually require that the interviewer have substantial professional training. There are many kinds of, and purposes for, interviews. For example:

- *Employment interviews:* for securing, developing, and training employees;
- *Induction interviews:* for orienting new employees;
- *Performance review interviews:* for training, and developing employees;
- *Counseling interviews*: for personal and personnel matters;
- *Correction interviews:* for disciplining and guidance of staff;
- *Grievance interviews:* reverse correction interviews;
- *Data gathering interviews:* to obtain special information;
- *Consulting interviews:* exchange of information and problem-solving with an expert;
- *Sales interviews:* for persuading another;
- *Order-giving interviews:* to assign tasks and procedures;
- *Exit interviews:* a debriefing of an employee upon separation.

From the above it can be seen that interviews are directed toward serving three basic goals:

- to increase understanding through information-giving and information-getting;

- to persuade; and
- to solve problems.

To be effective, interviews should be carefully planned. Objectives should be determined in advance, and thought should be given to major obstacles likely to arise. The strategy and tactics of the interview should be planned beforehand, and consideration should be given to some contingency plans in the event that certain events occur during the interview.

The beginning of the interview should establish a workable arrangement between the parties by establishing an appropriate atmosphere, stimulating interest and attention, and presenting the problem or goal of the interview. The body of the interview should pursue the above objectives.

The close of the interview should round out and gracefully terminate the interview. The gist of the interview should be reviewed or summarized; the bases for further conversations should be established if necessary; and appreciations should be expressed.

*Group Discussions:* The term "group discussion" describes an activity that enables a number of cooperative people to talk freely about a problem under the leadership of a member of the group. They have the common purpose of interchanging ideas for specific needs. Group discussion is sometimes confused with debate, but the two activities differ in purpose, in format, and in the attitude of the participants. *The purpose of debate is advocacy; the purpose of discussion is inquiry.*

In group discussion, the participants deliberate seriously with minimum restraints. They work in cooperation with one another in discussion at least until the group as a unit has reached a solution to a problem. Their purpose is to inquire in order to learn all aspects of a problem, and then to solve it. Although participants may disagree, their purpose is to sort out the areas of agreement in arriving at answers.

*Techniques of Group Discussion:* The techniques and formats of group discussion may vary, but the underlying purpose remains the same – to inquire into the essential aspects of a problem and to solve it. Some types of discussions, such as the *meeting,* or *round-table,* are not intended for audiences; others, such as the *panel,* the *symposium,* and the *forum,* are planned for audiences. Whatever the format, the participants should remember that they are acting as a group studying a question. It requires real skill on the part of all participants to pool relevant information, to move the discussion forward, to limit heated cross talk, and to stress areas of agreements.

*Criteria for group discussion:* Group discussion is useful only if the group has a real problem to solve and if its members all agree on what that is. Thus, stating the question in an effective way is important to promote fruitful discussion. Here are some criteria for worthwhile discussions:
- The problem should deserve a solution.
- The problem should be worth the time spent on it.
- The problem should be either timely or timeless.
- The problem should be able to be solved in the time available.
- The group should be competent to solve the problem.
- The problem should be stated in question form.

- The question for discussion should not be stated in a form demanding a "yes" or "no" answer, but in a form indicating a need for discussion. (Instead of: "Should the federal government control the press?" try: "What should be the role of the federal government in regulating the press?")

*Leading a discussion* requires some special skills. The discussion leader must insure the orderly, systematic, and cooperative consideration of the question. He tries to direct the course of the discussion without manipulating the group to accept any particular conclusion. He assures that every member of the group has an opportunity to participate, and that no one monopolizes the floor. He provides needed facts or calls upon others to provide them. He summarizes when needed and restates the issues under discussion. He strives to keep the emphasis upon agreement and cooperative thinking in order to avoid conflict.

A simple functional plan for discussion leadership might include the following steps for a problem-solving discussion:
- Introduction of the problem by the leader
- Defining potentially confusing terms
- Presentation of relevant facts by group members
- Specifying criteria for judging a good solution
- Presentation by members of possible solutions
- Analysis of solutions in relation to criteria
- Decision: which solution is preferred, or what additional information is needed before a decision can be made

*Forms of group discussion:* Several forms of group discussion are in common use. Each occasion for group discussion implies its own format for discussion that will best serve its own specific needs, purposes, and interests. The common formats include:
- The *round table* (or informal) group discussion is usually not observed by an audience. The preferred number of participants is from four to seven, although good discussions may be held with as many as fifteen or as few as three participants. The discussants should cooperate courteously in reaching a decision. Formal recognition to speak is not necessary. The outstanding characteristic of the round-table discussion is its informality.
- The *panel* is similar except for the presence of an audience. With an audience, the members are more formal in their presentations, speaking not only for themselves, but for the audience as well. If the audience participates by asking questions after the solution has been reached, the activity is called a *panel forum.*
- A *symposium* differs from the panel or round-table because all participants, perhaps three or four, are experts on phases of the question. The speakers give set speeches in order and are provided little opportunity for interchanging ideas with their fellow participants. The symposium is typically presented for the benefit of an audience. Often a panel follows a symposium, offering the participants an opportunity, after their individual presentations, to exchange ideas in a discussion format. When the audience is invited to ask questions of the participants, the activity is called a *symposium-forum.*
- The *forum* is an activity distinguished by audience participation. The forum may be used in combination with a panel, a symposium, a lecture, a debate, or any other form that may be useful to communicate basic information to the

audience prior to its participation. The leader, in conducting a forum, should explain the procedures to be followed by members of the audience in asking questions or making comments, including how to be recognized, how much time will be allowed, and the like.

Group discussion is an excellent means of pooling knowledge, reaching decisions, and informing the public. The public-service employee will find himself participating in group discussion both within his organization, at staff meetings and other groups, and for audiences as a means of informing public opinion.

**Speaking Before Groups**
The distinction between speaking IN a group and speaking BEFORE a group is not always apparent. If, as a member of a group, one speaks his piece for five full minutes without interruption, or if he rises and speaks from a standing position, is he speaking in the group or before it? While it is a popular notion that group speaking, or public speaking is characterized by a much higher degree of formality, and by one-way communication from the speaker to his audience, it is well to consider speaking before a group as simply dignified, amplified conversation. *Public speaking, at its best, seeks to establish a carefully planned conversational relationship with a group of persons.*

The public-service employee will find many occasions in which he will be called upon to speak before a group. The group may be his co-workers, as at a staff or committee meeting; his colleagues, as at a professional conference; or members of the public, as at a public meeting, or a meeting of a citizens' group. Whatever the particular occasion, the employee may be called upon to speak before a group for any of several purposes. The general principles of effective oral communication apply to public or group speaking, as well as to person-to-person speaking, and attention to these principles will aid in developing effectiveness in speaking before groups. Public-service employees commonly participate in speaking before groups for the purposes of informing, instructing, persuading, motivating, or entertaining.

*Speaking to Inform*
The primary purpose of the speech to inform is to convey information to listeners to clarify a point of view, a process, a method, an idea, a problem, or a proposed solution. By far the greatest amount of speaking before a group is done to convey information. The content may vary from relatively simple, concrete topics, such as how to complete a personnel form, to highly abstract topics, such as how a client-centered program will affect relations with clients.

Three general types of informing speeches are commonly used in public-service work:
- reports
- briefings
- informational talks

An *oral report* summarizes in orderly fashion a body of information, usually assembled by the person making the report.

A *briefing* is similar to a report, except that it usually occurs as a prelude to some imminent action. All the facts needed for decision-making actions are assembled immediately before the action, and conveyed to those who will be making the decisions.

The *informational talk* is less formal, usually delivered by a knowledgeable person without need for much formal preparation. An informational talk might be presented by the head of an agency about the agency's work to a group of new employees. A simple and typical four-part outline for information speeches consists of the following parts:

- Introduction – tell them what you are going to tell them
- Key Idea – tell them the main or central idea
- Body – tell them the details
- Conclusion – tell them what you told them

*Speaking to Instruct*

Almost every employee in a public agency at one time or another will be expected to teach or train others. This teaching will often occur in a group situation, and the employee will function as a teacher, speaking to the group, assigning practice, evaluating student work, and similar activities. Speaking for this purpose should generally follow the rules of good human relations, of course, but additionally should use certain principles of learning which will increase the effectiveness of teaching.

When speaking to instruct or train a group, the instructor should employ the following principles:

- *Include an advance organizer:* A summary of the tasks that will be learned, and a reason for learning them
- *Provide active practice:* Give the learners, or listeners, plenty of opportunity to practice what you want them to learn. Ask a lot of questions; hand out worksheets; break the group into "buzz" groups for discussion; get them actively involved.
- *Help them succeed:* Don't assign them work or ask them questions which they are likely to fail. Give them hints if necessary during practice, but help them succeed.
- *Give them plenty of feedback:* If they answer a question correctly, or turn in a correct worksheet, or make a correct contribution in some other way, let them know it right away. Not tomorrow, or next week, but let them know immediately.

If these principles can be incorporated into instructional talks and training sessions, they are likely to be more effective.

*Speaking to Persuade*

The public-service employee may find himself speaking to persuade a group from time to time. In ordinary work situations, he may wish to persuade his fellow workers to adopt a new policy, or a certain attitude toward their work. On other occasions, he may be speaking to members of the public, trying to persuade them favorably toward his agency, or to avail themselves of the agency's program.

Basically, there are three types of appeals that the speaker can make to his audience:

- *Logical Appeals:* Through the use of deductive reasoning (from general ideas to specific conclusion) and inductive reasoning (from specific data to a general conclusion), and the presenting of factual evidence to support this reasoning, the speaker appeals mainly to the listener's intellect and reason.

- *Psychological Appeals:* Through appeals to the listener's motivations, feelings and values, the speaker tries to get his listeners to WANT to adopt the idea being presented.
- *Personal Appeals:* Through his own personal effect, the speaker tries to influence his listeners – by characterizing his own reputation, appearance, personality and character in a way that will create a favorable and receptive climate for his ideas.

Beyond these types of appeals, the persuasive speaker will do well to attend carefully to the principles of good human relations discussed earlier.

*Speaking to Motivate*

Another occasion for speaking before a group is to motivate them – to excite, arouse, or spur them on. Usually such speaking is occasioned by some strong feelings in the speaker about his subject. He may, for example, feel that the staff of the agency is simply not attaching sufficient importance to certain areas of their work. At a staff meeting he might address the group and try to get them "fired up" about that work.

Speaking of this type generally follows the patterns of the persuasive speech, since we often are seeking to influence the listeners in a particular direction. Typically, however, its appeal tends to focus upon the psychological, since the speaker is usually more interested in affecting attitudes, motivations, and values than he is in affecting beliefs.

*Speaking to Entertain*

While not normally central to the duties of public-service employees, the entertaining speech is an occasional responsibility that may fall to almost anyone. At an annual dinner, a staff party, an agency picnic, one may be called upon to speak briefly to a group in a light and casual tone. When called upon on such an occasion, one should be especially aware that he need not be uproariously funny to be entertaining. *To entertain means simply to amuse or to divert.*

It is well to recognize that few persons have the practiced skills of a professional comedian to keep an audience laughing from start to finish. The occasional speaker who seeks to entertain an audience, to amuse and divert them for a few brief moments, does well to adapt his humor to the local and familiar experiences of his audience.
In general, the entertaining speech should attend to the principles of good human relations. The speaker should not develop humor at the expense of any person's dignity. While he may poke gentle fun at himself, rarely can one poke fun at others without injuring their dignity and self-esteem. As with other purposeful speeches, speeches to entertain may be organized around the four-part outline discussed earlier.

**STUDENT LEARNING ACTIVITIES**
- Prepare a list of principles affecting delivery, and a list of principles affecting human relations. Develop checklists for evaluating the speech of others based upon these principles.
- Participate in informal conversation with two others before the class. No topic should be decided in advance. Following the conversation, participate in a class critique of the conversation.
- Participate in two interview situations set up by your teacher. In one, function as the interviewer; in the other, as the interviewee.

- Participate in a round-table discussion on a problem assigned by your teacher.
- Participate in a panel-forum on a problem assigned by your teacher.
- Participate as a member of a symposium-forum on a problem assigned by your teacher.
- Prepare and present a 5-minute oral report on a topic assigned by your teacher.
- Prepare and present a 5-minute lesson on a subject assigned by your teacher.
- Prepare and present a 5-minute persuasive or motivational speech on a subject assigned by your teacher.
- Prepare and present a 5-minute speech to entertain the class.
- Participate in critiques of the speeches and discussions involving other students. Use principles of delivery and human relations as the basis for your criticism.

**TEACHER MANAGEMENT ACTIVITIES**
- Have each student develop checklists for critiquing oral communications based upon the principles of delivery and human relations discussed in the first topic. Through class discussion, develop a checklist evaluation form that will be used by the class for evaluating speech performance.
- Have students in groups of three participate in informal conversations. Topics should not be decided in advance. The setting should be informal as possible. But the conversation should be observed and evaluated by members of the class. "Buzz" groups may be formed, with teams of "evaluators" dropping into the groups.
- Assign interview situations to pairs of students, designating the interviews and the interviewees. Students should be given ten or fifteen minutes to prepare for their part of the interview. Interviews should be critiqued by the class.
- Assign students to round-table panel and symposium groups. Assign each a problem to discuss. Have each group discuss its problem before the class. Critique the discussions.
- Have each student prepare a five-minute report, a five-minute lesson on some subject, a five-minute persuasive speech, a five-minute entertainment speech, on topics you approve. Presentations should be evaluated by the class using the critique forms developed by the class.

**EVALUATION QUESTIONS**

1. Effective speakers have voices that:　　　　　　　　　　　　　　　　　1._____
    A. Have a pleasant pitch and volume
    B. Lack variety of pitch
    C. Have great volume
    D. Have a very high pitch

2. A competent speaker would:　　　　　　　　　　　　　　　　　　　　　2._____
    A. Look at the people in the front row
    B. Look at the people in the back row
    C. Look at all the people in the group
    D. Look at the people in the middle of the group

3. Looking at the audience is helpful to the speaker because:  3._____
    A. It helps the speaker watch for audience reaction
    B. It helps the speaker watch for signs of misunderstanding
    C. It enables the speaker to pick out signs of doubt
    D. All of the above

4. An effective speaker would:  4._____
    A. Look lively and sincere
    B. Keep his face as blank as possible
    C. Look overly composed;
    D. Look disinterested about the subject

5. Body language can indicate:  5._____
    A. Emphasis
    B. Firmness of purpose
    C. Indifference
    D. All of the above

6. These items would be included in a group of visual aids:  6._____
    A. Phonograph records and record player
    B. Charts, graphs, and maps
    C. Tape decks and cassettes
    D. All of the above

7. It is preferable for a speaker to use:  7._____
    A. Many abstract and general words
    B. Precise words
    C. Fancy words
    D. Round-about expressions

8. As a speaker, you should:  8._____
    A. Use your own language
    B. Pattern your language after someone else
    C. Imitate highly educated people
    D. Use the occasion to try out big words you are learning

9. Accomplished speakers:  9._____
    A. Deliver their speeches as fast as they can to economize time
    B. Deliver their speeches at a very slow rate
    C. Give very solemn speeches at a rapid rate
    D. Vary the rate within the speech to achieve variety

10. An effective speaker would:  10._____
    A. Speak rapidly without leaving any break between sentences
    B. Fill up the spaces by saying "ah"
    C. Pause occasionally
    D. Use "you know" to fill in

11. A good technique in human relations is to:  11.____
    A. Tell others they are wrong about everything
    B. Point out the other person's faults
    C. Admit your own mistakes
    D. Attack others personally

12. The most sought after people are those who:  12.____
    A. Tell others all about themselves
    B. Are good listeners
    C. Smile only when necessary
    D. Let others know how they feel about every subject

13. For a person who has recently been hired, it is preferable to:  13.____
    A. Be quick to show what others are doing wrong
    B. Be suspicious of others until they prove themselves
    C. Try to convince others to think as you do on every subject
    D. None of the above

14. A good technique in human relations is to:  14.____
    A. Ask the opinions of others
    B. Help other people get what they want
    C. Present your doubts in the form of a question
    D. All of the above

**Answer Key**

| | | | | |
|---|---|---|---|---|
| 1. A | 4. A | 7. B | 10. C | 13. D |
| 2. C | 5. D | 8. A | 11. C | 14. D |
| 3. D | 6. B | 9. D | 12. B | |

# BASIC FUNDAMENTALS OF WRITTEN COMMUNICATION

| CONTENTS | Page |
|---|---|
| INSTRUCTIONAL OBJECTIVES | 1 |
| CONTENT | 1 |
|   Introduction | 1 |
| 1. Business Writing | 1 |
|     Letters | |
|       Selet the letter type | |
|       Select the Right Format | |
|       Know the Letter Elements | |
|       Be Breef | |
|       Use Concrete Nouns | |
|       Use Active Verbs | |
|       Use a Natural Tone | |
|     Forms | 4 |
|     Memoranda | 5 |
|     Minutes of meetings | 5 |
|     Short Reports | 6 |
|     News Releases | 8 |
| 2. Reporting on a Topic | 9 |
|     Preparation for the Report | 9 |
|       What is the Purpose of the Report? | |
|       What Questions Should it Answer? | |
|       Where Can the Relevant information be obtained? | |
|     The Text of the Report | 10 |
|       What Are the Answers to the Questions? | |
|       Organizing the Report | |
|     The Writer's Responsibilities | 11 |
|     Conclusions and Recommendations | 11 |
| 3. Persuasive Writing | 11 |
|     General Guidelines for Writing Persuasively | 11 |
|       Know the Source Credibility | |
|       Avoid Overemotional Appeal | |
|       Consider the Other Man's Point of wiew | |
|     Interpersonal Communications | 12 |
|       Conditions of Persuading | |
|       The Persuassion campain | |
| 4. Instructional Writing | 13 |
|     Advances Organizers | |
|     Practice | |
|     Errorless Learning | |
|     Feedback | |
| STUDENT LEARNING ACTIVITIES | 16 |
| TEACHERS MANAGEMENT ACTIVTIES | 17 |
| EVALUATION QUESTIONS | 19 |

# BASIC FUNDAMENTALS OF WRITTEN COMMUNICATION

**INSTRUCTIONAL OBJECTIVES**
1. Ability to write legibly.
2. Ability to fill out forms and applications correctly.
3. Ability to take messages and notes accurately.
4. Ability to write letters effectively.
5. Ability to write directions and instructions clearly.
6. Ability to outline written and spoken information.
7. Ability to persuade or teach others through written communication.
8. Ability to write effective overviews and summaries.
9. Ability to make smooth transitions within written communications.
10. Ability to use language forms appropriate for the reader.
11. Ability to prepare effective informational reports.

**CONTENT**

INTRODUCTION

Public-service employees are required to prepare written communications for a variety of purposes. Written communication is a fundamental tool, not only for the public-service occupations, but throughout the world of work. Many public-service occupations require written communication with ordinary citizens of diverse backgrounds, so the trainee should develop the ability to write in simple, nontechnical language that the ordinary citizen will understand.

This unit is designed to develop the student's ability to communicate effectively in writing for a number of different purposes and in a number of different formats. Whatever the particular purpose or format, however, effective writing will require the writer:

- to have a clear idea of his purpose and his audience;
- to organize his thoughts and information in an orderly way;
- to express himself concisely, accurately, and concretely;
- to report relevant facts;
- to explain and summarize ideas clearly; and
- to evaluate the effectiveness of his communication.

1. BUSINESS WRITING
   Several forms of written communication tend to recur frequently in most public-service agencies, including:
   - letters
   - forms
   - memoranda
   - minutes of meetings
   - short reports
   - telegrams and cables
   - news releases
   - and many others

   The public-service employee should be familiar with the principles of writing in these forms, and should be able to apply them in preparing effective communications.

   Letters

   Every letter sent from a public-service agency should be considered an ambassador of goodwill. The impression it creates may mean the difference between favorable public attitudes or unfavorable ones. It may mean the difference between creating a friend or an enemy for the agency. Every public-service employee has a responsibility to serve the public effectively and to provide services in an efficient and courteous manner. The letters an agency sends out reflect its attitudes toward the public.

The impression a letter creates depends upon both its appearance and its tone. A letter which shows erasures and pen written corrections gives an impression that the sending agency is slovenly. Similarly, a rude or impersonal letter creates the impression that the agency is insensitive or unfeeling. In preparing letters, the employee should apply principles of style and tone which will serve to create the most favorable impression.

<u>Select the Letter Type</u>. The two most common types of business letters are letters of inquiry and letters of response - that is, "asking" letters and "answering" letters. Whichever type of letter the employee is asked to write, the following guidelines will simplify the task and help to achieve a style and tone which will create a favorable impression on the reader.

<u>Select the Right Format</u>. Several styles of letter format are in common use today, including:

- the indented format,
- the block format, and
- the semi-block format.

Modified forms of these are also in use in some offices. The student should become familiar with the formats preferred for usage in his office, and be able to use whichever form the employer requests.

<u>Know the Letter Elements</u>. Every letter includes certain basic elements, such as:

- the letterhead, which identifies the name and address of the sender.
- the date on which the letter was transmitted.
- the inside address, with the name, street, city, and state of the addressee.
- the salutation, greeting the addressee.
- the body, containing the message.
- the complimentary close, the "good-bye" of the business letter.
- the signature, handwritten by the sender.
- the typed signature, the typewritten name and title of the sender.

In addition, several other elements are occasionally found in business letters:

- the *attention line,* directing the letter to the attention of a particular individual or his representative.
- the *subject line,* informing the reader at a glance of the subject of the letter.

- the *enclosure notation,* noting items enclosed with the letter.
- the *copy notation,* listing other persons who receive copies of the letter.
- the *postscript,* an afterthought sometimes (but not normally) added following the last typed line of the letter.

Be *Brief.* Use only the words which help to say what is needed in a clear and straightforward manner. Do not repeat information already known to the reader, or contained elsewhere in the letter. Likewise, do not repeat information contained in the letter being answered. Rather than repeat the content of a previous letter, one can say something like, "Please refer to our letter dated March 5:"

An employee can shorten his letters by using single words that serve the same function as longer phrases. Many commonly used phrases can be replaced by single words. For example,

| Phrase | Single word |
|---|---|
| in order to | to |
| in reference to in | about |
| the amount of | for, of |
| in a number of cases | some |
| in view of | because |
| with regard to | about, in |

Similarly, avoid the use of adjectives and nouns that are formed from verbs. If the root verbs are used instead, the writing will be more concise and more vivid. For example,

| Noun form | Verb form |
|---|---|
| We made an adjustment on our books | We adjusted our books |
| We are sorry we cannot make a replacement of | We are sorry we cannot replace |
| Please make a correction in our order | Please correct our order |

Be on the lookout for unnecessary adjectives and adverbs which tend to clutter letters without adding information or improving style. Such unnecessary words tend to distract the reader and make it more difficult for him to grasp the main points. Observe how the superfluous words, italicized in the following example, obscure the meaning: "You may be *very much* disappointed to learn that the *excessively large* demand for our *highly popular recent* publication, 'Your Income Taxes,' has led to an *unexpected* shortage of this *attractive* publication and we *sadly* expect they will not be replenished until *quite* late this year."

Summarizing, then, a *good letter is simple and clear, with short, simple words, sentences, and paragraphs. Related parts* of *sentences and paragraphs are kept together and placed in an order which makes it easy for the reader to follow the main thoughts.*

<u>Be Natural</u>. Whenever possible, use a human touch. Use names and personal pronouns to let the reader know the letter was written by a person, not an institution. Instead of saying, "It is the policy of this agency to contact its clients once each year to confirm their status," try this: "Our policy, Mr. Jones, is to confirm your status once each year."

<u>Use Concrete Nouns</u>. Avoid using abstract words and generalizations. Use names of objects, places, and persons rather than abstractions.

<u>Use Active verbs</u>. The passive voice gives a motionless, weak tone to most writing. Instead of "The minutes were taken by Mrs. Smith," say, "Mrs. Smith took the minutes." Instead of "The plans were prepared by the banquet committee," say, "The banquet committee prepared the plans."

<u>Use a Natural Tone</u>. Many people tend to become hard, cold, and unnatural the moment they write a letter. *Communicating by letter should have the same natural tone of conversation used in everyday speech.* One way to achieve a natural and personal tone in the majority of letters is through the use of personal pronouns. Instead of saying, "Referring to your letter of March 5, reporting the non-receipt of goods ordered last February 15, please be advised that the goods were shipped as requested," say, "I am sorry to hear that you failed to receive the items you ordered last February 15. We shipped them the same day we received your letter."

<u>Forms</u>

In most businesses and public service agencies, repetitive work is simplified by the use of *forms*. Forms exist for nearly every purpose imaginable: for ordering supplies, preparing invoices, applying for jobs, applying for insurance, paying taxes, recording inventories, and so on. While the forms encountered in different agencies may differ widely, several principles should be applied in completing any form:

- <u>Legibility</u>. Entries on forms should be clear and legible. Print or type wherever possible. When space provided is insufficient, attach a supplementary sheet to the form.

- <u>Completeness</u>. Make an entry in every space provided on the form. If a particular space does not apply to the applicant, enter there the term "N/A" (for "not applicable"). The reader of the completed form will then know that the applicant did not simply overlook that space.

- <u>Conciseness</u>. Forms are intended to elicit a maximum amount of information in the least possible space. When completing a form, it is usually not necessary to write complete sentences. Provide the necessary information in the least possible words.

- *Accuracy.* Be sure the information provided on the form is accurate. If the entry is a number, such as a social security number or an address, double-check the correctness of the number. Be sure of the spelling of names, No one appreciates receiving a communication in which his name is misspelled.

## Memoranda

The written communications passing between offices or departments are usually transmitted in a form known as *"interoffice memorandum."* The headings most often used on such "memos" are:

- TO:       identifying the addressee,
- FROM:     identifying the sender or the originating office,
- SUBJECT:  identifying briefly the subject of the memo,
- DATE:     identifying the date the memo was prepared.

Larger agencies may also use headings such as FILE or REFERENCE NO. to aid in filing and retrieving memoranda.

In writing a memo, many of the same rules for letter-writing may be applied. Both the appearance and tone of the memo should create a pleasing impression. The format should be neat and follow the standards set by the originating office. The tone should be friendly, courteous, and considerate. The language should be clear, concise, and complete.

Memos usually dispense with salutations, complimentary closings, and signatures of the writers. In most other respects, however, the memorandum will follow the rules of good letter-writing.

## Minutes of Meetings

Most formal public-service organization conduct meetings from time to time at which group decisions are made about agency policies, procedures, and work assignments. The records of such meetings are called *minutes*.

Minutes should be written as clearly and simply as possible, summarizing only the essential facts and decisions made at the meeting. While some issue may have been discussed at great length, only the final decision or resolution made of it should be recorded in the minutes. Information of this sort is usually included:

- Time and place of the call to order,
- Presiding officer and secretary,
- Voting members present (with names, if a small organization),

- Approval and corrections of previous minutes,
- Urgent business,
- Old business,
- New business,
- Time of adjournment,
- Signature of recorder.

Minutes should be written in a factual and objective style. The opinions of the recorder should not be in evidence. Every item of business coming up before a meeting should be included in the minutes, together with its disposition. For example:

- "M/S/P (Moved, seconded, passed) that Mr. Thomas Jones take responsibility for rewriting the personnel procedures manual."
- "Discussion of the summer vacation schedule was tabled until the next meeting."
- "M/S/P, a resolution that no client of the agency should be kept waiting more than 20 minutes for an interview."

Note that considerable discussion may have surrounded each of the above items in the minutes, but that only the topic and its resolution are recorded.

Short Reports

The public-service employee often is called upon to prepare a short report gathering and interpreting information on a single topic. Reports of this kind are sometimes prepared so that all the relevant information may be assembled in one place to aid the organization in making certain decisions. Such reports may be read primarily by the staff of the organization or by others closely related to the decision-making process.

Reports may be prepared at other times for distribution to the public or to other agencies and institutions. These reports may serve the purpose of informing public opinion or persuading others on matters of public policy.

Whatever the purpose of the short report, its physical appearance and style of presentation should be designed to create a favorable impression on the reader. Even if the report is distributed only within the writer's own unit, an attractive, clear, thorough report will reflect the writer's dedication to his assignment and the pride he takes in his work.

Some guidelines which will assist the trainee in preparation of effective short reports include use of the following:

- A good quality paper;
- Wide and even margins, allowing binding room;

- An accepted standard style of typing;
- A title page;
- A table of contents (for more lengthy reports only);
- A graphic numbering or outlining system, if needed for clarity;
- Graphics and photos to clarify meaning when useful;
- Footnotes, used sparingly, and only when they contribute to the report;
- A bibliography of sources, using a standard citation style.

A discussion of the organization of content for informational reports follows later in this document.

## News Releases

From time to time, the public-service employees may be called upon to prepare a news release for his agency. Whenever the activities of the agency are newsworthy or of interest to the public, the agency has an obligation to report such activities to the press. The most common means for such reporting is by using the press release. Most newspapers and broadcasting stations are initially informed of agencies' activities by news releases distributed by the agencies themselves. Thus, the news release is a basic tool for communicating with the public served by the agency.

The news release is written in news style, with these basic characteristics:

- Sentences are short and simple.

- Paragraphs are short (one or two sentences) and relate to a single item of information.

- Paragraphs are arranged in *inverted order* — the most important in information appears first.

- The first or *lead* paragraph summarizes the entire story. If the reader went no further, he would have the essential information.

- Subsequent paragraphs provide further details, the most important occurring first.

- Reported information is attributed to sources; that is, the source of the news is reported in the story.

- The expression of the writer's opinions is scrupulously avoided.

- The 5 W's (who, what, why, where, when) are included.

News releases should be typed double spaced on standard 8 1/2 x 11 paper, with generous margins and at least 2" of open space above the lead paragraph. Do not write headlines - that is the editor's job. At the top of the first page of the release include the name of the agency releasing the story and the name and phone number of the person to contact if more information is needed. If the release runs more than one page, end each page with the word "-more-" to indicate that more copy follows. End the release with the symbols "###" to indicate that the copy ends at that point.

Accuracy and physical appearance are essential characteristics of the news release. Typographical errors, or errors of fact, such as misspelled names, lead editors to doubt the reliability of the story. Great care should be taken to assure the accuracy and reliability of a news release.

2. REPORTING ON A TOPIC

At one time or another, most public-service employees will be asked to prepare a report on some topic. Usually the need for the report grows out of some policy decision contemplated by the agency for which full information must be considered. For example:

- Should the agency undertake some new project or service?
- Should working conditions be changed?
- Are new specialists needed on the staff?
- Or should a branch office be opened up?

Or any of a hundred other such decisions which the agency must make from time to time.

When called upon to prepare such a report, the employee should have a model to follow which will guide his collection of information and will help him to prepare an effective and useful report.

As with other forms of written communication, both the physical appearance and content of the report are important to create a favorable impression and to engender confidence. The physical appearance of such reports has been discussed earlier; additional suggestions for reports are given in Unit 3. Basic guidelines follow below for organizing and preparing the content.

Preparation for the Report

*What is the Purpose of the Report?* The preparer of the report should have clearly in mind why the report is needed:

- What is the decision being contemplated by the agency?
- To what use will the report be put?

Before beginning to prepare the report, the writer should discuss its purpose fully with the decision-making staff to articulate the purpose the report is intended to serve. If the employee is himself initiating the report, it would be well to discuss its purpose with colleagues to assure that its purpose is clear in his own mind.

*What Questions Should the Report Answer?* Once the purpose of the report is clear, the questions the report must answer may begin to become clear. For example, if the decision faced by the agency is whether or not to offer a new service, questions may be asked such as these:

- What persons would be served by the new service?

- What would the new service cost?
- What new staff would be needed?
- What new equipment and facilities would be needed?
- What alternative ways exist for offering the service?
- How might the new service be administered?

And so on. Unless the purpose of the report is clear, it is difficult to decide what specific questions need to be answered. Once the purpose is clear, these questions can be specified.

*Where Can the Relevant Information be Obtained?* Once the questions are clear in the writer's mind, he can identify the information he will need to answer them. Information may usually be obtained from two general sources:

- *Relevant documents.* Records, publications, and other reports are often useful in locating the information needed to answer particular questions. These may be in the files of the writer's own agency, in other agencies, or in libraries.

- *Personal contacts.* Persons in a position to know the needed information may be contacted in person, by phone, or by letter. Such contacts are especially important in obtaining firsthand accounts of previous experience.

## The Text of the Report

*What are the Answers to the Questions?* Once the relevant information is in hand, the answers to the questions may be assembled.

- What does the information reveal? This activity amounts to summarizing the information obtained. It often helps to organize this summary around the specific questions asked by the report. For example, if the report asks in one part, "What are the costs of the new service likely to be?" one section of the report should summarize the information gathered to answer this question.

*Organizing the Report.* The organization of a report into main and subsections depends upon the nature of the report. Reports will differ widely in their organization and treatment. In general, however, the report should generally follow the pattern previously discussed. That is, reports which generally include the following subjects in order will be found to be clear in their intent and to communicate effectively:

- *Description of problem or purpose.* Example: "One problem facing our agency is whether or not we should extend our hours of operation to better serve the public. This report is intended to examine the problem and make recommendations."

- *Questions to be answered.* Example: "In examining this problem, answers were sought to the following questions: What persons would be served? What would it cost? What staff would be needed?"

- *Information sources.* Example: "To answer these questions, letters of complaint for the past three years were examined. Interviews with clients were conducted by phone and in person, phone interviews were conducted with the agency directors in Memphis, Philadelphia, and Chicago."

- *Summary of findings.* Example: "At least 25 percent of the agency's clients would be served better by evening or Saturday service. The costs of operating eight hours of extended service would be negligible, since the service could be provided by rescheduling work assignments. The present staff report they would be inconvenienced by evening and Saturday work assignments."

<u>The Writer's Responsibilities.</u> It is the writer's responsibility to address finally the original purpose of the report. Once the questions have been answered, an informed judgment can be made as to the decision facing the agency. It is at this stage that the writer attempts to draw conclusions from the information he has gathered and summarized. For example, if the original purpose of the report was to help make a decision about whether or not the agency should offer a new service, the writer should draw conclusions from the information and recommend either for or against the new service.

<u>Conclusions and Recommendations.</u> Example: "It appears that operating during extended hours would better serve a significant number of clients. The writer recommends that the agency offer this new service. The present staff should be given temporary assignments to cover the extended hours. As new staff are hired to replace separating persons, they should be hired specifically to cover the extended hours."

3. <u>PERSUASIVE WRITING</u>

Often in life, people are called upon to persuade individuals and groups to adopt ideas believed to be good, or attitudes favorable to ideas thought to be worthwhile or behavior believed to be beneficial. The public service employee may find he must persuade the staff of his own agency, his superiors, the clients of the agency, or the general public in his community.

Persuading others by means of written and other forms of communication is a difficult task and requires much practice. Some principles have emerged from the study of persuasion which may provide some guidelines for developing a model for persuasive writing.

## General Guidelines for Writing Persuasively

*Know the Credibility of the Source*. People are more likely to be persuaded by a message they perceive originates from a trustworthy source. Their trust is enhanced if the source is seen as authoritative, or knowledgeable on the issue discussed in the message. Their trust is increased also if the source appears to have nothing to gain either way, has no vested interest in the final decision. Then, the assertions made in persuasive writing should be backed up by referencing trustworthy and disinterested information sources.

*Avoid Overemotional Appeals*. Appealing to the common emotions of man—love, hate, tear, sex, etc.—can have a favorable effect on the outcome of a persuasive message. But care should be taken because, if the appeal is too strong, it can lead to a reverse effect. For example, if an agency wanted to persuade the public to get chest X-rays, it would have much greater chance of success if it adopted a positive and helpful attitude rather than trying to frighten them into this action. For instance, appealing mildly to the sense of well-being which accompanies knowledge of one's own good health, instead of shocking the public by showing horror pictures of patients who died from lack of timely X-rays.

*Consider the Other Man's Point of View*. To persuade another to one's own point of view, should the writer include information and arguments contrary to his own position? Or should he argue only for his own side?

Generally, it depends on where most of the audience stand in the first place. If most of the audience already favor the position being advocated, then the writer will probably do better including only information favorable to his position. However, if the greater part of the audience are likely to oppose this position, then the writer would probably be better off including their arguments also. In this case, he may be helping his cause by rebutting the opposing arguments as he introduces them into the writing.

An example of this technique might occur in arguing for such an idea as a four-day, forty-hour workweek. Thus: "Many people feel that the ten-hour day is too long and that they would arrive home too late for their regular dinner hour. But think! If you have dinner a littler later each night, you'll have a three-day weekend every week. More days free to go fishing, or camping. More days with your wife and children." That is good persuasive writing!

## Interpersonal Communications

The important role of interpersonal communication in persuading others—face-to-face and person-to-person communications—has been well documented. Mass mailings or printed messages will likely have less effect than personal letters and conversations between persons already known to each other. In any persuasion campaign the personal touch is very important.

An individual in persuading a large number of persons will likely be more effective if he can organize a letter-writing campaign of persuasive messages written by persons favorable to his position to their friends and acquaintances, than if his campaign is based upon sending out a mass mailing of a printed message.

<u>Conditions for Persuading</u>. In order for an audience of one or many to be persuaded in the manner desired, these conditions must be met:

- the audience must be *exposed* to the message,
- members of the audience must *perceive* the intent of the message,
- they must *remember* the message afterwards,
- each member must *decide* whether or not to adopt the ideas.

Each member of the audience will respond to a message differently. While every person may receive the message, not everyone will read it. Even among those who read it, not everyone will perceive it in the same way. Some will remember it longer than others. Not everyone will decide to adopt the ideas. These effects are called *selective exposure, selective perception, selective retention,* and *selective decision*.

<u>The Persuasion Campaign</u>. How can one counteract these selective effects in persuading others? One thing that is known is that *people tend to be influenced by persuasive messages which they are already predisposed to accept*. This means a person is more likely to persuade people a little than to persuade them a lot.

In planning a persuasion campaign, therefore, the messages should be tailored to the audiences. Success will be more likely if one starts with people who believe *almost* as the writer wants to persuade them to believe—people who are most likely to agree with the position advocated.

The writer also wants to use arguments based on values the particular audience already accepts. For example, in advocating a new teen-age job program, he might argue with business men that the program will help business; with parents, that it will build character; with teachers, that it is educational; with taxpayers, that it will reduce future taxes; and so on.

*The idea is to find some way to make sure that each member of the particular audiences reached can see an advantage for himself, and for the writer to then tailor the messages for those audiences.*

4. INSTRUCTIONAL WRITING

Another task that the public-service employee may expect to face from time to time is the instruction of some other person in the performance of a task. This may sometimes involve preparing written instructions to other employees in the unit, or preparing a training manual for new employees.

It may sometimes involve preparing instructional manuals for clients of the unit, such as "How to Apply for a Real Estate License," "How to Bathe your Baby," or "How to Recognize the Symptoms of Heart Disease."

Whatever the purpose or the audience, certain principles of instruction may be applied which will help make more effective these instructional or training communications. These are: *advance organizers, practice, errorless learning,* and *feedback*.

### Advance Organizers

At or near the beginning of an instructional communication, it helps the learner if he is provided with what can be called an "advance organizer." This element of the communication performs two functions:

- it provides a framework or "map" for the leader to organize the information he will encounter,
- it helps the learner perceive his purpose in learning the tasks which will follow.

The first paragraphs in this section, for example, serve together as an advance organizer. The trainee is informed that he may be called upon to perform these tasks in his job *(perceived purpose),* and that he will be instructed in advance organizers, practice, errorless learning, and feedback *(framework, or "map")*.

### Practice

The notion of *practice makes perfect* is a sound instructional principle. When trying to teach someone to perform a task by means of written communication, the writer should build in many opportunities for practicing the task, or parts of it. This built-in practice should be both appropriate and active:

- *Appropriate practice* is practice which is directly related to learning the tasks at hand.

- *Active practice* is practice in actually performing the task at hand or parts of it, rather than simply reading about the task, or thinking about it.

By inserting questions into the text of the communication, by giving practice quizzes, exercises, or field work, one can build into his instructional communication the kind of practice necessary for the reader to readily learn the task.

### Errorless Learning

The practice given learners should be easy to do. That is, they should not be asked to practice a task if they are likely to make a lot of mistakes. When a mistake is practiced it is likely to recur again and again, like spelling "demons," which have been spelled wrong so often it's difficult to recall the way they should be spelled. Because it is better to practice a task right from the first, it is important that learners do not make errors in practice.

- One method for encouraging correct practice is to give the reader hints, or *prompts,* to help him practice correctly.

- Another method is to instruct him in a logical sequence a little bit at a time. Don't try to teach everything at once. Break the task down into small parts and teach each part of the task in order. Then give the learner practice in each part of the task before giving him practice in the whole thing.

- A third way of encouraging errorless learning is to build in practice and review throughout the communication. The learner may forget part of the task if the teacher doesn't review it with him from time to time.

Remember, people primarily learn from what they do, so build in to the instructional communication many opportunities for the learner to practice correctly all of the parts of the task required for learning, first separately and then all together.

### Feedback

The reader, or learner, can't judge how well he is learning the task unless he is informed of it. In a classroom situation, the teacher usually confirms that the learner has been successful, or points out the errors he made, and provides additional instruction. An instructional communication can also help learners in the same way, by providing *feedback* to the learner.

Following practice, the writer should include in his instructional communication information which will let the reader know whether he performed the task correctly. In case he didn't, the writer should also include some further information which will help the reader perform it correctly next time. This feedback, then, performs two functions:

- it helps the learner confirm that his practice was done correctly, and

- it helps him correct his performance of the task in case he made any errors.

Feedback will be most helpful to the learner if it occurs immediately following practice. The learner should be brought to know of his success or his errors just as soon as possible after practice.

**STUDENT LEARNING ACTIVITIES**

- Write "asking" and "answering" letters, and answer a letter of complaint, using the format assigned by the teacher.

- Write memoranda to other "offices" in a fictitious organization. Plan a field trip using only memos to communicate with other students in the class.

- Take minutes of a small group meeting. Or attend a meeting of the school board and take minutes.

- Write a short report on a public service occupation of special interest to you.

- Write a 15-word telegram reserving a single room at a hotel and asking to be picked up at the airport.

- Write a news release announcing a new service offered to the public by your agency.

- Based upon hearing a reading or pretaping of a report, summarize the report in news style.

- View films on effective communication, for example, *Getting the Facts, Words that Don't Inform,* and *A Message to No One.*

- For a given problem or purpose, compile a list of specific questions you would need to answer to write a report on the topic.

- For a given list of questions, discuss and compile a list of information sources relevant to the questions.

- As a member of a group, consider the problem of "What field trip should the class take to help students learn how to write an effective news release?" What questions will you need to answer? Where will you obtain your information?

- As a member of a group, gather the information and prepare a short report based on it for presentation to the class.

- Write a report on a problem assigned by your teacher.

- Write a brief persuasive letter to a friend on a given topic. Assume he does not already agree with you. Apply principles of source credibility, emotional appeals, and one or both sides of the issue to persuade him.

- Plan a persuasive campaign to persuade a given segment of your community to take some given action.

- Write a short instructional communication on a verbal learning task assigned by your teacher.

- Write a short instructional communication on a learning task which involves the operation of equipment.

- Try your instructional communications with a fellow student to check for errors during practice.

**TEACHER MANAGEMENT ACTIVITIES**

- Have students practice letter writing. Assign letters of "asking" and "answering." Read them a letter of complaint and ask them to write an answering letter. Establish common rules of format and style for each assignment. Change the rules from time to time to give practice in several styles.

- Have small groups plan an event, such as a field trip, assigning the various tasks to one another using only memoranda. Evaluate the effectiveness of each group's memo writing by the speed and completeness of their planning.

- Have the class attend a public meeting. Assign each the task of taking the minutes. Evaluate the minutes for brevity and completeness.

- Encourage each student to prepare a short report on a public service occupation of special interest to himself.

- Give the students practice in writing 15-word telegrams.

- Have the students prepare a news release announcing some new service offered to the public, such as "Taxpayers can now obtain help from the Internal Revenue Service in completing their income tax forms as a result of a new service now being offered by the agency."

- Give the students practice in summarizing and writing leads by giving them the facts of a news event and asking them to write a one or two-sentence lead summarizing the significant facts of the event.

- Read a speech or a story. Have students write a summary and a report of the speech or story in news style.

- Show films on effective communication, for example, *Getting the Facts, Words that Don't Inform,* and *A Message to No One.*

- State a general problem and have each student prepare a list of the specific questions implied by the problem.

- State a list of specific questions and discuss with the class the sources of information which might bear upon each of the questions.

- Have small groups consider and write short reports jointly on the general problem, "What field trip should the class take to help students learn how to write an effective news release?" Have each group identify the specific questions to be answered, with sources for needed information.

- Have each student identify and prepare a short report on a general problem of interest.

- Assign students to work in groups of three or four to draft a letter to a friend to persuade him to make a contribution to establish a new city art museum.

- Assign the students to groups of five or six, each group to map out a persuasive campaign on a given topic. Some topics are "Give Blood," "Get Chest X-Ray," "Quit Smoking," "Don't Litter," "Inspect Your House Wiring," etc.

- Have each student identify a simple verbal learning task and prepare an instructional communication to teach that task to another student not familiar with the task.

- Have each student prepare an instructional manual designed to train someone to operate some simple piece of equipment, such as an adding machine, a slide projector, a tape recorder, or something of similar complexity.

- Have each student try his instructional communication out on another student, unfamiliar with the task. He should observe the activities and responses of the trial student to identify errors made in practice. He should revise the communication, adding practice, review, and prompts wherever needed to reduce errors in practice.

# EVALUATION QUESTIONS

## Written Communications

1. Which type of letter would be correct for a public service worker to send?

    A. A letter containing erasures
    B. A letter reflecting goodwill
    C. A rude letter
    D. An impersonal letter

2. Memos usually leave out:

    A. Complimentary closings
    B. The name of the sender
    C. The name of the addressee
    D. The date the memo was sent

3. A good business letter would not contain:

    A. Short, simple words, sentences, and paragraphs
    B. Information contained in the letter being answered
    C. Concrete nouns and active verbs
    D. Orderly placed paragraphs

4. In writing business letters it is important to:

    A. Use a conversational tone
    B. Use a hard, cold tone
    C. Use abstract words
    D. Use a passive tone

5. Messages between departments in an agency are usually sent by:

    A. Letter
    B. Memo
    C. Telegram
    D. Long reports

6. Repetitive work can be simplified by the use of:

    A. Memos
    B. Telegrams
    C. Forms
    D. Reports

7. In filling out forms and applications, it is important to be:

    A. Legible
    B. Complete
    C. Accurate
    D. All of the above

8. Memos should be:

    A. Clear
    B. Brief
    C. Complete
    D. All of the above

9. Minutes of meetings should not include:

    A. The opinions of the recorder
    B. The approval of previous minutes
    C. The corrections of previous minutes
    D. The voting members present

10. Reports are written by public service workers to:

    A. Assemble information in one place
    B. Aid the organization in making decisions
    C. Inform the public and other agencies
    D. All of the above

11. News releases should include:

    A. A lead paragraph summarizing the story
    B. Long paragraphs about many topics
    C. The writer's opinion
    D. All of the above

12. Readers of news releases and reports are influenced by the:

    A. Content of the material
    B. Accuracy of the material
    C. Physical appearance of the material
    D. All of the above

13. The contents of a report should include:

    A. A description of the problem
    B. The questions to be answered
    C. Unimportant information
    D. A summary of findings

14. People tend to be influenced easier if:

    A. They can see something in the position that would be advantageous to them
    B. They are almost ready to agree anyhow
    C. The appeal to the emotions is not overly strong
    D. All of the above

# KEY (CORRECT ANSWERS)

1. B
2. A
3. B
4. A
5. B

6. C
7. D
8. D
9. A
10. D

11. A
12. D
13. C
14. D

---

# WRITING EXAMINATION SECTION

*Question*

Your community is considering a proposal to ban driving by teenagers after dark. Write a letter, of about 200 words, to the mayor or other official in your community. In your letter, defend or attack the above proposal. State your opinion. Give two reasons for it, and explain each reason. *Write* only *the body of the letter.*

Your answer will be rated on the following:

Statement of your opinion

Your two reasons and the explanation for each

Your overall plan

Your paragraphing

Your sentence structure, spelling, punctuation, capitalization, and usage

*Rating Criteria*

The rating of a student's answer is to be based upon the criteria below with chief emphasis to be placed upon the following:

*Content* - The student's opinion about the issue is stated. The reasons for this opinion are given and are explained adequately.

*Organization and Development* - The student"s answer is developed according to an overall plan or pattern. The individual paragraphs are well-developed and knowledge of when to paragraph is demonstrated. Transitions between sentences and paragraphs are suggested.

*Mechanics* - In addition, emphasis is to be placed upon the *mechanics* of writing, which include observance of rules for sentence structure, spelling, punctuation, capitalization, and usage.

## SAMPLE WRITING ANSWERS
### ANSWER I

I believe that the proposal to ban driving by teenagers after dark is an extremely unreasonable request.

My first complaint is the totally restrictive effect this proposal could have on the older teenagers like myself. For instance, all job opportunities would be limited to daylight hours only. This would crush ambitious attitudes in many teenagers. Also, any kind of amusement would have to be crammed into the daytime, leaving houses full of cooped-up teenagers inside with nothing to do. These kinds of situations are not constructive or idealistic.

Secondly, this proposal is not realistic. I happen to live in a scarcely populated area where there is no mass transit system. Food stores and drug stores are located miles away from our house. If there were an accident in the house and I were the only one home at night, I would not be able to drive the injured party to the hospital, which is ten miles away. If this proposal were passed, it could be dangerous or hazardous to someone's health.

Ban driving by teenagers after dark? Ridiculous! Doing so would only work against, instead of for, our society and its people.

### ANSWER II

In response to the proposal made regarding the ban of teenage driving at night, I feel that this is a grave mistake. How are the young people of this community ever to learn to accept responsibility and maturity, when the simple act of driving a car at night is prohibited? Though teenagers, now, they will some day be adults and must learn to face certain accountabilities. If they have proven their ability to operate a car, and are confidantly given the priviledge to drive, then this priviledge should hold true for both the night and the day.

This proposal if made law, would be very bad for many proffessions. Think of the business lost by movie theaters, discotheques, and fast-food restarants in and around the community, if one of their biggest customers, teenagers were forbidden to drive at night. Also, think of the time that would be wasted by policemen tracking down "breakers" of this proposed law, while more serious crimes would be happenning.

I am sure this will be only one of many letters against this proposal. I hope, though, that you will take this letter and the statements made into consideration, for the topic at hand is a serious one to the teenagers and others of the community.

## ANSWER III

I am writing this letter to inform you that I am against the proposel to ban driving by teenagers after dark. I feel that teenagers are not the only ones who drive after dark that get in acidents, go through red lights, and speed.

I do realize that some teenagers do take advanteges of driving when they have a bunch of kids in a car. However, the majority of teenagers who do drive at night do not do things to disrupt our town. In most situations there are always a particular bunch of people who do abuse their privledges.

The reasons why some kids should be able to drive after dark are important. I know an eighteen year old girl who has to drive five miles one way to work at 8:30 pm. and has to drive back home at 12:30 am. Also in emergency teenagers should be able to drive at night.

I wish you would consider the points I have made in this letter to not to ban teenagers driving after dark.

## ANSWER IV

I think that kids should be able to drve a night even if they are 18 teen. When you are 16 teen you are alowed to drive at night if there is a licences driver with you. So there is no difference. If you live in the country you are pretty fare away from things to do. So it is important that they can drive at night. If they can't drive they would hang around in the towns and the might case some trouble. Some kids get jobs when they are in the teens. If they work at night, and aren't allowed to drive at night they might loss there job or they will have to have someone bring them. The car market might go down, because why would someone what to buy a car if the only time they can drive it was during the day. There would be less kids going to the movies, or shoping then they would not make money anymore. If would not be fare to teenagers to. When you were a teenager you could not wait to drive at night. It is un-constentutional becaus you are critasing the teenagers in America. In the winter time it gets dard earlyer so they would sit in all winter long.

# WRITING TEST
*SCORING KEY*

*Ratings of Sample Answers for the Writing Task*
<u>Sample</u>

| | | |
|---|---|---|
| I | Excellent | *Content* - excellent; opinion stated, reasons given and fully explained *Organization and Development* - excellent; plan evident and well executed, knowledge of paragraphing demonstrated, transitions used<br>*Mechanics* - excellent; no errors in sentence structure, spelling, punctuation, capitalization or usage |
| II | Very Good | *Content* - very good; opinion stated, reasons given and explained *Organization and Development* - very good; plan well executed, knowledge of paragraphing demonstrated, transitions used Mechanics - very good; several basic words misspelled, a few errors in punctuation |
| III | Minimally | *Content* - weak; opinion stated, reasons Acceptable given but not fully explained *Organization and Development* - weak; plan evident, paragraphing not well developed, transitions lacking<br>*Mechanics* - very good; some basic words misspelled, error in usage |
| IV | Very Poor | Content - poor; opinion stated but presentation of ideas incoherent *Organization and Development* - poor; plan not evident, knowledge of paragraphing lacking<br>*Mechanics* - poor; run-on and incomplete sentences, many basic words misspelled, many basic rules in punctuation, capitalization, and usage not observed |

www.ingramcontent.com/pod-product-compliance
Lightning Source LLC
Chambersburg PA
CBHW082036300426
44117CB00015B/2500